Powell's   Fragmentation & Memory (NoDJ)
75.00/4.98   NDJ
Theology & Religion   74634

FRAGMENTATION AND MEMORY

KARMEN MACKENDRICK

Fragmentation and Memory

MEDITATIONS ON CHRISTIAN DOCTRINE

FORDHAM UNIVERSITY PRESS
New York ♦ *2008*

Copyright © 2008 Fordham University Press

All rights reserved. No part of this publication may be reproduced, stored in a retrieval system, or transmitted in any form or by any means—electronic, mechanical, photocopy, recording, or any other—except for brief quotations in printed reviews, without the prior permission of the publisher.

Library of Congress Cataloging-in-Publication Data

MacKendrick, Karmen, 1962–
  Fragmentation and memory : meditations on Christian doctrine / Karmen MacKendrick.
    p. cm.
  Includes bibliographical references and index.
  ISBN 978-0-8232-2949-9 (cloth : alk. paper)—ISBN 978-0-8232-2950-5 (pbk. : alk. paper) 1. Baltimore catechism. 2. Catholic Church—Doctrines. I. Title.
BX1968.M315 2008
230′.2—dc22

2008022288

Printed in the United States of America
10 09 08   5 4 3 2 1
First edition

FOR ALAN, WHO ALWAYS REMEMBERS

CONTENTS

Acknowledgments	ix
Introduction: *On Having Forgotten*	1
1. The One and the Many	9
2. The Sin of Origin	32
3. From Trauma to Revelation: *Forgiveness*	55
4. Poppies and Rosemary: *Love*	84
5. Dismembered Divinity: *Saints' Relics*	106
6. Eternal Flesh: *The Resurrection of the Body*	132
Afterword: *On Returning to Memory*	149
Notes	153
Works Cited	179
Index	189

ACKNOWLEDGMENTS

It is a source of recurrent pleasure and occasional surprise to me that so many smart and interesting people are so willing to be engaged in my projects. They have made this book much better than it would have been without them—though even that is to make the doubtable assumption that it would have been possible at all.

Among those who listened and gave me feedback throughout the process, I owe particular thanks to a few. I have been thinking together with Bruce Milem and Virginia Burrus, though in different ways and often on different matters, for so long that I have undoubtedly begun to credit myself with ideas and insights that were originally theirs. I hope that I haven't done so too egregiously here, and I thank them for their sheer smarts and their continued generosity. My friend and former colleague Jennifer Glancy has likewise been exemplarily generous and precise in her thinking, both to my benefit.

Helpful conversations with Elliot Wolfson provided both essential insights and valuable references. Catherine Keller was helpful in her enthusiasm and her questions, particularly about the forgiveness chapter.

I am grateful to James Dahlinger, S.J., both for his knowledge of Catholic doctrine and for the quiet discretion with which, I nonetheless suspect, he concerns himself with the well-being of my soul. Jim, Virginia, and Bruce were among the friends who helpfully accompanied me on the exploratory relics trips central to Chapter 5. On others, Marcos Bisticas-Cocoves, James Digiovanna, Colette Copeland, and Boris Belay were both helpful and pleasant companions. Among the wider circle of friends less immediately involved in this particular text, I owe particular

ACKNOWLEDGMENTS

thanks to Ellen Feder and Carol Siegel for the sheer persistence of their supportiveness.

Peter Manchester and Mark Jordan provided the most helpful manuscript readings I could possibly have desired. Their careful and exact thinking has grounded my speculative flights here and kept me from some thoroughly embarrassing errors, and their enthusiasm has come as a relief to my perpetual authorial anxiety.

Helen Tartar, with her exquisite editorial sense, has been kind in the face of my worries and sensitive in the face of my prose. I am privileged to be able to work again with her and with the rest of the staff at Fordham.

I've had the opportunity to work out parts of my thinking here through the presentation of early chapter versions in a number of venues. For this my thanks go to the International Association for Philosophy and Literature (and especially to Anne O'Byrne, for organizing the session), the philosophy department at Gettysburg College, the Wayne State University Humanities Center, the Humanities Center at Harvard, and the University of Western Ontario. LeMoyne College provided me with an opportunity to present ideas and, through the Research and Development program, with funding to visit a number of different reliquary sites. Carolyn McTiernan, assistant to the Provost, deserves special mention for finding me even more funding than had originally been granted. An earlier version of Chapter 6 appeared in an issue of the journal *Discourse* on the topic of "material spirit," and I appreciate the request of the issue editor, Carl Good, which led to its writing.

Finally, Alan Griffin deserves more thanks than I can give here: He patiently photographed every relic we encountered, conducted online research, rescued my hard drive, and endured my wide variety of writing-induced moods with a sweetness well beyond the requirements of spousal tolerance.

FRAGMENTATION AND MEMORY

INTRODUCTION
On Having Forgotten

> This truth *is going*, in bringing to me the last words, the words that are always last, it is going to free me from speaking. *I can no longer speak*: this happens, this is still happening, an inexplicable prayer.
> —Jean-Luc Nancy, "To Possess Truth in One Soul and One Body"

> If a book could for a first time really begin, it would, for one last time, long since have ended.
> —Maurice Blanchot, *The Writing of the Disaster*

Invariably, I have forgotten how to write.

This invariant fact, emerging early in every writing project, is, nevertheless, just as invariably a surprise. I always forget that I have always forgotten. Beginning to write anything, I realize that I have no idea how to do so—how to draw together (sculpturally or choreographically or musically) the frequently dissonant elements whose togetherness is somehow going to be the point of the book. I have, in other words, forgotten writing, both before and after writing; forgotten how I have done and how I will do something that, in fact, I do nearly every day. The process is perhaps a bit less astonishing now than it was when it happened in earlier iterations—eventually less astonishing, at any rate; I come slowly to remember, every time, that I have forgotten before. Still, the initial surprise is there.

That surprise, and the subsequent fragmentation, re-collection, and even coherence of the written work provided the formative impetus and question for this text. Here I return persistently to memory, to forgetfulness, and to the forgotten in memory—and to all of these as traces of the

INTRODUCTION

eternal in (relation to) time. And here I remember something else: this set of themes emerges, for me, in writing of anything at all, as if it were central to the very possibility of using words.[1] The present text is another form of telling and untelling, the presentation of old and even stodgy questions in theology with an eye (and perhaps an ear) to the ways in which they, too, unwork themselves. Of course there are organized writers, people who write on schedule and always know what to read, whose finished projects are, clearly, expanded versions of their initial proposals and not surprising diversions; people for whom writing is work (perhaps pleasant, perhaps painful) and not, to use Maurice Blanchot's expression, worklessness or unworking (*désoeuvrement*). For the rest of us, the writing process itself breaks apart, departing the conscious, readily accessible levels of memory, leaving only a trace in the text. It is as if the productive unravels the processual; as if making the thing-of-the-book, the work, also unworks the process, the working. And yet, of course, to unravel is a process too. Given all this, the surprise of writing becomes the fact that it does gather together at all. The surprise is not that one writes (that one is writing), but that one has written; that a work (or even a body of work) has somehow brought itself into existence while the writer was engaged in anxious distraction. Writing inscribes an admixture of gathering and breakage.

Here, I have tried to make that paradoxical mix itself thematic, particularly in terms of its functions in and as time. As I hope the following chapters will show, such a broken and re-collected time is implicated, interleaved, with eternity; the more particular themes are those of philosophical theology, where discourse has most often attended to the eternal, where paradox is most often developed as something other than contradiction.

The following chapters attempt, then, to address what it is in time that breaks in, what breaks up, what draws together: the ways in which time is not only laid out in a line (or even a circle). Elusive as writing always is, there is something especially slippery in this conceptual set. Because it is, in some measure, about its own unworking, the effort to work it out, its "betrayal" in the work, must be delicately managed. "In the effort to discern time," writes Elliot Wolfson, "the mind comes to the rim of reason, the limit of language."[2] Yet all writing must somehow be writing about time: the process of moving disparate ideas together, those ideas' arrangement, the structuring of order and transition in the text is about nothing more than it is about time. We are always writing at the very edge of writing's possibility, even when we give the illusion of writing without forgetfulness, or puzzlement, or questions.

ON HAVING FORGOTTEN

Here the question itself becomes thematic. Each chapter begins in an endeavor to read dogmatic or doctrinal declarations, presented here in their starkest question-and-answer form, from the old Baltimore catechism of the Catholic Church. I have employed the older catechism deliberately, for its questioning form and its association with repetition, and for its sheer exemplary dogmatism, to ask if even here there might be something more, something evocative and elusive and intriguing that might give us cause to pay attention yet again. This text was formerly for catechumens an object of memory, rote memorization achieved by repetition, another form of the repetition of the question—and indeed, each question in it gives rise to more, as the terms of each response are rendered more precise. Its aim is as much call and response as the inculcation of dogma. Thus, the catechism is at once thought at its most dogmatic, to be committed to memory rather than explored in query, and yet thought that consists of nothing but questions, thought in which each answer is the source of more questions. This constant opening onto questions is vital here: my aim is not to reinforce dogma but precisely to show what it is that resists formulaic finality, however evidently orthodox, worn out, and used up its source may be. I have read just a few of the hundreds of catechismic questions and answers here in terms of fragmentation and memory—that is to say, also, in terms of the eternity of the world and the divinity of the mundane. I should emphasize that this is not a work *about* the catechism, but one in which catechismic formulations provide a useful kind of shorthand; it is there that we find the starkest form of several of the questions most fundamental to a consideration of memory and fragmentation.

The idea of taking on tired texts is hardly novel. Writing of the worrisome upsurge of a particularly narrow, knowledge-asserting version of Christianity, Jean-Luc Nancy notes in "Of Divine Places" that:

> In the end, something resists. To all of the harshest and most justified criticism of Christianity—of its political and moral despotism, its hatred of reason as much as of the body, its institutional frenzy or its pietistic subjectivism, its traffic in good works and intentions, and ultimately its monopolization and its privatization of the divine—to all of that something puts up a resistance, beneath the horizon of everything: something that, it is not impossible to claim, has [in spite of all the mumbo jumbo] left upon the form of the *Pater noster* . . . a mark that is difficult totally to erase: a generous

INTRODUCTION

abandonment to divine generosity, a supplication out of that distress to which the divine alone can abandon us—the divine or its withdrawal.³

The catechism lacks the prayer's elegant concision, but perhaps in its wearied words, as well, is an opening, a resistance to the foreclosure, to the rigidity of the very orthodoxy it seems to impose. Despite their ready fit with my own obsessions, I have been, as one must, rather wary of taking up these dogmatic or doctrinal subjects. Those discussed here have drawn me by their very strangeness or, more exactly, by my sense that ideas that seem so bizarre probably harbor interesting paradoxes—mine is not, as will be readily evident, a particularly dogmatic approach.

This series of meditations is linked not only by the common centrality of fragmentation and memory to each but also by a common tendency among its topics to destabilize various senses of law, by the importance to each of the dialogical, and by the curious structuring of time and of the subject who knows temporally. The opening chapter will set forth a less personal history of the linked topics of memory and fragmentation, in a review of the classic philosophical version of recollection and fragmentation—the problem of the one and the many—in which we find early considerations of the relations of temporal and eternal, as well. Both the problem and its solutions open onto the issues that structure the rest of the text, which moves first to a consideration of original sin as an ostensibly "primary" fragmentation that in fact complicates or even undoes the notion of primacy or of origin. The theoretical considerations of original sin come fairly directly from the works of Augustine, but they are read through curious comments that Gilles Deleuze makes on the nature of sin in his reading of Leibniz, and through a Deleuzean questioning of origin more generally.

A chapter on sin seems to demand a following chapter on forgiveness. Forgiveness, I argue, alters the relational temporality of forgiven and forgiver while illuminating the time of the promise, to which forgiveness is sacramentally linked. Here I follow Elliot Wolfson to argue that forgiveness is given as always already promised. This chapter considers the transformative effects of forgiveness on the structure of our temporality psychoanalytically (using theories of trauma) as well as theologically.

The following chapter takes up the perpetually uncomfortable topic of love, seeking common elements in the theological and interpersonal senses of the term. Jean-Luc Nancy's understanding of love as the renewal (rather than, or perhaps *as*, the fulfillment) of a promise of futurity is read alongside the very curious infolded time of the Eucharist as a manifestation of both love and memory; the exploration of the promise begun in the previous chapter is further developed here. Together, these lines of thought underlie the argument for the possibility that in and through an act of both memory and mourning, love opens time too, and reenfolds time and the eternal.

Continuing the move toward a more explicit corporeality begun by the question of the Eucharist, the next chapter takes a slightly different approach, taking on through the analysis of numerous examples the question of the religious roles played by saints' relics. Three experiences of memory, I argue, are evoked here: the historical, the communal, and the sacred. Each draws other times into a slippery present; each draws fullness of life into a fragment (of time and of flesh both), and each unsettles our notions of identity as a tidy individuality. Nancy, again, is helpful here, particularly in his understandings of the workings of history and community and their relations to identity.

The final chapter takes up corporeality most directly, in a discussion of the doctrine of bodily resurrection. As with other strange doctrines, this one may have theologically intriguing or revealing things to tell us even if we find its usual dogmatic interpretations a little bizarre. Deleuze's theories of both repetition and sensation help to work out the chapter's understanding of corporeal time for an argument that bodily resurrection may be read as eternal, rather than enduring, life.

While I have long been intrigued by the eternal as the disruptive outside of time, the outside that cuts through, in this set of meditations I have been drawn as well to the ways in which the eternal is, if not precisely *proper* to time (propriety implying a certain staying in place), nonetheless found in living in time. I don't mean to identify the temporal and eternal altogether, but to take up the notion of "a temporal flow of experience in which eternity is nonetheless present."[4] As Wolfson says, glossing the Kabbalist Moses Cordovero, "From this perspective it can, nay must, be said that the 'secret of eternality' is not in opposition to temporality, but rather is a more subtle manifestation of time, a timeless time."[5] This time seems to me proper as well to the version of Christianity that Friedrich Nietzsche presents in the misleadingly titled *Anti-Christ*: "Blessedness is . . . the *only* reality—the rest is signs for speaking of it."[6] Nietzsche argues that Christ exemplifies "the profound instinct for how one would have to *live* in order to feel oneself 'in Heaven', to feel oneself 'eternal' . . . this alone is the psychological reality of 'redemption.' "[7] In this sense, eternality is not merely an abstract, inexperienceable

INTRODUCTION

dimension to be understood in theoretical physics, but (at least potentially) as much a part of living as is time. To trace that lived dimension through its displacements and disruptions is also to reread the catechismic questions for signs of the immanent, and eminently disruptive, reality of blessedness.

All of these considerations, I think, finally point to the importance of memory and fragmentation in understanding what it means to mean, in reading a handful of puzzling and peculiar philosophical/theological topics, but perhaps still more in reading ourselves in those puzzles, finding in these considerations of dogma something intriguingly nondogmatic, something perpetually and importantly open, something paradoxical, something we come to each time as what we had forgotten.

As we read ourselves into those questions, they tell us something about thinking and writing too. Blanchot remarks upon "[t]he separation put to work in the act of writing: how much passivity, how much worklessness are needed to respect it, and, doing so, to betray it. In the ethical obligation, in the demand of the historical struggle, in the eschatological affirmation, nothing allows one to decide if the altered manner in which the distance seems to propose itself does not restore it to the demand that excludes it from any affirmation, pure or impure."[8] This passivity does not imply not-working; the act of writing is performed not in my absence, but in my respectful betrayal of the separation between writer and written, and between the text and itself as well.

Thus writing is always a process involving fragmentation (though never fragmentation alone). The respectful worklessness of writing breaks apart within the process of remembering and the production, nonetheless, of the work, a work that must be more than simply breakage; more, even, than fragments. In their essay "Noli Me Frangere," Philippe Lacoue-Labarthe and Jean-Luc Nancy write, "It is a mistake, then, to write in fragments on the fragment. . . . But what else is there to do? Write about something else entirely—or about nothing—and let oneself be fragmented."[9] One lets oneself be not only separated, but fragmented; the text will pull itself apart even as one pulls it all together. These movements are neither successive nor simply contrary, but always mutually implicated, always at work in a double pull on writing and thought. Disintegration pulls at recollection, eternity at time, the already-given at the future-promised, the flesh at the word.

As all this suggests, writing must also be drawn to what fragments writing, what cuts across it from some outside, explodes its limits from within, says itself in silence and stutter. This draw toward fragmentation is especially evident when writing is drawn to paradox—to seeming contradictions that resist singular resolution. Paradox fragments, pulling apart from an always elusive common point toward which the opposing lines of thought (such as time and eternity, language and silence, pain and pleasure) are nonetheless drawn.[10] The challenge of writing about paradox is to trace faithfully the double movement toward and away from this gravitational point, even while it consistently eludes saying.

We misunderstand writing and fragmentation, however, if we undertake to fragment writing as if it were a task we might accomplish, as if we could *produce* the fragment: "Above all, we must not believe that we could know how to fragment, that we could know ourselves in fragments, that we actually could fragment. No one fragments, unless perhaps it is the *Noli me frangere* that all writing utters: don't fragment me, don't wish to fragment me—fragmentation goes on, and I'm fragmented enough; anyway, it's not up to you."[11]

Perhaps all writing is, as Catherine Keller says of theology, "an incantation at the edge of uncertainty."[12] At this edge, we look out and we ask, the answers opening onto more questions. "The fact is," writes Deleuze, "that every thing has its beginning in a question, but one cannot say that the question itself begins. Might the question, along with the imperative which it expresses, have no other origin than *repetition*? Great authors of our time (Heidegger, Blanchot) have exploited this most profound relation between the question and repetition."[13] Georges Bataille makes questioning the redeeming quality of philosophy:

> Philosophy takes on a strange dignity from the fact that it supposes infinite questioning. It's not that results gain philosophy some glamour, but only that it responds to the human desire that asks for a questioning of all that is. No one doubts that philosophy is often pointless, an unpleasant way of employing minor talents. But whatever the legitimate biases on this subject, however erroneous . . . the "results," its abolition runs into this difficulty—that exactly this lack of real results is its greatness. Its whole value is in the absence of rest that it fosters.[14]

Certainly the same questions keep returning; I have not answered them, and perhaps the work at hand is not to answer, only to enter them into conversations. Every work has its beginning in a question, but it is not done, not finished, in an answer. Writing of the infinite or eternal, the gathered and the broken, seems necessarily to remain unfinished (the

INTRODUCTION

doubleness of the French *infini* is suggestive here), not permitting completion. Perhaps the task of this work is to point to certain questions, to the ideas and the experiences that raise those questions, or to work by a sort of negation (as theology so often does) of too-simple answers. Perhaps the work of writing is, as Blanchot suggests, unworking, and most so when it touches upon what disintegrates or renders not whole, and what recollects or draws impermanently together. We begin with both many and one.

1

THE ONE AND THE MANY

24. Is there only one God? Yes, there is only one God. *I am the Lord, and there is none else: there is no God besides me. (Isaiah 45:5)*
25. How many Persons are there in God? In God there are three Divine Persons—the Father, the Son, and the Holy Ghost. *Going, therefore, teach ye all nations; baptizing them in the name of the Father and of the Son and of the Holy Ghost. (Matthew 28:19).* . . .
33. Can we fully understand how the three Divine Persons, though really distinct from one another, are one and the same God? We cannot fully understand how the three Divine Persons, though really distinct from one another, are one and the same God because this is a supernatural mystery.
—*A Catechism of Christian Doctrine*, Revised Edition of the Baltimore Catechism, Part 1, Lesson 3

Footnotes to Plato

What is found at the historical beginning of things is not the inviolable identity of their origin; it is the dissension of other things. It is disparity.
—Michel Foucault, "Nietzsche, Genealogy, History"

As the introduction has already hinted, the effort to clarify conceptually the thematic commonality of this text proves exasperating, perhaps appropriately so. How can one say together, and in some kind of order, discussions of fragmentation and scatteredness in time? How does one remind oneself and one's readers of what seems always to participate in forgetfulness? The brief and highly selective glance at history offered in this introductory chapter is one way into the questions of memory and fragmentation, a not quite nostalgic survey of the pull of the question of the one and the many, and the force of that question—and then the shattering of the difficult but relatively orderly problem of the one and the many into the fragments of post-Nietzschean philosophy and its curious temporalities, temporalities that, for all their evident postmodernity, turn out to have considerable resonance with much older ways of thinking.

American pragmatist William James writes, at the outset of the twentieth century:

> A certain abstract monism, a certain emotional response to the character of oneness, as if it were a feature of the world not coordinate with its manyness, but vastly more excellent and eminent, is so prevalent in educated circles that we might almost call it a part of philosophic common sense. Of *course* the world is one, we say. How else could it be a world at all? Empiricists, as a rule, are as stout monists of this abstract kind as rationalists are.[1]

Beyond this abstract intellectual assumption, James suggests of the presumptive experiential monism underlying unitive "mystical" states that there is an affective benefit as well: "*An Absolute One, and I that One*—surely we have here a religion which, emotionally considered, has a high pragmatic value; it imparts a perfect sumptuosity of security."[2] Indeed, as Bataille will later note, "to no longer wish oneself to be everything is to put everything into question. Anyone wanting slyly to avoid suffering, identifies with the entirety of the universe, judges each thing as if he were it."[3] *Monism*, a general term covering a wide range of beliefs in different kinds of oneness or unity, is as old as Western philosophy, and James's remarks suggest part of the reason. Philosophy, as both Plato and Aristotle famously claim, begins in wonder,[4] and when we wonder about the world, amazed by it and attempting to make sense of it, one of our deepest impulses is to try to cover the dizzying range of evident phenomena with the elegance of a single principle: to make one of many. There is a great intellectual security in this simplicity, an elegant absence of confusion. Likewise, in its religious versions, a sense of unity may indeed, as James suggests, impart tremendous affective security; to *be* the Absolute One certainly bolsters me against the insecurity of being only my usual contingent, inessential self.

But monism, especially in this second sense, is also terrifying; to be "I" cannot be to be identical with any absolute one, but can only be my own distinction from it—and threats to this distinct ego boundary are likely to be disturbing.[5] Thus, if we are serious and absolute monists, we have no way of being that "we" at all, and certainly no way of being a cluster of "I's." (This is perhaps one reason why in the history of philosophy there have been precious few absolute monists—though not, to be sure, none at all.) Monisms are tempting, but beneath that temptation they are disquieting, as well. Still, this disquieting temptation is an enduring one; in the self-evident multiplicity of human existence, we continue to try to gather the fragments of knowledge and experience. This particular form of wonder has a long history. "Newcomers who came to Plato's Academy to hear his famous Lecture on the Good were shocked to find that instead of a discussion of the good life, Plato was exploring the most basic problem of arithmetic, the relation between the numbers one and two"[6]—one, and the many in its minimal form. Granted, this problem of the one and the many is not much of a conversation-starter today. But I think we see in this classic problem—one of the foremost philosophical issues in the ancient world—something of the intensity and persistence of our desire to gather together.

In a way, the problem of the one and the many is still *the* problem, and not only of philosophy. It is the problem of all of our laws: how do we gather disparate facts, or disparate situations, or disparate peoples, under coherent principles? The laws of science turn the disorganized sets of data into knowledge; the laws of states turn the disorganized series of individual behaviors into a governable set; the laws of ethics constrain into manageable, sometimes single, options the indefinite range of possibilities for human action.

But, to give this orderly discussion a more theological twist, the law also kills.[7] And so a query into fragmentation, into breaking (we do not merely ignore or disobey laws, we *break* them) is not merely a query into disintegration, loss, and death:[8] it is a query into life, as the resistance to what kills. What, if anything, escapes; what resists? I do not intend here to consider the value of deliberate law breaking in the legal sense. Certainly such a consideration is possible, and such a justification more or less strong depending upon the laws themselves and one's ethical or political position. But I want instead to concern myself with the kinds of fragmentation that do not depend upon the breaking of a prior whole: with what lies outside as uncontainable, or incomplete, or open.

The problem of perfect containment begins together with Western philosophy. The Milesian monists, among the earliest known Western philosophers, each believe that everything is made of a single material

THE ONE AND THE MANY

substance—such as water, or air, or indeterminate primal matter.[9] They often attribute divinity to the one substance; we have here not a materiality from which divinity is distant nor even matter to which the sacred is superadded, but inherently *divine stuff*. As later philosophy becomes increasingly complex, the association of unity with divinity recurs, in various forms (usually moving away from materiality), but persistently. Only rarely, though importantly, do we see hints of primary complexity or differentiation (the richest of these enfold one and many together).[10]

The persistent association of divinity with unity, in turn, may lead us to wonder about the contrary possibility of sacred fragments. As much of this text will suggest, I suspect that we have undervalued the broken—but that is to get ahead of ourselves. And in fact, even if we cannot remain in the sumptuous securities of monism (even, perhaps especially, if we *do* value breakage), we may find that the notion of the divine or sacred character of stuff—that is, of the material universe—makes its own strange kind of sense, as the present text's frequent recurrence to the bodily suggests.[11]

In addition to early material monisms, the more conceptually difficult numerical monism of the Eleatic philosophers claims that there is not merely a single formative substance but, in fact, a single One: one thing, perhaps, except that without differentiation it is difficult to see just what the concept of "thing" might entail. One of the most famous of the ancient Eleatic philosophers, Parmenides, famously admits that while in Truth there is only one single, unchanging, and indescribable unity, "for the mortals passing through them, the things-that-seem must 'really exist,' being, for them, all there is."[12]

This suggests less a dual reality of multiplicity and unity than a dual *perspective*—one from the point of view of unchanging eternity, one from the transient slippage of time. The former is unquestionably the one that Parmenides' goddess urges us to value as the way of Truth, but it is an inhuman truth.[13] Parmenides cannot, of course, be a Neoplatonist—as he is pre-Socratic, this would require some impressive chronological maneuvering—yet this sense of two simultaneous, overlapping perspectives on "what is" will arguably be shared by the much later school. And indeed *Doxa*, "the way of subjectivity," which forms the poem's second half, begins with a statement that we might easily, if we did not know better, attribute to Plotinus, probably the best-known Neoplatonic philosopher: "Wherever I begin, it is all one to me, for there I shall return again."[14] That is, we may find our way from one to many or back again from anywhere; all is, at once. (Much later than Plotinus, T. S. Eliot

THE ONE AND THE MANY

begins his poem "East Coker" by declaring "In my beginning is my end" and finishes it with the line "In my end is my beginning."[15] It's an enduringly fascinating thought.)

Parmenides' student Zeno emphasizes the impossibility of motion (which requires multiplicity of place), creating a delightful paradox when, at the opening of Plato's dialogue entitled *Parmenides*, he declares motion impossible after he and his teacher have just *traveled* to Athens and Parmenides has "gone out" of the room for a while.[16] This dialogue, one of Plato's most complex and baffling, may also act as our entry into Plato's incalculably influential thought.

In some way or another Parmenides is clearly an influence on Plato, though *which* of those some or other ways is a lot less evident.[17] The notoriously difficult *Parmenides* exemplifies not the absolute monism of its namesake but the increasingly precise and complex philosophical method of gathering and division—implicitly, then, of fragmentation and (re)collection—of Plato's later dialogues.[18]

This is not necessarily the kind of thought we most readily think of as Platonic. The better-known version of Plato is the one that emerges from a straightforward reading of a middle text like the *Republic*, with its famous allegories of the line (509d–11e) and the cave (514a–17c), in which an unchanging Real seems to elude the sense perception we mistake for reality. The lowest reality is that of fleeting images such as reflections or shadows, just barely surpassed by that of material things known sensually, and the highest reality is that of the Forms, pure abstractions known only by intellectual contemplation, from which the reality of all lower entities is derived. Thus, for instance, the shadow of a bed is minimally real; the bed itself real but not enduringly so (or rather, enduring only briefly); the Form of the Bed utterly real, which is to say that it has no dependence upon time, or space, or perception at all. Here the Forms appear as perfect exemplars, paradigms only imperfectly copied in the sensory realm. At Reality's pinnacle is the highest Form, either Beauty or Truth or Goodness (or all three in some unnameable trinitarian unity), which is somehow formative, if not precisely generative, of all that is. As Forms are perfect exemplars of the qualities for which they stand, the Form of Beauty, for example, is also the most beautiful thing in existence. (The puzzles of formation, generation, and causality between Forms and multiple objects will be taken up by Aristotle and by Platonists and Neoplatonists later, and of course continue to provoke Plato scholarship to this day.) This is Platonism as it is most often received: an affirmation of the Truth and the value of what is stable

THE ONE AND THE MANY

and universal, and, if not an active devaluation of the somatic and sensual, at the least a tendency thereto.

Even here, though, there are hints of irony or even self-subversion. Socrates' demands for directness, his arguments against images, are indirect and imagistic, suggesting not a singular truth but a complex interplay. The same Socrates who approaches Truth by metaphoric indirection condemns poetic language, going so far as to banish the poets from his perfect city (*Republic* 605b–8a)—shortly before presenting, as one more argument for justice, a poetic myth, a myth about the ways in which good and bad souls are sorted out for reward or punishment in an immortal afterlife.

The possibility of sorting becomes increasingly important for Plato, but it never becomes as tidy as we might expect. The later dialogues increasingly emphasize the importance of collection under a particular definition or kind and division along the lines of difference. As Alexander Nehamas and Paul Woodruff note, considering the *Parmenides* with other late dialogues:

> The method of collection and division depends on the idea that the Forms are closely connected with one another and that to know a Form is to know its connections: to divide a Form (itself an impossible task according to the middle theory attacked in the *Parmenides*, which asserts that each form is indivisible) is to determine the Forms to which it is related as a genus is related to its species. According to the late dialogues the Forms constitute a great network of essentially interrelated objects.... The Forms of the middle theory are, as the *Parmenides* insists, "separate" both from each other and from their many instances.... But when the *Philebus* [another late dialogue] discusses collection and division it leaves us with an impression at least that the connections between the world of Forms and the world of sensible objects are much more intimate. Division of a form, for example, may end precisely when we reach the countless objects that fall under it.[19]

Whatever emphasis on unity we might find in Plato, then, is clearly rendered strange, and strangely multiple, in the greater context of his work; it becomes a unity of relation and of collection.

Indeed, the *Parmenides*, with its strange, structurally repeating puzzles, sometimes seems to make the very notion of Form nonsensical, whatever sort of Form we may have in mind. The most famous of these puzzles is the "third man" argument: that the Form of the Large must itself be

THE ONE AND THE MANY

large (indeed *the* L/large), and so there must be some Form by which the Form of the Large is large, and so there must be some Form by (virtue of) which the Form that forms the Form of the Large is large, and so on (132a–b). Though it first appears as an attempt to gather together in some decisive fashion, this dialogue with a famous monist becomes instead a kaleidoscope of complication and multiplicity. The one does not simply become many, but it seems to become relational among the many. Rather than the stillness of Forms as we usually think them, we find fragmentation and (re)collection in motion.

In another late dialogue, the *Sophist*, an older, almost-offstage Socrates cedes the floor to a student of Zeno's identified only as the Eleatic stranger. Here an argument purportedly for the unity of Being is presented entirely through a series of increasingly exact and minute *divisions* enunciated by the visiting Eleatic philosopher, divisions that are meant to allow the proper subject matter and methods of philosophical discussion to be determined. The dizzying divisions of the stranger's logic in the *Sophist* leave us a bit clearer, maybe, as to how to distinguish philosopher from Sophist (one of the dialogue's purported purposes), but rather more befuddled about the nature of Being (its other stated intent) than we would have been before beginning to read. It seems likely that Plato, whose writing seldom appears to be accidental, is in fact performing the interplay of gathering—of recollection—and division, even as his characters discuss it.

This interplay adds another layer of dialogue, the structure of Plato's most famous and philosophical works. The dialogues don't simply pit one speaker against another, and certainly don't always have "winners": for instance, Parmenides, who is clearly wrong, who has traveled to Athens although he has declared that movement is impossible, is never really, definitively refuted (or affirmed) in the dialogue bearing his name. Rather, the Forms themselves are left, as it were, as an exercise for the reader, drawing her into the ongoing openness of the conversation. As Nehamas and Woodruff note of the *Phaedrus*, to question the dialogue is to continue asking the dialogue's questions.[20] And this, of course, is both to enter into and to continue the process of dialogue itself. Questions open onto more than answers.

This is so even when a dialogue is, like the *Sophist*, only barely, nominally, dialogical. Here Plato draws our attention to the very fact of interchange—the Stranger is asked whether he wants to give a monologue or to have an interlocutor, and he chooses the latter (with the provision that his respondent be well mannered).[21] We immediately note, however,

15

that the "interlocutor's" role, played by the eager student Theatetus, is entirely that of yes-man, with the occasional request for elaboration. Nowhere does he argue or even suggest a theory that might in turn be argued against. Evidently, then, the *Sophist* presents, to all intents and purposes, one speaker, on oneness (or unity), even though that oneness is known by precise division.

But, in fact, it can't.

Because a dialogical, dialectical truth, a Socratic or a Platonic truth, is *not* one, cannot be just one—must be not merely two but at least three, the dialogue itself a third between its speakers. Even the singular Forms become implicated in relations. Knowledge, even remembered knowledge, may in some strange sense be "in" me but can only be awakened in relation or connection—in dialogue. (For instance, the famous memory of the slave boy in the *Meno*, where Socrates most clearly affirms knowledge as memory, is awakened only by Socrates' questions.[22]) Memory is not only drawn out of us but also draws us in—as when, in the *Phaedrus*, we respond to the memory of the beauty of the heavens in our response to the beauty of boys.[23] The *Phaedrus*, in fact, is so rich in considerations of memory, unity, and fragmentation that it merits a slightly more extensive consideration here.

The structure of this work is somewhat odd, consisting of an introductory setup that displaces the stubbornly urban Socrates into the beauty of the countryside, a speech delivered by Phaedrus (but written by Lysias) praising the attentions of one who does not love over those of one who does, a speech by Socrates condemning love as a form of madness; and a second speech by Socrates, who, having reconsidered, praises love's madness as a divine and useful force. The text then ends with a more dialogical consideration of rhetoric, where a comparison between speaking and writing seems to favor the former.

The *Phaedrus* is most famous for the third speech, delivered by Socrates under what he himself declares to be divine inspiration. The body of this speech again takes the form of a myth, a simile, which Socrates is careful to identify as such (246a–b). This is a slightly mischievous move, since he has earlier suggested that it's simply too exhausting to come up with rational accounts of myths (229b–e), and this speech is in fact an exaltation of reason, though—importantly—reason under the influence of love's madness.

The soul is represented as a charioteer (generally taken to be the character of reason) guiding two horses, one amenable though spirited and one disorderly and impatient. The chariot-soul circles the heavens in the company of the gods, enjoying, depending upon how well the charioteer can guide his horses, a more or less clear view of the Beautiful itself. With a small distraction, however, the soul stumbles, and falls into fleshly form.

But the corporeal world too contains reminders of the gods and the world of Beauty. These reminders are embodied in those whose beauty makes us love them—not in a mild and contemplative way but with desperate desire. In the madness of eros, the soul "seethes and throbs . . . like a child whose teeth are just starting to come in" (251c); "the whole soul is stung all around, and the pain simply drives it wild—but then, when it remembers the boy in his beauty, it recovers its joy. From the outlandish mix of these two feelings—pain and joy—comes anguish and helpless raving: in its madness the lover's soul cannot sleep at night or stay put by day" (251d–e). But this desire, when reined in by reason, acts too as the memory of the love of the gods and the glory of Beauty itself (252d–55a). The painful/joyous awakening of memory in desire joins with the dispassionate work of reason to create the best, richest, and most virtuous life for both lover and beloved.

Each soul must be incarnated again and again; souls can even go from human to animal or vice versa. With each incarnation, as memory is more and more perfected, the soul becomes more nearly perfect itself, until it attains the ultimate human form—that, of course, of the philosopher—and finally may remain in the heavenly bliss of contemplation.[24]

Here, in the third speech, memory (stimulated by desire) as a source of knowledge is evoked explicitly, but the invocation of memory actually begins much earlier in the dialogue. Before any of the speeches is delivered, Phaedrus, who has been delighted by Lysias's speech on love, has been coyly pretending that he knows only the gist and not the text of the speech. Socrates does not believe him, declaring that he knows perfectly well that Phaedrus will surely have memorized the speech, and "if I don't know my Phaedrus I must be forgetting myself—and neither is the case" (228a). In fact it turns out that Phaedrus has a written copy of the speech with him, from which he is persuaded to read.

It's possible to read Socrates' statement as just a hyperbolic declaration of how well he knows Phaedrus. But given the dialogue's obsessions with memory, we may permit ourselves at least to wonder otherwise. Socrates does indeed forget himself in this work, and repeatedly. He gives his first speech (against love) and then worries that he has neglected his "divine sign," by which he always knows if he has done rightly or wrongly; he has neglected, if not forgotten, to consider that love is a god

THE ONE AND THE MANY

(or godlike) and ought to be praised. Socrates himself claims of this first speech, in which he suggests that love is a form of madness and so best avoided, that it comes from what he has forgotten (which may include love poetry; 253c–d). More telling still is the forgetting that comes later, when Socrates tries to recapitulate his second speech and must ask Phaedrus, "but now tell me this—I can't remember at all because I was completely possessed by the gods: Did I define love at the beginning of my speech?" (263d). Not only does Socrates forget himself, maybe he *doesn't* know (doesn't properly remember?) Phaedrus, since he is so confident that Phaedrus has memorized when in fact Phaedrus will read—a distinction given more weight by the opposition between writing and memory in the last portion of the dialogue, as we shall note below. We may already begin to mistrust Socrates' memory, and perhaps we are meant to do so.

But what seems more certainly to be implied is that Socrates forgets himself and Phaedrus, or remembers himself and Phaedrus, together. To follow the Delphic injunction and know oneself is never to know only oneself. And to know is to remember. Thus implied is the dialogical nature not only of learning but of memory, which is never only my own, and of identity, which is never given in solitude.

Nor do we speak alone. Socrates' first speech is not directly addressed to, but nonetheless repeatedly directs itself toward the "beautiful boy," who is the object of Lysias's speech as well. Someone must draw out our words; both Socrates and Phaedrus coyly require the other to talk them into delivering their speeches (speeches they clearly want to make), and Socrates' second speech seems to be demanded by the divine inner voice—with a little help from Phaedrus, to whom Socrates declares, "I'm sure you've brought into being more of the speeches that have been given during your lifetime than anyone else, whether you composed them yourself or in one way or another forced others to make them. . . . Even as we speak, I think, you're managing to cause me to produce yet another one" (242a–b). Speaking is drawn out of us not only by the urgency of what we have to say but by the urgency of some other's need to hear.[25] Even though the boy evoked in the second speech is fictitious, or at any rate absent, the need to address the speech to him remains strong.

This does not, to be sure, render his absence irrelevant; that Socrates is speaking to no one present may be one of this impious speech's flaws. The address of the absent, in fact, turns out to be one of the most important problems Socrates has with writing, as opposed to speaking: because writing is indiscriminate in its dissemination, it cannot address itself with adequate precision and so may be read by someone who has no need to "hear" it, who won't benefit by it, who maybe won't even understand it properly. Speaking, on the other hand, can adapt itself to the one to whom it is directed, thus maximally benefiting its hearer.[26]

Another of writing's flaws, according to Socrates, is the way in which it substitutes for memory. The working of erotic madness on memory is a kind of duplication or bringing back again rather than simply a reminder that something once was, but writing is mere reminder. In yet another myth, in which the Egyptian god Theuth presents the art of writing to King Thamos, Socrates has Thamos declare, "You have not discovered a potion for remembering, but for reminding; you provide your students with the appearance of wisdom, not with its reality" (275a–75b).

Like most who write, I am inclined not to concur with Socrates' devaluation of most writing—and we must suspect that Plato, always a writer, was a bit suspicious of it himself. (Socrates, famously, only speaks, though he is probably able to read.) Further, hints in the text do link memory to writing: for instance, Phaedrus reminds Socrates that speakers may avoid writing precisely to avoid memory, "you are surely aware yourself that the most powerful and renowned politicians are ashamed to compose speeches or leave any writings behind; they are afraid that in later times they may come to be known as 'sophists'"(257d). We have already seen that Socrates, speaking, seems to forget rather a lot—himself, since he gets Phaedrus wrong in thinking him a speaker from memory and not a reader from the page, the sources of his first speech, the content of his second. In another work, he claims, "I'm a forgetful sort of man ... and if someone speaks at length, I lose the thread of the argument."[27] To trust in speech rather than in writing, then, seems no improvement to memory. The sole exception would be the memorized speech—but such a speech would share the fault of being inadaptable to its audience.

Writing, like speaking, may well be drawn out by the urgency of its own message, or by the desire of another to hear, but it may also be seduced into being by its own medium, by the demand of words to be set down. Because words don't exist in abstraction, but in communication, this too is the demand of address, its specificity no longer that of persons but of communities (those bound by the reading of a common language). Here too, writing gathers and breaks apart, performs collection—whether under definition or under memory—and fragments. Once more, to question is to enter into questioning, not because we forget the answers but because we are drawn by further memory.

19

THE ONE AND THE MANY

We are drawn into relation. The One to the Many, the whole to the fragmentary, the single to the multiple, and the slipping to the staying are relations of priority but also (less expectedly) of time, a temporality complicated by memory. Plato's sense of the soul's immortality does not, as it might at first seem, imply a first learning; rather, it ties learning and forgetting into a constantly breaking circle, just as the souls in the *Phaedrus* circle Beauty, break away, fall, and rise. In "Plato's Forgetting," Petar Ramadanovic notes, "The learning and relearning are not successive events (even the linearity of experience is contested by true knowing). So, true knowledge demands another move of thought beyond possession and presence: a tying down in and by memory whose hold holds without authority, as we see in the many examples of Socrates' failure to recall the source to which a truth belongs."[28] This circle fragmented by paradoxes of repetition and forgetfulness is surprisingly near to that of the Nietzschean return as both Pierre Klossowski and Maurice Blanchot read it,[29] a connection that will be further discussed below. It is also essential to the theories of emanation at the heart of the school of Platonic interpretation that will be labeled Neoplatonism.

From a Sort of Neoplatonism . . .

> What if *beginning*—this beginning, any beginning, The Beginning—does not lie back, like an origin, but rather opens out?
> —Catherine Keller, *Face of the Deep*

> Thus the One fails divinely to come about, but passes and becomes as it passes, remembering itself but exceeding itself anew, coming to pass and brimming over in remembrance itself.
> —Jean-Luc Nancy, "Hyperion's Joy"

Neoplatonic thought offers us some of the most intriguing "solutions" to the problem of the one and the many, solutions that do not so much resolve the problem as productively alter its terms, with memory playing a vital role. (In fact, a large part of the appeal of Neoplatonism is the poetry of its ontology, and its quite poetic insusceptibility to problem solving.) I must emphasize that, as with Plato, I shall not begin to do justice to this thought here: Neoplatonic systems tend to be gorgeously complex, even baroque, impressively difficult, and frequently, often deliberately, elusive. I want only to indicate a few crucial ideas that will point in turn toward some productive complications in the intersections

THE ONE AND THE MANY

of memory and forgetting, fragments and wholes, complications that resonate with the work of later theorists.

Neoplatonism, despite the variety of its forms, might be read as a monism as pronounced as Parmenides'. In Plotinus's version, at the center of everything (analogically and possibly ontologically, rather than spatially or materially) is The One, the source of all, which is yet not itself an entity.[30] Struggling with definition in *Ennead* 6.9 ("Of the Good, or the One") he writes:

> What then must The Unity be, what nature is left for it?
> No wonder that to state it is not easy. . . . Generative of all, The Unity is none of all; neither thing nor quantity nor quality nor intellect nor soul; not in motion, not at rest, not in place, not in time: it is the self-defined, unique in form or, better, formless, existing before Form was, or Movement or Rest, all of which are attachments of Being and make Being the manifold it is.[31]

And later, "We must therefore take the Unity as infinite not in measureless extension or numerable quantity but in fathomless depths of power."[32]

The causality by which this source creates is difficult to conceptualize, lending itself better to metaphor than to direct predication. Arthur Hyman writes, "Dissatisfied with a cosmogony that explains the origin of the world on the analogy of the production of an artifact by a craftsman, Plotinus formulated the theory of emanation: The world proceeds from an ultimate principle, the One or the Good, like streams of water from a spring or like sunlight from the sun, like heat from fire, like cold from snow, or like perfume from something scented."[33]

The One, Plotinus insists, properly eludes all predication, since to predicate anything of it is to leave something (that predicate's opposite) out of it, and The One excludes nothing. After all, exclusion, making an inside and an outside, a same and a different, must minimally be numbered two. Yet Plotinus, if not *exactly* predicating of The One, does nonetheless attribute goodness to it, and joy—so much goodness and joy, in fact, that The One cannot remain in its perfect self-containment and overflows itself into multiplicity—first, into "intellect." As Margaret Miles summarizes:

> The One emanates its undifferentiated rays to intellect effortlessly, spontaneously, and without diminishment. In intellect, thought as

well as the forms of everything that exists originate. Far from being a realm of abstraction, intellect 'reduces'—as a cook reduces a sauce to its most potent flavors—the powerful but undefined energy of the One, using it to make the world we see and experience. . . .

[The One] does not love as an act of intention, since it has no activity of any kind. But there is a sense in which the One *is* love: It is pure gift, supplying to every living being its own particular life, intelligence, and beauty.[34]

From there, "Intellect, in turn, beams its myriad forms to the common soul of all living creatures. At the level of soul, a further differentiation occurs; soul transforms the forms it receives from intellect into bodies. Bodies are created and supported in life by the One's continuous creative power circulating through the universe."[35]

The reasons for this emanation are not rationally clear, though they seem affectively sound; the overflow of joy and joyful desire is unfamiliar to very few of us. In addition, however, "Invoking what has been called 'the Principle of Plenitude' and what might be called 'the dynamism of existence,' Plotinus holds that whatever is perfect produces something other than itself."[36] Thus the perfection of unity is the source of multiplicity: a One not flowing into Many would be less perfectly One. The dependence of multiplicity on unity may be mirrored by that of unity on manyness.

Depending upon emphasis and focus, readings of Neoplatonism may take two distinct directions, possibilities we also find in Plato (coming especially out of the *Phaedrus* and the *Symposium*). The first, formative of most impressions of Neoplatonism (like Platonism, this thought too has its simplified "received" form), emphasizes the distance between Reality and Goodness, on the one hand, and materiality, on the other. Still acknowledging the ultimate goodness of the source, this line of thought nonetheless focuses negatively on materiality, particularly human corporeality and material temptations to it, and insists upon a turn against, or at least away from, the flesh in the search for the highest good, which lies in the opposite direction from materiality. The second, which I admit to finding far more appealing, emphasizes the element of this source—divinity, often as not—in even the "lowest" materiality. Potentially, all of creation is a path to the divine; or more surprisingly still, all of creation is divine already. To foreshadow some of the following chapters, I think that this second perspective may in some ways be a better fit for the myths of Christianity, with its incarnational and decidedly corporeal foundations, than the antimaterial, antisomatic strain that has historically dominated so much of Christian tradition, even (or perhaps especially) in its Neoplatonic versions. Of course, as Miles points out, body is not a particularly strong obsession, positively or negatively, for Plotinus; the Neoplatonically influenced traditions that come to be called Gnostic are more negatively focused on the body, while Christianity, at least in its other early versions, is more positively so.[37] In fact, neither Neoplatonism nor Christianity is as hostile to the body as most of us have tended to assume. (It does remain somewhat less usual to suggest that there may be eternity to corporeality, by, as I would do here, reading the corporeal not as dead matter but as flesh already in complex relation with word.[38])

It is true that Plotinus understands true knowing and true happiness in abstraction from the body.[39] To know the best life is to withdraw from the distractions of fragmentation into a kind of remembering—a remembering of the state "prior" to dismemberment or separation, which must also be prior to selfhood, since unity erases the self's individuality. It is thus also an active forgetting of all that one is, or knows. Thus we *return* in a reverse flow—or in the same circle—toward the always joyfully overflowing, always seductively drawing One from which we "first" flowed out. For Plotinus, "Soul has two different kinds of memories, those which reach soul through body and those occurring within the soul. . . . Soul is defined by its memories: it 'is and becomes what it remembers'" (4.4.3).[40]

That remembering and forgetting turn out to be so close here is less surprising if we recognize the peculiar temporality of emanation. The One itself does not participate in temporality; it does not endure, but is (without being) eternally. It "is" less as an eternal *thing* than as, perhaps, the perspective of eternity. Thus emanation and return are described in time, by temporal creatures, as successive processes. But time too is a mode of differentiation, of before and after; in the eternal, remembering and forgetting likewise *are*. The whole is already broken, and the fragmentary regathered.

Like Parmenides, Plotinus suggests a shift in perspective rather than an alternate reality; what is from the perspective of time the flow of emanation from and return to the One is from the perspective of eternity all in the circle of the divine. What's more, the "knowledge" or "experience" of this eternity, terms made problematic by the absence of the individuated knowing subject, can break into time[41]—sometimes, as I shall argue here, as flesh.

We tend to conceive eternity as static or staying, and this unchangingness is central to the canonical Platonic sensibility and thus to

Christianity as it develops under a strong Platonic influence. But Neoplatonism, including its Christian variants, offers us another option, a vibrantly living eternity as the fullness of life or (to be Aristotelian) flourishing.[42] And this eternity is not whole, or not simply whole; not the all at once but the outside of every time, which is just as much found enfolded within time's slippery moments. As C. Lee Miller notes, in Neoplatonic thought traditionally, "Eternity stands as the intensification or enfolding of the order or *ratio* or intelligibility that unfolds in time, and this means that God's presence touches temporal duration in such a way that the latter is never eternity, but neither is it nothing but time."[43] This intersection is the space of collection and recollection, of Neoplatonic memory (in the mode that so fascinates Augustine), but also the no-space pinpoint break in time, the disruptive, the fragmenting.[44] Having "known" it, we cannot put time back into the fixity of its line; we know other possibilities; we have lived revelation and seen the meaning of time transformed. We return to ourselves with a knowledge for which there is no proper place (not in our memories, not in our words), and so all of our knowing is perpetually unsettled. But more, we are both ourselves, always, and beside ourselves, ecstatic, in this unsettledness.

Multiplicity, the overflow but also the fragmentation of unity, is as near as we come to a sense of "origin"—the origin as fragmentation, a fragmentation into multiplicity that is the perfection of unity. For human beings, origin is in the loss of unity—a point that Plotinus does not make and might not like but that is implicit in the distinction between oneness and the multiplicity of individual selfhood. For Plotinus, the best and happiest of human being is in the recollection of fragmentation into this unity, but this recollection is also the forgetful loss of humanity. The sense of the eternal further undoes questions of priority; the emanation is the return is remembrance is forgetting; the One is and is not the many. The combination of joy and desire overflows, withdraws, and draws in. In the tractate "On Beauty," Plotinus writes (with the *Phaedrus* clearly in the background):

> Therefore we must ascend again toward the Good, the desired of every Soul. Anyone that has seen This, knows what I intend when I say that it is beautiful. Even the desire of it is to be desired as a Good.
>
> And one that shall know this vision—with what passion of love shall he not be seized, with what pang of desire, what longing to be molten into one with This, what wondering delight! If he that

THE ONE AND THE MANY

has never seen this Being must hunger for It as for all his welfare, he that has known must love and reverence It as the very Beauty; he will be flooded with awe and gladness, stricken by a salutary terror; he loves with a veritable love, with sharp desire; all other loves than this he must despise, and disdain all that once seemed fair.[45]

The forgetfulness of time and the memory of the eternal are not exclusive but co-occurrent truths.[46]

With repetition, as the very thought of eternal recurrence suggests, comes fragmentation, the opening up of the answer into new questions. All possibilities, all recurrences, are at once present and absent in the brokenness of these recyclings. My stories and images gathered here are not simply of memory but conspicuously of repetition. In each, some "first" is repeated: a first sin (in the chapter on original sin), a first promise (in the chapters on forgiveness and on love), a first life (in the chapters on relics and on resurrection)—but in each the repetition troubles our reading of the first, including our reading of it *as* the first.

Recurrence extends to the sense of our selves. Constantly rebroken, forgotten, regathered (since memory is never once and forever), we are never the same selves twice, never even quite stable in our boundaries. We retain a longing for unity, oneness, for the attained ascent of Diotima's ladder.[47] But all we ever get is the pleasure and ache of the approach; philosophy is not the attainment but the love of wisdom, the desire for more of it.[48] When eternity breaks through, it breaks with the order of time and the possibility of speaking—that is, the closest we get to unity or to the "wholeness" of eternity is further fragmentation. Something always breaks, is broken, whether it breaks away from the eternal or from time itself.

Here, as Ramadanovic has it of the *Phaedrus*, "mneme and anamnesis do not (only) mark the presence of the past . . . as memory does in Aristotle, but (also) an irreducible alterity that evades, escapes, and undermines presence. The question of forgetting . . . is, then, one of the pastness of a past that was never present as such, and is only through a recalling of what has never been in the senses or in the mind. At the same time, this is also a question of a certain faithfulness of memory."[49] *Faithfulness*, like faith, is not simply a presentation of statements as factually true but a complex reach through to the other side of presence. If the addressee of writing is not so literally present as that of speaking,[50]

THE ONE AND THE MANY

we may still write with a kind of faith—in our readers, in the need for hearing, or simply in our words.

Memory is not simply my own; it needs inter-locution, speaking with, in order to be re-called. It needs, that is, to be open to the outside. As Derrida notes, "more than one, it is always necessary to be more than one in order to speak, several voices are necessary for that . . .—Yes, granted, and par excellence, let us say exemplarily, when it's a matter of God."[51] Memory's faithfulness becomes crucial for us. We generally think of memory as something like the present-ation or making-present of the past. And yet, because I cannot own memory (and so it cannot be in a simple way my own), there remains (or there always fails to remain, to stay) that which always eludes the present, goes ungathered, and thus evades the gathering up of the universal. The process of collection and division is not finally, or finitely, completeable; philosophy never coheres into a system without aporia. There is always, already, the forgotten, something that tugs at memory as having come before us, before those of us who remember.

Mutually implicated with memory, forgetting too is constructive. As Marita Sturken writes, "Forgetting is not a threat to subjectivity but rather a highly constitutive element of identity; indeed it is a primary means through which subjectivity is shaped and produced."[52] There is here a certain resemblance to Nietzsche's notion of "active forgetting," which is perhaps more of a selective remembering and releasing, a retelling of one's own stories (choosing from among the multiple narratives of history) to elide or neglect those elements most inimical to flourishing.[53] As we continue to be, we go on forgetting.

In the canonical, excessively stable version of Platonism, active forgetfulness, which opens the future by unchaining it from the past, makes no sense; there is one narrative of Truth. But Plato himself is subtle enough to forget. Multiplicity and singularity are mutually implicated both for Plato and for his Neoplatonic interpreters, and the "truth" of memory always "only" remembered—and thus always primally forgotten, because to remember (rather than to know, or perceive) must be to recall after an absence, however brief.[54] The fragments of human knowledge are always imperfectly sutured across us as we speak together, until we are lost in a space beyond our own beginnings. Knowledge recollected isn't identical with knowledge simply possessed; it is lost and then refound. Plotinus writes of those who see the Good, or the One, or God: "they see God still and always, and that, as long as they see, they cannot tell themselves they have had the vision; such reminiscence is for souls that have lost it."[55]

THE ONE AND THE MANY

Through Fragments of Saying . . .

> Words strain, crack and sometimes break . . .
> —T. S. Eliot, "Burnt Norton"

Loss implies incompleteness, partiality, fragmentation. Incompletion is always different, always other than the whole that it must presume without being in too simple an opposition to it.

The *Phaedrus* tells us that speaking gathers together in an act of recollection: "But a soul that never saw the truth cannot take human shape, since a human being must understand speech in terms of general forms, proceeding to bring many perceptions together into a reasoned unity. That process is the recollection of the things our soul saw when it was traveling with god" (249b–c). Recollection is fundamental to the collective generalization that is language; in words, we gather. Meaning, then, is here acquired by the gathering of multiple perceptions into a unity of form—but this unity is relational, impermanent, and incomplete.

Language, as this sense of generalization already tells us, is itself a means of collection. There are so many *things*, and—as if unavoidably—we cluster them. We say of many that they are not quite the *same thing* (then they could not be many) but the same *kind of* thing: men, or fruit-bearing plants, or cups of coffee. But how legitimate is this clustering, and how do we *know*—how does an encounter with a cup of coffee so readily and necessarily subsume itself into a more general appreciation for coffeeness as such? Do we know because we recognize a reality of participation, or because we conveniently cluster by ontologically insignificant resemblance? How does a language that functions, as it must, by differentiation also function, as it must, by alliance? How do we speak of things—what are we remembering about coffee, and what are we neglecting to recall (or actively forgetting) when we give to one cup of coffee the same designation as another? While I will not attempt a full answer to these questions of language, I do want to hold to the insight that we must, even to speak, be engaged in the double play between many and one, and between forgetting and memory. Our thinking, our sense of self, and our knowledge of the world are structured by these tensions.

And so too, especially in the monotheistic faiths with their emphasis on word and on text, is our theology. As Louis Mackey notes of Augustinian (and thus also Neoplatonic) Christianity, "The distance between the single eternal divine Word and the fragmentary and transient words of men puts their relationship beyond conception: merely to name the relation iterates their difference and indefinitely defers their reunion."[56]

THE ONE AND THE MANY

Whom do I address when I address my god—particularly when this address explicitly invokes not only a presence but an absence (as it does in the Eucharist)? Still recognizing the power of words to collect (or the recollective power of naming), Augustine (famous, like Socrates, for denigrating rhetoric with rhetorical brilliance) begins also to see the fragmentation of language, the loss and slip inherent in the very words that gather.

What gathers together—whether ontologically, verbally, or a bit of both—must gather into a present—but something always eludes the present, eludes presence. *Memory* plays here a role not unlike that of the form in its *gathering* or unitive function, but it is complicated by its presumption of a necessary prior forgetting.[57] (Again, we do not remember what is constantly present, but only what has, however briefly or intermittently or recently, vanished; more, we know that some element, even if it is only some interpretation or story, is always excluded by any recalling or retelling.) Memory's unitive function makes fragmentation phenomenologically vivid—its gathering and unifying always remind us at the same time of the elusively ungatherable, both of what is lost and of what is transformed by remembering. If we take seriously the notion of prior fragmentation and forgetfulness, not merely conceptually, but as a way of troubling ontology, too, then the problem of the one and the many itself shatters (reappearing as a multiplicity of fragments, as many different questions). It shatters, but it doesn't go away: there is something vital about gathering, too, something coeternal (not infinitely enduring, but caught in that same infinite/simultaneous circling) in memory and forgetfulness. Memory gathers, but it also multiplies; making again, raising again, summoning again the lost and recalled moment. Remembrance, of course, is not identical with loss, nor the remembered with the lost. But I (along with many of those I cite in this text) have long suspected that what memory gathers is not the broken bits of a prior whole but an always-prior brokenness. The gathering is all we have; if writing only reminds, it is because it gathers together in mind, in memory, as a re-collection.

Into a Fleeting Sort of Present

> Then's now with now's then in tense continuant.
> —James Joyce, *Finnegans Wake*

In fragmenting, in repetition, the One becomes many, which is also to say from outside time that it *is* many—but to say the One is many implies no sameness, no identically retained, reiterated form. Only the always-already of difference—even repetition demands distinction between one recurrent element and the previous or the next—and of the scattered, not only broken but fallen away from itself (this notion too, as I've indicated, is implicit in some readings of Nietzsche's eternal recurrence, particularly Klossowski's).[58] A casual reading of eternal recurrence suggests simply that we are caught in a loop; due to the infinite extension of time and the conserved finitude of matter, all formations and all sequences of formation must eventually happen again. Nietzsche's ethical reading is a complication; he argues that we should live so that the repetition of our lives exactly as they are is a joy we can affirm, instead of a burden by which we are crushed. Klossowski, however, elegantly points out an important and deeper complication here. The affirmation of the eternal return must be all-encompassing; as Nietzsche notes, one does not have the ethical option of affirming a partial return, or getting only the good bits back.[59] For Nietzsche, this must change one's approach, and one's response, to one's life: one ought to live so as to be able to say *yes* to living this life, even in the face of its pains. But Klossowski further points out that this yes saying must affirm the return not only of *this* sequence but of the incredible multiplicity of other possible sequences that split off from every moment. That is, to affirm a moment so intensely that one affirms the eternal recurrence of a lifetime is not only to affirm all of a given sequence (this life) but the "whole" of the eternal return, meaning every possible sequence, including those that resemble(d) this life up to this point but then diverge(d). It is to affirm an eternal splitting of one's life, one's self; to affirm the impossibility of affirming by making possible the absence of the affirming self. In common with other French Nietzscheans, especially Deleuze, Klossowski reads repetition as something quite other than more of the same. An eternity of repetition is the shattering of time.

The difference between such notions and what Neoplatonism, perhaps more optimistically, offers us is this: to the flow of emanation and return is added the complication of Nietzsche, of the origin as absence and falling away; and the absence of the origin too, the complication in the flowing back. The *durchbrechen* (literally "breaking through"), with which Christian Neoplatonist Meister Eckhart names the return, is also a sense of the eternal recurrence, the already-multiplicity of shattering and breaking away—of divinity fragmented throughout the creation from which it is never wholly separate, while never being wholly present therein. As Blanchot notes, the I who returns in Nietzschean recurrence is never quite oneself: "the exigency of return, *excluding from time any present mode*, will never free up a now in which the same would amount to the same, to the selfsame in myself."[60] It is not only the obviously other voices that multiply collect "my" memory, but even those I might consider my own. Thus altering sharply our experience of the full present and the univocal past, this shattered return must transform the future, too. Blanchot writes:

> For there is *the future*, the one within the ring [the circle of recurrence] that offers itself to repetition as a temporal instance, and there is *the future* itself of "Everything returns"—the to-come now carried to the greatest power of lack; that to which, in its uncertain non-coming, we who are not in it, being henceforth deprived of ourselves, as of all present possibility, say: welcome to the future that does not come, that neither begins nor ends and whose uncertainty breaks history. But how do we think this rupture? Through forgetting. Forgetting frees the future from time itself.[61]

The transformations of time by memory and forgetting, by breakage and recollection, are crucial to the analyses that follow. Forgetfulness that frees the future must, I shall argue, be connected to remembering; we must both remember and forget, not so much selectively as mutually. We must think not only the rupture of time but the mending, the redemption, of the fracturing quality of time itself. We must gather fragments but also recognize the divinity that impels their fragmentation. My own efforts to think this, obviously enough, take the form of writing. To cite Blanchot one last time in this introduction, we may note (granting that the full complexity of the *Phaedrus* may not be represented here):

> the huge divide that opens up . . . between Plato and Moses: for one, writing, which is external and alien, is bad because it makes up for the loss of memory and thus encourages the failings of living memory. . . . For Moses, writing assuredly guarantees memorization, but it is also (or primarily) the "doing," the "acting," the exteriority which precedes interiority or will institute it—in the same way that Deuteronomy, in which Moses begins the whole story over again in the first person, redoubles and prolongs the difficult Exodus.[62]

In the chapters that follow, I take up stories, and tell them as true, tell them for the truth that myths have in them. Multiplicity and temporal

THE ONE AND THE MANY

stretch belong to stories, stories we tell ourselves and struggle to tell (perhaps in writing), stories started over in a different person, imperfectly repeated with bits of them lost, to memory, to forgetting—forgetting that fragments but forgets fragmentation too, giving us the optimism to remember, to gather together again, to shore up against infinite loss the promise of another recurrence.

2

THE SIN OF ORIGIN

57. What has happened to us on account of the sin of Adam? On account of the sin of Adam, we, his descendants, come into the world deprived of sanctifying grace and inherit his punishment, as we would have inherited his gifts had he been obedient to God. *But, by the envy of the devil, death came into the world. (Wisdom 2:24)*
58. What is this sin in us called? This sin in us is called original.
—*A Catechism of Christian Doctrine*, Revised Edition of the Baltimore Catechism, Part 1, Lesson 5

The Persistence of Separation

[N]o one is responsible for an emergence; no one can glory in it, since it always occurs in the interstice.
—Michel Foucault, "Nietzsche, Genealogy, History"

Glossing what he calls the "strange and wondrous" Leibnizian theory of damnation, Gilles Deleuze writes in *The Fold*, "the damned, Judas or Beelzebub, does not pay retribution for a past action but for the hate of God that constitutes the present amplitude of his soul and fills it in the present. He is not damned *for* a past action, but *by* a present action that he renews at every moment."[1] Such damnation, then, partakes not only of an unexpected agency—one can only damn oneself, and that by an insistent (hateful) relational mode—but also of a peculiar temporality. It consists not of a singular event and subsequent reiteration of response (an indefinite continuation of punishment), but of a single moment amplified to an ever-renewed present, eternity as the staying now, the persistent-recurrent accomplishment of an act of fury and hatred. It is thus a direct contrast to vibrantly living eternity and so to

THE SIN OF ORIGIN

the (more positive) images of eternal life.[2] Eternal damnation partakes of a deeply strange temporality, in which the moment is infinite, too, all of time "gathered" into an instant or the instant exploded into all of time: "For eternity must not be thought as those moments of time taken together, but rather as coexisting with each single moment so that eternity again sees only its (whole, immeasurable) self in each single one."[3] So too, I will argue, does "original" sin.

Most commonly, if we think of it at all, we think of damnation as a judgment, the working out of divine justice and thus in every case the rightful penalty for wrongful behavior (though perhaps, at the same time, this must read as a failure in divine mercy). Unlike grace, in many respects its contrary counterpart, damnation is presumed to follow the law—unless we believe in complete predestination, which is easier to render logically coherent than is a theory holding together free will and divine power, but affectively and phenomenologically remains a lot less satisfying. (In fact, under predestination a divine law is still followed, but its preestablishment makes it difficult for human beings to understand its workings: they are either too obscured or incomprehensibly simple.) Dogmatically, damnation occurs when a mortally sinful moment is not regretted in time to prevent a divine judgment of guilt requiring punishment.[4] (This is the point of frequent sacramental penance and reconciliation: to lessen the odds of dying with unshriven sins on one's soul by doing the necessary penance as promptly as possible. Of course, the next chapter will complicate this notion just a bit.) So, on this view, damnation is simply a legalistic penalty, something impersonal.

It's clear that the Leibnizian theory (as Deleuze reads it) is different from this relatively simple relation of cause and effect, different in ways that seem to me to render it more philosophically and theologically coherent than a straightforward reading of the dogmatic version. Leibniz's is not the withdrawal of the divine love for the human, nor even divine refusal to express that love by rescuing a given human person from damnation. Rather, it is the *infinitely renewed* human refusal of love for the divine, either a destruction or a perverse misdirection of the full force of the desire and the joy that we might turn toward divinity. (Indeed, by making of hate a focus that consumes the attention entirely, it is a refusal to love or delight in any aspect of what is.) Thus, there is nothing impersonal about it, nor anything like the necessity imposed by law; it is a wholly personal grudge held by the damned. It is likewise a refusal of reciprocal divine desire. Its time is that of repetition; if it has a first moment, a "decision" to hate or an onset of hatred, that moment seems

33

THE SIN OF ORIGIN

very nearly irrelevant, certainly nothing in proportion to the act of the infinite present. (It shares this repetitive temporality, as I shall note in the next chapter, with trauma.) Leibnizian damnation is the in(de)finite repetition of some "original" sin, but that origin is here either missing or, at a minimum, almost irrelevant, impossibly disproportionate to the stubborn continuation of hate.

But what about that missing original? Here, it seems, we have already forgotten. And perhaps that is exactly it: forgetfulness itself, or rather a particular kind of forgetfulness, is that primal privation, a falling away that makes it possible (though not necessary) for us to cling to the memory of hate instead. More commonly, it keeps us from the full memory of love or of joy. While damnation refuses to let go, original sin seems unable to hold on; it is a reiterated movement of forgetting and falling away. Its repetition lies in forgetfulness itself; to "escape" it demands a turn in attention, a different distractedness. In original sin, we lose the capacity for dwelling in the eternity of the present proper to time—for the affirmation of the present that might say *yes* to eternity. So, like Deleuze's Leibniz, I want to look at sinfulness, but in this case the "original" version, as a matter of attention and desire, a turn in their direction, a kind of relation.

Definitionally, as I shall explain in more detail below, we cannot get out of or beyond original sin, but I want to look at what it might mean to get before or behind it, which will also mean getting before or behind our selves even as we remain those selves, the "we," who cannot evade it. This is a complicated move, an ecstasy in which we are at once outside ourselves and yet remain ourselves. Pseudo-Dionysius the Aeropagite attributes this kind of duality even to God:

> And we must dare to affirm . . . that the Creator of the Universe Himself, in His Beautiful and Good Yearning towards the Universe, is through the excessive yearning of His Goodness, transported outside of Himself in His providential activities towards all things that have being, and is touched by the sweet spell of Goodness, Love and Yearning, and so is drawn from His transcendent throne above all things, to dwell within the heart of all things, through a super-essential and ecstatic power whereby He yet stays within Himself.[5]

This loss of self and of time is not the destruction of either, but rather their radical transfiguration.

THE SIN OF ORIGIN

To make sense of such a reading, I would begin before the beginning, in the notion of origin as we saw it in the last chapter, the start as schism, creation as an overflow, with individuation an act of separation. Meister Eckhart says of this preorigin that "I was what I wanted and wanted what I was,"[6] a state altered only in my own willful going out from divinity, when desire and fulfillment are separated, in the separation of I and God that gives identity to each.

Original sin is arguably an "original" breaking away. Here the human will splits from the divine; the consequent fall into finitude is echoed in other persistent separations. Original sin is generally understood as the human heritage of the sin of Adam and Eve described in the third book of Genesis, in which the couple give in to the urgings of the serpent, eat of the tree of knowledge though God has forbidden them to do so, and are consequently condemned to labor and to mortality.[7] As the doctrine develops, the persistent trace of original sin is supposed to be manifest in the tendency to sin actively or individually; that is, it shows up as the *disposition* to sin (a tendency Augustine labels *concupiscence*, a term sometimes used with a more narrowly lustful connotation).

This splitting away of human from divine in the loss of Paradise is instigated by a turning away of the desire once divinely directed. We are told in the *Catechism* that the original sin is one of turning the will toward selfhood, the preference for one's own self over God:

> In that sin man *preferred* himself to God and by that very act scorned him. He chose himself over and against God, against the requirements of his creaturely status and therefore against his own good. Constituted in a state of holiness, man was destined to be fully "divinized" by God in glory. Seduced by the devil, he wanted to "be like God," but "without God, before God, and not in accordance with God."[8]

The preference here is not for one entity (self) over another (God). Rather, to turn desire away from God is to lose not (or not only) some external divinity, but (also) what is sacred in oneself, one's own (at least potential) divinization. This is an idea traceable back at least to Plotinus: "God—we read—is outside of none, present unperceived to all; we break away from Him, or rather from ourselves; what we turn from we cannot reach; astray ourselves, we cannot go in search of another; a child distraught will not recognize its father; to find ourselves is to know our source."[9] This image of division is also an image of finitude, of parts and fragments turned away from the infinite—with finitude itself, or mortality, as the consequence. In this distraction of desire, we are divided from our proper infinite-finitude: "It is only inasmuch as I am infinite that I am limited,"[10] declares Blanchot. Original sin is the fall (or perhaps more exactly, the turn) into only finitude, a loss of awareness and experience in the loss of attention and desire for and of the infinite, for eternity.

In the highly influential Augustinian understanding, original sin is an inheritance that is also a deprivation—postlapsarian humanity is deprived of immortality and of goodness understood as the ability not to sin. What is inherited is the consequence of a primal disobedience, Adam and Eve's consumption of the fruit of the tree of knowledge, which God has forbidden them to have. Immediately after this consumption, they feel shame, a dissociation from their own bodies—and they also note a novel disturbance in their disobedient flesh, as a punishment that answers to their own disobedience.[11] (That is, the punishment for disobedience is further disobedience, the instant multiplied and amplified.) Disobedience multiplies as the will divides; I cannot get my flesh to obey me (think of how often we will our bodies to do what they somehow cannot, even beyond the stirrings of involuntary arousal that worry Augustine);[12] I cannot even get my own *will* to obey me,[13] and I cannot get that will to reharmonize perfectly with God, such that to obey God would be to do as I will. Our wills multiply spilt, we are disharmonious with ourselves, and so we cannot quite be happy, let alone good.

Though only "actual" or individual (not original) sin is usually regarded as a perversity of will—because it, unlike original sin, entails the will's power of decision making[14]—the nature of original sin suggests that we might see willfulness at work even here, in this seemingly unwilled state of finitude. As original sin is often interpreted as the tendency to sin individually, so too might this original turn be the tendency to will individually, closed off from what might complicate and alter the will in its presumption of autonomy. (Thus, too, the refusal of human relationality, the unshakeable self-centeredness of which the next chapter will make much more, might be seen as a variant, or a trace, of original sin.)

Thus, original sin rather obviously fails to fit into the usual relation of fault and forgiveness. Technically, it is "forgiven" at baptism (also, not irrelevantly, a joining of the child to the community of the church, an entry into a new mode of relation and connection).[15] But the notion of lingering concupiscence essential to its definition suggests that this forgiveness (whatever it may mean) is neither the sin's "removal" nor the end of the matter. Even the most doctrinally dogmatic admit that original

THE SIN OF ORIGIN

sin is elusive of definition: it is not, but it somehow entails, mortality, concupiscence, and the absence of inborn sanctifying grace.[16] It is sin without the voluntary, deliberate element essential to every other definition of sin—though I shall suggest that it is related to this element in its alteration of the very means of volition, the will. It is supposed to be inherited from Adam, but by somewhat uncertain means; it is interpreted in Catholicism as a stain upon the soul, by Orthodox Christianity as an absence within it. (Other versions of Christianity tend to give the notion less emphasis, though they may also insist upon a fallenness or corruption of humanity.) Out of this complexity I would make a fairly simple suggestion: original sin metaphorizes not an action but a distraction and the loss that comes with it; it is "overcome" or met by an entanglement of memory and of forgetting, a turning from small distractions to the full divine force of desire, strong enough to open selves and times.

The tale told in the third chapter of Genesis is not self-evidently a story of transmissible sin. The idea that Adam not only lost for humanity the possible inheritance of a lovely home but also passed on the sinfulness of that "first disobedience" is drawn more directly from Paul, who declares in his letter to the Romans, "through one person sin entered the world, and through sin, death, and thus death came to all, inasmuch as all sinned" (5:12).[17] Thus he clearly connects death to the emergence of sin, and specifically to an original sin as performed by one person and inherited by all subsequent persons. Later in this chapter he declares that this sin does not die with Adam: "through the disobedience of one person the many were made sinners" (5:19).[18] Evidently it is not only good that overflows to the many from one.

The nature of our participation in this sin of Adam, the heritage of disobedience, which is also a distraction from the eternity "proper" to time, is a trifle vague. Setting down the official form of the doctrine, the Council of Trent in the mid sixteenth century declared that "sin is transmitted to all by generation [*propagatione*], not by imitation."[19] It is, in other words, what we *are*, and not what we do. The *Catholic Encyclopedia* follows both the Council of Trent and the work of Thomas Aquinas here: "It is true that, considered as 'a moral deformity,' 'a separation from God,' as 'the death of the soul,' original sin is a real sin which deprives the soul of sanctifying grace."[20]

What's more, as Augustine emphasizes, it is as a counterpart to grace, indeed, as that which necessitates grace, that original sin maintains its place in Catholic orthodoxy—without original sin, we need no grace, only discipline (to refrain from active sin)—indeed, we need only *self-discipline*, which grants us an independence from God that could be

THE SIN OF ORIGIN

dogmatically troubling, as it leaves our sinfulness or sinlessness altogether up to us.[21] Augustine points out that a doctrine of original sin is required if the sacrament of infant baptism is to make any sense—"And therefore the new birth would not have been appointed only that the first birth was sinful."[22] The doctrine and the sacrament are bound up together, and both together with a concept of grace as an unmerited redemption of temporal creatures. Thus too original sin, even if understood as coming under the law, keeps law from being comprehensive. There is no set of penal acts to perform that suffices for redemption, not because the sin is so immense but because it is outside the economy of law—an economy of order without openness, without room for grace.

The relation to memory is perhaps subtle. Original sin is dogmatically supposed to be ineluctable, as being inborn. It is thus older, or simply other, than our "individual" memories. But I do want to suggest that a kind of memory, awakened in desire and joy, might also be read as the almost-memory of that ante-origin; in some odd way, the "memory" of the prelapsarian state *is* the return to that state, as forgetfulness is/was its loss. More exactly, because to "remember" that state is to remember before the origin of selfhood, in the forgetting of self is the memory that returns us before ourselves. For us, original sin would then be unavoidable and insurmountable after all; but memory, especially memory awakened in desire, suggests to us that there is more to us than ourselves. Original sin is a fragmentation caught up in a distraction both of and from desire. But this is not a simple before and after; these complexities of memory are mutually implicated, caught up in the folds of one another.

This will necessarily alter the sense of guilt and its attachment to original sin. If the original sin is the split into finitude, the split of the ante-original "God" and "I," then the guilt of the "I" is simply that of solitude, at once my own and God's. Jean-Luc Nancy links finitude to separation, but notes too that our sense of solitude requires something more:

> Finite identity is not that of the separate individual. On the contrary, it is trembling separation itself, the alteration of monadic substance and closure—impartation and affection. Only the infinite identity of the Subject could ensure an actual individuality. In the realm of finite identity, by contrast, one is never born alone, although one is not born collectively. One never sleeps alone. And one never dies alone. But solitude does still exist: it is the infinite consciousness of finite identity.[23]

THE SIN OF ORIGIN

Solitude exists as the consciousness of this separation, of infinite from finite, of human from divine; as the infinite consciousness of finitude and the finite consciousness of infinity. We might claim an equal guilt for the human and for God in this schism, admittedly a theologically startling move[24]—or we might maintain God as otherwise than being (not a guilty entity, requiring the individuation that entities do), as desire and drawing, as what does not turn away.[25] To return to God is to return to undiminishable—infinite—desiring delight, to be unable (because so perfectly unwilling) to turn distractedly away. Human desire is satiable; original sin is thus ineluctable, because we will always be distracted from the intensity of wanting and of joy. In ordinary time, our present only passes; it is only in our own divinity that it intensifies.

Or, to complicate the matter differently, we might say that that first turn is *my* turning away—turning my will toward myself, turning my desire away from perfect harmony with delight, splitting the will into mine and God's.[26] It is my amplification of the moment of distraction. But if I turn away out of self-love (a love of my own will and desire placed, as the catechismic definition has it, above God's will—which we may read here as, perhaps, no more than a lapse in the tight attentiveness of that desire to itself) and if my love is God's love (when, before the turn, we are indistinct one from another, or simply when my will is in perfect harmony with God's and so with itself), then this turn, giving me my-self and God god-self, is not simply bad, unless we want to call all of creation bad, and I would rather not. (Nor would the God of Genesis, who saw that it was very good (1:31).) The negative aspect distinguishing creation from sinfulness is the persistent turn of attention away from divine joy into scattered smaller satiable pleasures, allowing no moments in which the joy of eternity can break through into those pleasures, transforming them and so us into something even more astonishing than pure infinity, into infinite and finite at once. We remain only finite where we have forgotten how to forget ourselves, and time.

It would seem reasonable to argue that desire, the mortal echo of this prelapsarian wanting, reflects a quest for wholeness, for mending the self and drawing together the scattered pieces of time into an eternal now. (This is to some extent a theological restatement of the Freudian, or Platonic, notion that Eros seeks to make new wholes.) Indeed, within Christian traditions, as Carolyn Walker Bynum has noted, wholeness is often linked to redemption, while falling to pieces signifies the decay and decadence of the damned.[27] But I would argue, again, that there is as well a redemption of fragmentation: the first fragmentation (provoking

THE SIN OF ORIGIN

separation from the divine) is mended (but not rendered whole) by another fragmentation (rendering the self lost in its openness to divinity); we redeem time in forgetting ourselves, and we forget ourselves only when we are not wholly contained, not self-contained and whole, within the boundaries of our skins and our egos.

From the *Phaedrus* to the Fall

> The origin always precedes the Fall. It comes before the body, before the world and time; it is associated with the gods, and its story is always sung as a theogony.
> —Michel Foucault, "Nietzsche, Genealogy, History"

Stories of falls are, of course, much older than the doctrine of original sin. We have already encountered the source of one of the most important, Plato's *Phaedrus*, in which the soul fallen from the heavens forgets the perfection it knew there, only to be later reminded by earthly beauty.

In the *Phaedrus*, the immortal soul "traverses the whole universe, though in ever-changing forms."[28] The perfect soul journeys in the heavens well above the world, but every soul is for the first many millennia of its existence imperfect, lacking in self-control, and so, Socrates declares, its "wings sink down until it can fasten on something solid, and settling there it takes to itself an earthy body which seems by reason of the soul's power to move itself. . . . [W]hat we must understand is the reason why the soul's wings fall from it, and are lost."[29] Ideally, we recall, souls just continue to circle about in the heavens, rising to the contemplation of the highest forms and descending only so far as the realms of the gods. The soul's fall into flesh is a descent gone too far:

> Whatsoever soul has followed in the train of a god, and discerned something of truth, shall be kept from sorrow until a new revolution shall begin, and if she can do this always, she shall remain always free from hurt. But when she is not able so to follow, and sees none of it, but meeting with some mischance comes to be burdened with a load of forgetfulness and wrongdoing, and because of that burden sheds her wings and falls to the earth, then thus runs the law.[30]

Thus runs the law—the fall into mortality, brought about in distraction, in which the soul "burdened with forgetfulness" turns its attention away from the joyful contemplation of divinity. As Blanchot declares

THE SIN OF ORIGIN

(evoking those Pauline discussions of law, sin, and death): "The law kills. Death is always the horizon of the law: if you do this, you will die. It kills whoever does not observe it, and to observe it is also already to die, to die to all possibilities."[31] In the *Phaedrus*, memory runs counter to law to draw even the incarnate soul upward, back toward the heavens of its origin: "a recollection of those things which our souls beheld aforetime as they journeyed with their god, looking down upon the things which now we suppose to be, and gazing up to that which truly is."[32] The law kills, but memory gives life, redeems the time in drawing across it.

As Eckhart glosses this, or a similar, passage: "Now at this point we hear Plato, the great priest, speaking to us of great things. He speaks of a purity which is not in the world. It is neither in the world nor outside the world; it is neither in time nor in eternity; it has neither an exterior nor an interior dimension. But from this God, the eternal Father, derives the abundance and the depths of his whole Godhead."[33] In Eckhart, of course, there is a decided shift away from the Platonic emphasis on successive lives, and indeed, perhaps even more importantly for Christian thought, a shift away from the clear distinction between this and the heavenly worlds. Yet for him as for Plato the best and highest life—and so for Plato, in a nearly Buddhist touch, the last of the soul's incarnations—is that of a kind of contemplation intertwined with memory. Once we truly remember the highest realms, we will find ourselves once again at home. The memory of having been there becomes all there is to being there; the memory does not recreate a past but perspectivally shifts and amplifies a now. And significantly, while falling away is certainly compatible with the preexistence of the soul (as for Plato), the image of descent seems more applicable still if the soul's existence as such comes about only in falling, if identity is attained only in separation. To be a self, to have finite identity, is already to have fallen away, a happy fault, but at the same time the source of discontent.

What tugs at our memories eludes us; we remember having forgotten, maybe, or, returned (at once after and at the same time) from ecstasy or joyous self-forgetting; we remember having remembered, yet not, not exactly, as us. This elusion, this self-forgetting, like the ecstasies described in mysticism, does not permit staying, but it does suggest the possibility, not of remaining indefinitely long in time, but of being other than temporal too. The way out of the dissatisfaction of finitude is into this joyful desire, fed by its own gratification. One does not desire this divinity, this God, as one desires a thing; rather, one and thing make no more sense here, and desire defies the poles of subject and object.[34]

As I've suggested, Eckhart's notion is still more philosophically and even theologically radical than Plato's tale of successive incarnations; it is

THE SIN OF ORIGIN

a tale of broken (or, from another perspective, illusory) boundaries, in which time and the eternal, inside and out, cross over into one another—and so, in this ultimate purity, do human and divine (thus the purest is the ultimately mixed). For Eckhart, the remembering of divinity is the forgetting of temporality: "The soul which is to be born in God must fall away from time as time must fall away from her."[35] But in fact, we recall, this "God" is for Eckhart not distinct from the soul—at least not once the divine is remembered (in which remembering the terms lose their meaning). It is forgetfulness that allows delimitation.[36] This forgetfulness he links to Adam's disobedience:

> When the soul is united with God, then it . . . forgets itself there, as it is in itself, and all things, knowing itself in God as divine, in so far as God is in it. Thus far it possesses a divine self-love and is inseparably united with God so that it enjoys nothing but him and delights only in him. . . . When Lord Adam broke the commandment, he was driven out of Paradise, and our Lord set two guards before its doors.[37]

The soul's self-forgetting comes about before and after the Fall. The original sin is the forgetting not of what was once remembered but of that which precedes memory because it precedes the remembering self-possessed subject, a pre-self self-love without pride or even self. The forgetfulness that makes time (a "first" forgetfulness, which in turn makes firstness) can, redemptively, be followed by a "second" turn into the forgetting of time, opening the space for us to remember beyond mortal memory. Until then, until we forget again, we remain fallen, our memories imperfect. But if postlapsarian self-forgetting forgets time, then before and after (and so "until") no longer hold. Divine desirous joy is undistracted present delight amplified like an inverse damnation, the inversion of origin by separation. It is the lived sense of this world as blessed.

Freedom

> Grant me now and in the future to follow gladly as you do with me what you will.
> —Augustine, *Confessions*

In this joy is a curious freedom. For Augustine, Adam had, and lost for all of us, the capacity to avoid sin altogether (we can, he acknowledges, still avoid it ourselves in *many* given instances, but not all, with the assistance of grace). Our misdirected desire, or at least our tendency to misdirect our desire, remains with us, even if the guilt for original sin is wiped away with baptism. Yet for Augustine there is a possibility even beyond Adam's capability: to attain, in the full memory of God, the state of *inability to sin*. "The first freedom of the will, given to man when he was created upright at the beginning, was an ability not to sin, combined with the possibility of sinning. But this last freedom will be more potent, for it will bring the impossibility of sinning."[38]

This slightly alarming notion, which must sound personally and ethically worse to most of us than original sin ever did, demands that we look more closely at the Augustinian view of freedom, so that we can understand just what it is that we are supposed to have lost in that first sin, how it is that our turn to self-mastery has somehow left us unfree, and what possible benefit we gain or regain in the incapacity for sinning.

In his furious arguments against Pelagius and his followers (who, to oversimplify, denied original sin), Augustine declares original sin to be not only the tendency to sin, but even the will's potential for disobedience generally—that is, as Elaine Pagels points out, in some sense *freedom as such*, the soul taking, as Augustine declares in *City of God*: "a perverse delight in its own liberty," disdaining God's service. Paralleling Lucifer's rebellion to Adam and Eve's inability to resist temptation, Augustine writes, "The cause of evil is the defection of the will of a being who is mutably good from the Good which is immutable. This happened first in the case of the angels and afterward, that of man."[39] This "defection of the will" is mythically manifest in the seduction of Adam and Eve by the fruit-loving serpent, made possible by their willingness to be distracted, the insufficiency of their attention and their need.

Once delighted in, this freedom *as such* too readily becomes a new enslavement, bondage to finite desire in a soul that should instead desire the infinite, and desire infinitely. Pagels writes:

> What earlier apologists had celebrated as God's greatest gift to humankind—free will, liberty, autonomy, self-government—Augustine characterizes in surprisingly negative terms. Adam had received freedom as his birthright, but nonetheless, as Augustine tells it, the first man "conceived a desire for freedom," and his desire became, in Augustine's eyes, the root of sin, betraying nothing less than contempt for God. The desire to master one's will, far from expressing . . . the true nature of rational beings, becomes for Augustine the great and fatal temptation: "The fruit of the tree of

THE SIN OF ORIGIN

knowledge of good and evil is personal control over one's own will."[40]

To complicate matters, Augustine does elsewhere celebrate the value of free will as a gift from God[41]—and he does not, of course, advocate a hedonistic abandonment of self-control or attempted self-mastery in favor of self-indulgence. Freedom is a great gift, but an ambiguous one, incorporating necessarily the possibility of its own misuse. For Augustine, real freedom is precisely proper desire—not desire temporally moderated, but desire directed in infinite intensity toward an infinite object; the desire not to be master of one's own will but to want so violently that the deliberative will is divinely overtaken. We attain Augustinian redemption not in mastering our desires but in being mastered by desire for the infinite, giving over our freedom to its force—a force destructive of will that can never be imposed wholly against it, since the force that overtakes us is our "own" desire. The temporality of the will is transformed; we too will from always. Time is transformed with it. This is a transformation and not a simple merging; as Cusanus notes, "human nature cannot pass over into essential union with the divine, even as the finite cannot be infinitely united unto the infinite, because it would pass into identity with the infinite, and thus would cease to be finite."[42]

Such a redemptive loss goes beyond Adam's ability not to sin, into that disturbing *inability to sin*. This is freedom transformed, self-forgetting, the conversion or turning again out of original forgetfulness. Only here can we be, in the Augustinian sense, truly free, free beyond the rather simple (if often terribly difficult) matter of deliberation and decision in making choices. When the whole *time* of willing is changed, its freedom lies not in being able to deliberate, follow through, and in consequence satisfy itself, but in overflowing every instant—not merely following, but simultaneously enacting, as Nietzsche also says of true freedom, "laws that precisely on account of their hardness and determination defy all formulation through concepts." "What is essential 'in heaven and on earth,'" Nietzsche adds, "seems to be, to say it once more, that there should be *obedience* over a long period of time and in a single direction."[43] Seeming to come back under law here, such freedom evades all that we can *understand* as law—that is, all universally applied, comprehensible sets of rules.

Pushing Augustine still further, Eckhart will declare, in his instructional talk on sin, that "we should be wholly established in God, and it is astonishing how much this inflames us with so great and so strong a love that we strip ourselves entirely of ourselves."[44] He gives this notion of being stripped of self a vivid metaphorical elaboration:

THE SIN OF ORIGIN

> For love is just the same as the fisherman's hook: the fisherman cannot lay hold of the fish unless it is attached to the hook. If it has swallowed the hook, the fisherman can be sure of his fish, whichever way it turns, this way or that, he knows he will get it. . . . Whoever lands on this hook is caught so fast that foot and hand, mouth, eye, heart and all that makes us what we are, must become God's possession.[45]

Stripped of self and possessed by God—these are the metaphors of desire too intense to be bound by the limitations imposed by distinction, of a will so perfectly (not) its own that its desire is intensified by its very satisfaction, a will caught up by joy. It is not a self abandoned to a God as distinct from itself, but a troubling of that distinction altogether.

This is not, however, the only way in which Eckhart pushes the idea of separation and jointure into stranger territory. In his sermon on the beatitudes, cited earlier, he goes on in the discussion of "my first cause": "But when I emerged by free choice and received my created being, I came into the possession of a God for, until creatures came into existence, God was not 'God,' but was rather what he was."[46] Oliver Davies, in translating this passage, provides a valuable gloss on the phrase "when I emerged by free choice," noting of an important earlier translation, "Walshe renders this difficult phrase: 'But when I left my free will behind . . .' but it seems to me Eckhart's meaning is that God's free will (through which the creation came about) was my free will since, prior to the Creation, I was in God and was one with God."[47]

This view, which does seem to me more consistent with Eckhart, makes it strikingly difficult, as I remarked earlier, to assign much *blame* for original sin, especially given the theological difficulties of blaming God (but then, the guilt of the born-to-sin infant is scarcely less problematic). It suggests that in fact, as in Leibnizian damnation, the sin and the penalty are the same: distraction, partiality, finitude, the incoherence of the will. In "breaking through," I do not get back lost parts of myself, but return to an atemporally precedent joy, in which oneness makes no more sense than any other number (after all, there cannot be "one" unless there are "none" and "many").

At issue is less some sort of problematic, difference-erasing unification than the transfiguration of desire and the shattering of subjectivity. Blanchot notes: "The 'One' is what least authorizes union, even with the infinitely distant. . . . The rigorous exactitude and the impossibility of the One (which is not unity) do not even allow for transcendence as its essential orientation. It has no horizon."[48] Such unqualifiedness is neither transcendent nor immanent; it simply doesn't fit the categories. We do not attain to unity with God as two entities joined together but to forgetfulness of self, and so of God. Our wills are no longer split within themselves; they direct their full force to divinity no longer intelligible as purely transcendent. Our bodies no longer resist our desire; they are taken up in it. Our time is broken open to what complicates and breaks it. But how do we remember how to forget, how to get back before ourselves?

Immaculate Flesh

> The incarnation of human subjectivity guarantees its spirituality.
> —Emmanuel Levinas, *Ethics and Infinity*

To make sense of getting back before ourselves, perhaps we may begin at our more literal beginnings. Augustine's understanding of original sin entails a view of propagation that demands the inheritance of acquired traits and an understanding of reproduction in which the entire person is contained in the paternal sperm, the mother serving only as receptacle and bearer. Thus, from our fathers, we inherit the flaws that Adam acquired.

Thomas Aquinas, who shares this view, draws out some of its curious implications. He uses it, for instance, to argue back to the claim that the original sin *must* be Adam's and not Eve's, as only the paternal sin could possibly be transmissible: nothing is transmitted to the infant from the mother.[49] No other sin is transmitted, however, as "actual" or individual sin always involves decision, and so cannot be passed to another individual.[50]

Given the theory of seminal transmission, one might reasonably assume that original sin would be present at the moment of conception; however, since Augustine also argues that the soul does not enter the fetal body until at least the forty-sixth day after conception, he would seem to be arguing either that matter is inherently sinful—as he sometimes does seem to do, a pretty clear holdover from his Manichean days—or, as seems more likely, that there is a sort of waiting period before sin's inheritance, the time between the formation of innocent matter and quickening by the maculate soul. There remains a trace of this ancient sense of dual conception in one of the key doctrines stemming from that of original sin, that of the Immaculate Conception.

THE SIN OF ORIGIN

Mary's freedom from original sin was made official dogma by Pope Pius IX in 1854, when he declared her state to have been made possible by a temporally peculiar causality in which Christ's grace preserved her "exempt from original sin."[51] This exemption does not occur (whatever the nuns may have told you) when her parents manage to procreate without desire. (To be sure, Augustine does hint at something like this in his discussion of *Christ's* conception: "Since he himself was begotten and conceived in no pleasure of carnal appetite—and therefore bore no trace of original sin." This does not, however, imply an absence of either pleasure or desire, as we shall soon see. Intriguingly and rather ingeniously, Augustine also suggests that Christ is sinless because Mary was not inseminated—remember, the sin is contained in the sperm.[52]) Rather, according to the Encyclopedic analysis of this official—and, in fact, officially infallible[53]—declaration:

> The term *conception* does not mean the *active* or *generative* conception by her parents. . . . The question does not concern the immaculateness of the generative activity of her parents. Neither does it concern the passive conception absolutely and simply (*conceptio seminis carnis, inchoate*) which, according to the order of nature, precedes the infusion of the rational soul. The person is *truly* conceived when the soul is created and infused into the body. Mary was preserved exempt from all stain of original sin at the first moment of her *animation*, and sanctifying grace was given to her before sin could have taken effect in her soul.[54]

This analysis clearly depends upon the dual-conception theory. Thus possessed of a stainless soul, Mary is often given the status of a second Eve, a new beginning, with her son rather oedipally playing Adam's role as the founder of a new world of redemptive possibilities. It's like do-overs for all of humankind, a second shot at the grace of which we deprived ourselves. Augustine also links the sinless conception of Christ to a seamless will. Peter Brown writes:

> Only in the virgin birth of Christ had Mary recaptured Eve's first harmony. Overshadowed by the Holy Spirit, Mary had felt not the slightest eddy of uncontrolled feeling at the moment when she conceived Christ: the physical sensations associated with the sexual act had been fully consonant, in her case, with the untroubled movement of her will. . . . For Augustine, Mary's conception of

THE SIN OF ORIGIN

Christ stood . . . for an act of undivided obedience. It recaptured the ancient harmony of body and soul, in which the soul was not the maimed thing that it so soon became.[55]

As Brown also emphasizes, Augustine does not argue that there would be some superiority to conception without bodily pleasure, some sanctity bestowed by numbness. Undivided obedience carries no reluctance, no grimness; instead, Mary's will is wholeheartedly, and joyfully, joined to God's—and to her own body. (The separation of will from flesh is, we recall, a consequence of original sin, which Mary lacks.) Why would we ever will less than joy? For Eve and Adam, too, Augustine "saw no reason why conception should not depend upon a moment of intense pleasure, and he was quite prepared to allow that such pleasure might have occurred in Paradise—no small imaginative feat for a late antique person of an ascetic lifestyle. What concerned him was that, after the fall of Adam and Eve, this pleasure had gained a momentum of its own, and that it clashed with the intentions of the will."[56] Sinless delight does not exclude the flesh.

It is important that joy in the flesh is not condemned; it is no "solution" to original sin to deny the physicality of pleasure. Matter is innocent. It is only matter fused with soul that can be maculate, sinful. Augustine's deep suspicion of the flesh seems to be a manifestation both of his own interior struggles with what contemporary pop psychology would undoubtedly call sexual addiction[57] and, as I suggested above, from his lingering, if officially renounced, Manichean streak.[58] But this suspicion runs counter to his stubborn theological insistence on the beauty and goodness of all that God has made, the absence of evil in existence.[59]

And after all, early Christianity insists upon the resurrection not of the spirit but of the flesh (as Chapter 6 will emphasize). Some later writers even go so far as to link Mary's immaculate character precisely to the flesh, via a rather lovely variant myth: "Some writers of [the eleventh through thirteenth centuries] entertained the fantastic idea that before Adam fell, a portion of his flesh had been reserved by God and transmitted from generation to generation, and that out of this flesh the body of Mary was formed."[60] Aquinas, by contrast, argues that Christ's flesh, and so presumably Mary's, must have been descended from Adam's in the more usual way, as only this makes sense of the doctrine of redemption. That is, if Christ took on fleshly form in order to redeem flesh, that flesh must have been first in need of redeeming.[61] Similarly, Brown notes that:

THE SIN OF ORIGIN

"Late antique Christians placed a heavy stress on the fact that the flesh of Christ and that of his virgin mother were utterly continuous with human flesh. Theirs had been human flesh 'reformed' in the strict sense: the flaws that rendered the body so burdensome, and so difficult to control in ordinary men and women, before it melted into the glory of the Resurrection, were already absent in the flesh of Christ and in the circumstances of his birth from Mary."[62] In these arguments, contrary to one another though they are in some respects, flesh remains central: it is in and as bodies (matter already "meaningful" in its entanglement with word) that we retain the memories both of divisive distraction and of salvific possibilities. The eternity that beckons us from within time, as grace's counter to damnation, as the absence of the origin of sin, is not something discorporate; it is another dimension of living enfleshed.

Were we to refuse to see the figure of Christ as genuinely corporeal—a fairly popular heresy, as it eliminates all sorts of irksome paradoxes—then the Incarnation and Resurrection myths would become (at least relatively) uninteresting. There is no great mystery, let alone philosophical interest, in the apparent reanimation of a three-day-old corpse, *if* the body was never more than a meat puppet for the God inhabiting it anyway. Gods no doubt can come and go from bodies as they please. Original sin belongs neither to unfallen soul nor to innocent, inanimate stuff, but to living matter, as the unique finitude of living creatures. Finitude is not the legislated penalty for but the nature of the sin; it is separation not by decision nor by renewed determination, but rather by distracted forgetfulness, by the failure and the limitation of desire, which redemption forgets in turn. The continuation of original sin is separation from the sacred, distinguishing it from oneself and refusing it from others and from the world. The question becomes, then, how to forget, and how to remember, in the flesh. (In addition to my suggestions here, I shall argue in the next two chapters that both love and forgiveness are also modes of opening onto some dimension of this sacrality.)

Redemptive Desire

> I have
> Immortal longings in me.
> —William Shakespeare, *Antony and Cleopatra*

The notion of a serpentine seduction of the will in the Edenic context of a forgotten primal or preprimal scene might lead us to consider early seduction theory, the conception of an infant trauma of being seduced that is, in the manner of trauma, repressed into unconsciousness but that triggers the emergence of symptoms when elements of later experience come too close. The forgetfulness that repeats original sin, however, is not the forgetting of a seduction—a drawing toward, a moving with—but of its opposite, a turning away. Luckily, as the counter to concupiscence, as the divinity in our temptation, we remain seducible. Even when our attention is distracted, there remains a trace in memory, a trace of the infinite in finite desire, a divine insatiability. Here too, just as in the inverse case of trauma (of which more in Chapter 3), there are reminders, triggers—mortal moments of beauty, joy, revelation, reopening the possibility of a divine seduction.[63]

In this, the "prescription" for living suggested by the dogma of original sin returns us surprisingly near to one of Augustine's philosophical ancestors. Plotinus calls for "a strenuous and patient spiritual discipline, a discipline that cumulatively embeds a particular way of seeing into a person's feeling and thinking,"[64] which enables one, all importantly, to attend to beauty: "Plotinus began his authorship with the suggestion that no one can adequately understand the world who has not been startled and instructed by its beauty (*Ennead* 1.6). For Plotinus, beauty was not an aesthetic category, in the usual sense of the word. To notice beauty is not to make a judgment about a particular object. To perceive beauty is to experience the universe as a gift."[65]

As human, again, we are constituted precisely by our limits. Yet we have, when we listen for it, a paradoxical desire to exceed those limits, thus a push toward our own fearfully redemptive destruction.[66] Augustine's will wills freely beyond what we can possibly understand as freedom, wills its own overtaking not as the desire to evade responsibility but as the desire to perfect itself by becoming (one with) God's will, in an impossible perfection of subordination.

Against the notion that all desire is a distraction from higher matters, I would say that desire is what draws us "upward," exploding the limits of the self preserved by its own forgetfulness, by turning and falling away. Thus the sin of origin lies not in wanting something more or something other than God but in not wanting enough, in the inadequacy of desire in and for the world that makes distraction possible. To prefer oneself is to prefer ego security over every risk. Its fault is a matter of intensity rather than direction, though direction can make intensity more or less likely: desire turned to the "wrong" directions will be either too widely scattered or too readily satiable. And because our desire is always, in time,

THE SIN OF ORIGIN

satiable and inadequate, we will and do always fall back, distractedly, into ourselves—but we are not only in time.

The misdirection of desire, then, is not toward temporal objects as such but more exactly toward a particular temporality between desire and object, one in which satisfaction follows upon and ends desire, in which joy is simply laid out in time.[67] The desire for God works in a different temporality, with neither satiation nor weariness following joy—at least for Augustine, who declares in the *City of God* that God "will be the goal of all our longings; and we shall see him for ever; we shall love him without satiety; we shall praise him without wearying."[68] Augustine's theology tends not toward a complete, finished, or total satisfaction, but toward an escalation of both desire and joy, in and through which we are constantly drawn toward God, out of finitude. But we do not desire such a God as a unique object: rather, our desire for the divine, our return to our own divinity, is possible in many desires (though perhaps not in every desire). God here is not a thing desired but a way of desiring, of being drawn through to the other side of satiation and human weariness. Or, as Plotinus, again, puts it, "We encounter the extraordinary with astonishment, though we should be astonished at . . . ordinary things too."[69]

Thus we can read original sin into a loop of forgetfulness and memory in which redemption, or at least the possibility thereof, is inherent. The "origin" is a "first" forgetting, a lapse of attention and desire like that of an imperfect lover, a distraction, and hence a separation. Hence, too, it is a first fragmentation, a splitting not only of self but of will (such that it no longer is what it wants or wants what it is; such that wanting and being are no longer identical). This is a happy fault, though not in the usual sense of setting up the Incarnation: this cutting off gives us ourselves, and the cutting across of self that we find in both forgiveness and love (subjects of the next two chapters) is never unambiguous.

We do not remain drawn into self-fragmenting desire for a long time; but perhaps in this desire we can break out of time, once and over again. Perhaps the joyful instant, as I shall argue again in Chapter 6, may be amplified to eternity, too. And perhaps, even in ourselves, we retain the memory of the immemorial, the outsideness of selfhood. Perhaps we regret, or perhaps we don't even notice, our distractibility, the condition of our existence not merely as matter, but as creatures of time, time in which we forget, in which we are, if inconstantly, unfaithful, time in which we are solitary. But occasionally, re-minded, reanimated, we are moved to remember. Occasionally, something pulls on our memories, triggers an ec-stasis in our minds and our flesh: an illuminating idea, an electrifying touch, the sensuous curve of a musical movement, an uncontainable joy. Occasionally, we stand astonished in the world.

We stand, but we cannot stay. The infinite, self-fulfilling yet self-sustaining desire of Eckhart's "first cause" is not enduring but eternal. We do not remain in desire but fall back into time, forgetting, possibly to be pulled back to desire by the nagging sense of which Augustine also writes, our certainty that we remember forgetfulness itself, a certainty that, oddly, gives us hope: "When at least we remember ourselves to have forgotten, we have not totally forgotten. But if we have completely forgotten, we cannot even search for what has been lost."[70]

Once we are reminded—by the beauty of the world, by our own intellectual inspirations and dissatisfactions, by anything that catches at our breath—of the intensity of the divine love we had forgotten, Augustine suggests, we are drawn into an infinite and reciprocal desire—from which only *we* ever fall away, in an indefinite repetition of our origin in forgetting. Brown writes that, in Augustine's reading, "With Adam's Fall, the soul lost the ability to summon up all of itself, in an undivided act of will, to love and praise God in all created things."[71] What we lose in falling away is this kind of joy, a joy that overflows into praise without satiation or distraction, without some divided part of the will wandering off or away from this desiring delight.

Our image of divine love or divine desire is the impossible perfection of our own. That is, our conception of divine love differs from that of human love in being infinite, not only in the intensity of its desire but in the constancy of its memory—and in the perfection of the link between the two. Though it is easier to speak of self and of God, the guilt-inducing "original" split is not between one entity and another, but within an infinite desire, rendering finitude by forgetfulness. Yet this split is not everything; there is in us an infinite divine desire that draws us out of ourselves, but we are at the same time (another shift in perspective) fallen in our finitude. We forget. We can delight and desire recurrently but not continuously: our distractibility may be limited, but it is perpetual. Distraction is the very condition of finitude. It is in this sense that original sin is the sin of origin, the forgetfulness that is our own existence, our boundaries, ourselves. We overcome it only in self-loss, and thus the condition is for us—as us—inescapable, left behind only by getting out of ourselves. And this self-loss, the loss not of difference but of intentional, temporally oriented subjectivity, is also our loss of the distinctness of God.

THE SIN OF ORIGIN

This finitude is what *we* are, but self-loss comes in multiple modes. The way out of sin is the way out of self, but a way out that remains proper to the self, an ecstasis proper to time, an alongsideness and not a destruction. (We are all too capable of such destruction, for others as well as ourselves, capable of making the world so ugly that its blessedness is nearly obscured, if never altogether obliterated: it is against this that we are called to stand astonished.) Even joyous destruction is not all sunlight and flowers: we're no less lost for all that, and a disaster is disastrous however joyfully named. We don't have the option of surviving angelic combustion. And, after all, one of the radical elements of Christian theology is that of a God who, in human form, *dies*—is destroyed—at human hands, and this very finitude is considered evidence of divine love. Again, if the son given to the world were simply infinite, the sacrifice of the crucifixion would be a bit of a parlor trick, the resurrection no more than sleight of hand. Love playing as the converse of solitude plays also between finitude and infinity.

We are redeemed in the flesh not only when, like St. Teresa, we envision cherubic spears ripping our entrails; or, like St. Lutgarde, gulp blood and fluid from the side of the crucified God; or, like St. Catherine, climb into the wounded side of Christ's body, but when our desire shatters us, takes us out of time, forces us, if not to hold a single thought beyond time, to recur to it as an act beyond any will of our own in a perfect harmony with divine will and with human body—when matter becomes formed by Word and is Flesh, and material and soulful can only improperly, or at best analytically, be distinguished.

Original sin is about distractibility, the limits of both memory and attention; it is about forgetfulness in the division of that attention from itself. It is not the forgetting of what was once remembered, but forgetfulness at the very origin of the possibility of memory, the beginning of selfhood in a lapse of attention. It is a Deleuzean repetition without a first,[72] a forgetfulness prior to memory, a turning away that constitutes us. Like many saints (mystics and ascetics alike), Augustine may pray for continence,[73] but never for the repression or elimination of desire; indeed, he prays to God to intensify his love, though his descriptions of that love already sound so nearly insatiable. The problem with so much of our desire, again, is that it is so readily satiated, leaving us secure in ourselves with the kind of need-no-more satisfaction that follows a good meal. Both asceticism and mysticism have modes of seeking desire beyond limit. Asceticism plays with the intensification of desire and the powerful pleasure of its denial;[74] mysticism with the self-shattering beyond satisfaction and language alike. Both are approaches to time's redemption. Insatiable desire, always pushing past the "I" who would claim it, is our experience of, our openness to, divinity. What Augustine seeks from God is not satisfaction but shattering, *more*, back beyond the limits of mortal memory.

"Redemption," in this model, occurs in the desire we desire to have—or equally by which we desire to be possessed—an infinite and unwavering desire that we can constitute only as sacred. It is immanent, not transcendent; it is within and not beyond living. This tension between the possibilities and the experience of finite human desire, yearning for our own divinity but perpetually distracted by the mere existence of chocolate in the world, must be a tension between memory and loss. Our own infinite desire for desire faces the limits of our memories, our responsibility for the loss of desire, the guilt of our own finitude, the weakness of our own flesh. Time contains the germ of its own redemption, its own rupture; "salvation beckons the release from time through time."[75] When we forget ourselves we return beyond memory to a desire so utterly obsessive and so perfectly satisfied that it breaks freedom's bond to finitude, so perfectly insatiable that it breaks the self-containment of those of us who would make desire our own.

We are nagged by what precedes and eludes memory, forgetfulness as a feeling of having forgotten. The reminders of the sacred may come from anywhere; for Augustine, as for Plato and Plotinus, they often emerge in beauty, which pulls at our language and our flesh alike.[76] The sublime, with its hint of menace, may be a still more potent source; for each, as Rilke says, "we are so awed because it so serenely disdains to annihilate us."[77] Perhaps we understand our desire as the search for some primal, mythical wholeness; perhaps we see it as the quest for joyous annihilation. But the way to that wholeness, indeed the very meaning of it, is through further fragmentation, through desire pulling on or pushing through subjectivity until the latter breaks—desire created by beauty, sublimity, pleasure, in the context of their insatiability; desire that feeds on satisfaction rather than being extinguished by it. The separated self may be incomplete, but it is also excessively self-sufficient or self-contained; breaking through the wall of the self requires a remarkable force upon our absorbed attention. Open again, we are pulled back to the before of memory, to the fire of joyful desiring—not in finding a missing piece of ourselves, but in losing the tidiness of individuation. And returned to ourselves from and even alongside our own absence, we are complicated, enfolding within our selves perpetual reminders of forgetfulness, fiery sparks of the divine.

3

FROM TRAUMA TO REVELATION

Forgiveness

379. What is the sacrament of Penance?
Penance is the sacrament by which sins committed after Baptism are forgiven through the absolution of the priest. . . .
384. What must we do to receive the sacrament of Penance worthily? To receive the sacrament of Penance worthily, we must: first, examine our conscience; second, be sorry for our sins; third, have the firm purpose of not sinning again; fourth, confess our sins to the priest; fifth, be willing to perform the penance the priest gives us. *But if the wicked do penance for all his sins which he hath committed and keep all my commandments and do judgment and justice, living he shall live, and shall not die. (Ezekiel 18:21)*
—*A Catechism of Christian Doctrine*, Revised Edition of the
 Baltimore Catechism, Part 3, Lesson 29

A Promise Created with Time

The archive has always been a *pledge*, and like every pledge, a token of the future.
—Jacques Derrida, *Archive Fever: A Freudian Impression*

We begin again, or not at all.
Catherine Keller, *Face of the Deep*

If we begin with the question of sin, whether original or derivative, an obvious consequent question is that of forgiveness. Forgiveness is an elusive notion; as the opening catechismic questions indicate, it appears sacramentally as reconciliation (formerly designated penance, itself an interesting terminological shift), and it is understood to obtain between persons as well as between human and divine—though all of its modes are often, following Alexander Pope, given the latter designation.[1] If we follow Deleuze's Leibniz, then it would seem that God's forgiveness must be our own: that is, in forgiving God we must find ourselves forgiven (the resonance of this claim with Christian Neoplatonism is perhaps obvious: "God and I, we are one in this work"[2]). I want to argue that we find in forgiveness, given or received, a call of eternal memory and the eternity of the opened future. Divine forgiveness is the to-come already given (precisely in its unspecificity), making human forgiveness possible. What becomes particularly strange and intriguing in this opening, then, at least for the purposes of this text, is the question of *when*. When is forgiveness offered, and what does its giving do to time?

Given this particular fascination, I would like to focus on a startling and rich textual moment, one that occurs in the catechism shortly after this definition of penance or reconciliation has been given: God, we read, is *bound by a promise* to sacramental forgiving. "Certainly," the *Catechism* declares, "God *could* forgive our sins if we confessed them to Himself in secret, but He has not *promised* to do so; whereas He has promised to pardon them if we confess them to His priests."[3] In this wording we find, however inadvertently, the temporal peculiarity of forgiveness; it is linked not to the orderly and successive time of the punishment (following upon transgression, preceding freedom from debt), but to that of the promise, which complicatedly enfolds past and future—which, by its past, allows the future of time. This fold is characteristic of the promise, which, as Nancy points out, does not bring about what it promises (to make a promise does not performatively effect the promised result), and yet is instrumental in causing, or in allowing, what is promised to come about.[4]

Viewing forgiveness as promise emphasizes its relation to the future; the idea of God's promise, a promise that would have to be made (have to have been made, have to be coming up for the making) not some time ago but from eternity, must alter it further. In his essay "Fore/giveness on the Way: Nesting in the Womb of Response," Elliot Wolfson unfolds (among other complexities) the temporal implications of kabbalistic readings of forgiveness and atonement via an analysis of the meanings of Yom Kippur. While we obviously can't conflate Kabbala and catechism, there are nonetheless useful conceptual parallels between the sacramental promise and the linking of forgiveness to "the symbol of the covenant."⁵ Like the sacrament, the covenant has in this context a "legalistic background" but goes beyond it: "covenant is the sign that brings forth memory, that which calls to mind, and thus breaks open the path to forgiveness."⁶

There is a great deal here that resonates with both sacramental and what we might call mundane forgiveness: the legalism taken up and gone beyond, the contrast with forgetfulness (with which forgiveness, as I shall note in more detail below, is frequently but wrongly conflated), and the transformation of time in the release of the future. Divine forgiveness, Wolfson argues (and I would follow him here), is fore-given, given already or given before, already enfolding and folded into any time in which we might have need of it. As Wolfson notes, the infinity of time, paralleling that of God, is "expressed in the ceaseless cycle of renewal and regeneration of the moment."⁷ I want, in fact, to argue that divine forgiveness is given to us *as* future, time's dimension of possibility. The future is the possibility of the new, "the predictably unpredictable possibility of each moment, the persistent presence of the unprecedented present that makes possible awaiting the past in recollecting the future."⁸ The promise of forgiveness is precisely this: the possibility of novelty (or of natality, the world born again).

To get more clearly at this possibly strange notion, I will look briefly to a pseudepigraphic accounting of the world's origin that is nonetheless, I think, quite compatible with the canonical claim of the promise (I have chosen this account simply because it is more vivid and straightforward). Here we read again of divine mercy as precedent to the creation that would require it. Indeed, it is only with mercy that the world can be maintained in existence at all: our world "would have had no permanence, if God had executed his original plan of ruling it according to the principle of strict justice. It was only when he saw that justice by itself would undermine the world that he associated mercy with justice, and made them to rule jointly. Thus from the beginning of all things prevailed divine goodness, without which nothing could have continued to exist."⁹

But the need for mercy and its granting as the infiltration of forgiveness into justice appear prior even to this sustaining. In the same account, God reassures the doubtful Torah about the creation of sure-to-be-sinful humanity:

> [The Torah] was skeptical about the value of an earthly world, on account of the sinfulness of men, who would be sure to disregard

her precepts. But God dispelled her doubts. He told her that repentance had been created long before, and sinners would have the opportunity of mending their ways. Besides, the Temple service would be invested with atoning power. . . . Finally, the messiah was appointed to bring salvation, which would put an end to all sinfulness.[10]

And again, "The grace and lovingkindness of God revealed themselves particularly in His taking one spoonful of dust from the spot where in time to come the altar would stand, saying, 'I shall take man from the place of atonement, that he may endure.'"[11]

Atonement is built in to this idea of forgiveness, co-created with mercy. As Wolfson notes of the kabbalistic account, "The mystical efficacy of repentance is such that it is indistinguishable from redemption."[12] In these accounts, as in the catechism, we are made in such a way that we may be forgiven; even when we have (originally?) turned away, we have the capacity for turning back, for return or conversion. That is, humanity is created capable of repentance, able to open the dialogue with the divine. Before the world's creation, God has made redemption possible, left open the space for forgiveness and thus for return to divinity.

We find a perhaps unexpected resonance in Augustine's account of the first creation story in Genesis. Here change itself, the very possibility of being otherwise, is found at the beginning of creation. Augustine attributes eternity and immortality properly speaking only to God,[13] but at the same time he gives us the conceptual apparatus to consider other possibilities. Like the changeless heaven, the formless earth, the earth at the outset of creation itself, is not within time:

> I find there are two things created by you which lie outside time, though neither is coeternal with you. One of them is so given form that, although mutable, yet without any cessation of its contemplation, without any interruption caused by change, it experiences unwavering enjoyment of your eternity and immutability. The other is so formless that it has no means, either in movement or in a state of rest, of moving from one form to another, which is synonymous with being subject to time.[14]

The world, that is, is created with both form and mutability, the capacity to slip between form and form, the capacity for novelty: it is so

FORGIVENESS

created that, even in carrying forth memory, it does not have to retain the past in perfect re-creation. Instead, to return to the divine is the creative possibility of remembrance, found within change itself (and this even though it is clear that Augustine is more strongly valuing the immutable).

To continue in the same pseudepigraphic account: "In the beginning, two thousand years before the Heaven and the earth, seven things were created . . . [and the last of these was] a Voice that cries aloud, 'Return, you children of men.' "[15] Here is a Neoplatonic echo of a sort that Augustine or Eckhart would recognize; before we are, and so before we are turned away, we are called to return; we find that call in our memories, urging us to turn back from the small joys of distraction to the greater joy. Thus forgiveness opens onto joy, repentance, and atonement, or onto the delight of redemption. But when we return, when we remember, it is not only the past we find opened.

To be able to atone—to be made for atonement, even—is to be called to return and able to hear the call (to be, that is, attentive to the very existence of possibility). As Louis Mackey notes, the inbuilt possibility of atonement is found in the very extension of time: "All things that come into being in time pass away in time. The exigence of temporality is ineluctable: 'Thou shalt surely die' (Genesis 2:17). But time is not only loss. The procession of creatures toward nothingness, though relentless, is differential and gradual, delaying the divine judgment and thereby leaving, as we say, time—time for repentance and conversion, the time of narration."[16]

We have the option not only of telling, but of retelling, of changing the story by transfiguring its meaning into one that allows a more open "ending," folded back onto the antememorial. Every human act of forgiveness, Wolfson suggests, echoes a (pre)originary divine forgiveness, "the giving before that engenders being in the concealment of its disclosure. . . . When forgiveness is granted below the primordial act of fore/giveness is reenacted. . . . The giving before of fore/giveness is occasioned by the act of repentance, the turning back to the source."[17]

Before we have forgotten, before we have even been distracted—or rather, before and after, always already, always awaiting—we are remembered, the promise holding open the space to hear the voice calling for return, repentance turning our ears toward the sound of it. But this listening, as I shall indicate in a later section of this chapter, demands a kind of speaking from us as well: as in the *Phaedrus*, the call is drawn by the need to hear.

The Christian mythic version of forgiveness, picking up on the idea that "Finally, the messiah was appointed to bring salvation," would seem to be more temporally linear, if still curiously so—and, as I shall unsurprisingly suggest, only seemingly so. It is also a repetition, as Mackey has it: "Recalling and foregrounding a beginning already made in Genesis (3:15), John's repetition of a creation narrative—a repetition in the eternal past—introduces the story of redemption. An iteration of the wor(l)d already present at its first beginning, redemption repeats creation. And the repetition is the true beginning, the origin of the origin."[18]

The Incarnation as the entry of God into time is generally read as part of a redemptive process: having effectively condemned itself in its originally sinful progenitor, humanity needs some way to negotiate between unavoidable original sin and undesirable eternal damnation. How, that is, can a people sinful at its center nonetheless be redeemed? Some grand sacrifice, on an unimaginably large scale, seems to be demanded. And so, the story goes (a story whose familiarity easily covers over its deep strangeness), God takes human form, and in this form takes on the sins of humanity as if they were his own guilt; that is, he, by the enormousness (and, perhaps, the enormity) of his sacrifice, atones for the accumulated and anticipated transgressions of humanity. (As I shall emphasize in the next chapter, this guilt, at the same time, is impossible on at least two grounds: first, the necessary innocence of divinity in the Christian model; second, the nontransferability of guilt before the very law that can punish or judge it.) The assumption of guilt is an act of love culminating in an extraordinary sacrifice in the crucifixion. The Christian twist on the appointment of the sin-ending messiah is to make the messiah and the sacrifice the same (of which curious move the next chapter will make more).[19] With the "end of sinfulness" comes not a stasis of bliss but the newly uncondemned opening of time, the future possible.

Were it not for the last, this story could read at first as a straight causal account laid out in time, even if the causes and effects thus recounted are a bit surprising. But to read it thus is to assign to the workings of the divine will an order in time, the Father precedent to the Son, human sinfulness to sacrificial redemption, the promise (the messiah) to the achievement of the promised (freedom from sin), with an intervening legal or at least legalistic process of trial, condemnation, and punishment by death.

One might counter that even if all three divine persons are coeternal and consubstantial, the Incarnation comes later than God's existence, and the crucifixion after that—that these remain purely temporal events. But it seems to me not only richer but more in keeping with the sense of divine eternity to suggest not that the eternal divine enters time (becomes simply temporal) and an orderly process then atones for the worst of human sin but rather that eternal forgiveness too enters time in the divine body; that forgiveness is at once eternal and prior, yet given in the flesh. (The "happy fault" of the Fall would not guarantee an incarnate redeemer in consequence, then, but would carry implicated within it the redemption of mortal flesh.) It is not only that forgiveness is promised, but that forgiveness is itself a promise, an opening of the future. It promises the future *as* future, as something other than the past again. Divinity does not suddenly cease to be eternal when it is also in time; the time of the sacrificial crucifixion must also be the nontime of eternal will. Salvation is "appointed," forgiveness promised, prior even to the appearance of the human-formed God whose trial and death are supposed to be the means of that forgiveness. If this is not simply the deterministic playing out of a prophecy, then it is a folding up and a bursting out of time, the future into the fore-given past, the present into the eternal, the promise into the open.

We don't always notice that forgiveness is given in flesh. In the semantic move from penance to reconciliation there has been likewise a movement away from the sometimes spectacular visible and physical penitential acts that once extended to such lengths as the hair-shirts and self-flagellation of the most intensely ascetic saints, or to less extravagant but often lengthy penalties imposed from without.[20] Penance was (or is) corporeal not because flesh, as opposed to soul, was (or should be) regarded as evil, but because flesh is not opposed to soul at all. Reconciliation tends to prescribe gentler penitential acts, such as prayer; Christianity generally, its North American forms particularly, has become much too squeamish about both flesh and pain to allow more overt mortification to continue (not entirely a bad thing, to be sure). But we still feel forgiveness in the body too, as a lightness in the muscles, a sharpness in the senses, a capacity for response when we are no longer closed off from the world. And Christianity still grounds the possibility of forgiveness in the Incarnation, in its corporeal sacrifice.

Forgiveness famously mends, restoring the rifts in communication, community, and communion, and so seems unlinked to fragmentation. But this very mending cracks open time: in it, eternity breaks through. Or, we might say, forgiveness breaks open what might otherwise be a seamless future, multiplying its possibilities, because the refusal of forgiveness closes off futures. Forgiveness unbinds the moment from the trauma of the past, and time from a precondemned stasis of same-again.²¹ As a *relational* transfiguration, forgiveness opens once-foreclosed possibilities *between* (notably between subjects who do not, quite, retain the perfect distinctness of their individual selves). It allows us again to approach one another; it allows (though it does not by any means impose) proximity, even intimacy. We may think of forgiveness as mending rifts, but we err in thinking of it as closing off or filling up spaces.

To work toward an understanding of this temporality and relationality, this connectivity which is also an unbinding, we might do well to look at forgiveness in contrast to the order of law.

Forgiveness Outside the Law

> [T]he law is a calculated and relentless pleasure, delight in the promised blood, which permits the perpetual instigation of new dominations and the staging of meticulously repeated scenes of violence.
> —Michel Foucault, "Nietzsche, Genealogy, History"

At first, as we've noted, sacramental forgiveness seems legalistic. The *Catholic Encyclopedia* emphasizes this character, declaring reconciliation "a judicial process in which the penitent is at once the accuser, the person accused, and the witness, while the priest pronounces judgment and sentence."²² Sin is understood as a break both in law ("an utterance, a deed, or a desire contrary to the eternal law"²³) and in the relations between human and divine and among humans in community.²⁴ For the sacramental forgiveness of sin, a fairly rigorous set of prior requirements applies: examination of conscience, sorrow for sins committed (those discovered, remembered, or recognized upon that examination), resolution to avoid future sin, confession of sin to a priest, and acceptance of penance as assigned by the confessor.²⁵ Upon the penitent's expression of willingness to perform the penance, and presuming his belief in the penitent's sincerity, the priest grants absolution or, more precisely, is said to act as the vehicle of God's granting absolution.

But in fact other sacraments are first associated with penance and penitence:

> Private confession evolved during the Middle Ages and became dominant in the modern church; other rituals preceded and were contemporary with it; still others are emerging today. Baptism was

the first sacramental ritual to be clearly associated with the forgiveness of sins. . . . When the mass came to be understood and experienced as a sacrifice, the bread and wine were often seen as a sin offering, and in the Middle Ages theologians such as Thomas Aquinas spoke of devout participation in the sacrifice as a purification from personal sinfulness.[26]

It is clear that atonement runs deeper than legalism.

Indeed, in this seeming law-governedness there are, as I've indicated, deep peculiarities: the efficacy of the law is grounded not, as usual, in force, punishment, and death but in a promise; its guarantee is not one of penalty for law breaking but of forgiveness for such breaking. But what is promised is itself elusive, neither an object nor even a particular event: it is simply forgiveness, which is to say, the opening of possibilities, in the space between forgiven and forgiver and more fundamentally still in the world, laid out between subjects in time. Forgiveness promises the future in all its uncertainty. It is in this way that it inverts damnation's foreclosure, its "meticulously repeated scenes." It is not simply that forgiveness is a promise or is promised but that into the very concept of both promise and forgiveness is built a complex temporality that pulls the two together. Not every promise promises forgiveness, but all forgiveness entails a promise, and divine forgiveness makes possible in advance the option of promising at all.

Considered as a judicial procedure, reconciliation, for all its orderly requirements, is oddly slippery. This slipperiness appears, I suspect, precisely because the sacrament does not deal with restitution (not even symbolically or by penance)—such restitution belongs to justice. It deals instead with forgiveness, and thus must vibrate between justice (which can only be governed by law, whether of the canon, ethical, or statutory variety) and mercy (which cannot come under law at all). The essential atonement does not somehow make up or pay for the wrongdoing; penance here is not a repayment.

Within the realm of law, it is important that justice and mercy remain distinct; guilt belongs to justice. Hannah Arendt is critical of the Christian response to the Holocaust on just these grounds:

> It seems to me that a Christian is guilty before the God of *Mercy* if he repays evil with evil, hence that the churches would have sinned against mercy if millions of Jews had been killed as a punishment for some evil they committed. But if the churches shared in the

guilt for an outrage pure and simple, as they themselves attest, then the matter must still be considered to fall within the purview of the god of *Justice.* . . . Justice, but not mercy, is a matter of judgment.[27]

The outcome of sacramental forgiveness is not justice (the ideal outcome of law), with its restoration of right balance. It is integration, defragmentation, the mending of a rupture. And it is a promise that at once calls back to memory and sets the future free of the sameness of the past; it is the opening of the possibilities of futurity. Thus it is about the move from an induced fragmentation back to a prior wholeness. In this case, what has been broken and restored is a pair of communities—the larger community of the Church, the smaller community of the person with God. These two reconciliations are held to happen, necessarily, together.[28] At the same time, this return does not restore the same, does not present again the already known; instead, it reestablishes relational possibility and the chance of future community. The "whole" is interconnection, but not totality.

Blanchot suggests a distinction between sacramental and other forms of forgiveness: "And if forgiveness come from others, it only comes; there is never any certitude that it can arrive, because in it there is nothing of the (sacramental) power to determine."[29] Yet even the more certain (promised) arrival of sacramental forgiveness only comes, only gives us the future (yet to come), only presents us with possibility and not with fact, with the promise and not with the law. Forgiveness has the power to open a once-foreclosed future; this openness is the inverse of determinism. Forgiveness reinscribes the trace of the grace given by mercy, its relation to the law an unpredictable, immeasurable exceeding.[30] Or, more exactly: unlike law, whose function is precisely determination, forgiveness does not determine, even if it is granted; it sides not with the determinate but with the possible. It is divine in sharing the opening-up quality of the sacred, which is the creation of possibility, the chance to change form, the making of spaces: it is given in time as the future.

In *The Writing of the Disaster,* Blanchot presents an initially surprising argument *against* forgiveness. "Do not forgive," he writes. "Forgiveness accuses before it forgives. By accusing, by stating the injury, it makes the wrong irredeemable. It carries the blow all the way to culpability." He adds: "I cannot forgive—forgiveness comes from others—but I cannot be forgiven either, if forgiveness is what calls the 'I' into question and demands that I give myself, that I subject myself to the lack of subjectivity."[31] While I would value the terms otherwise (that is, I would still

FORGIVENESS

insist upon a positive value for forgiveness), I do think Blanchot is quite right to note that forgiveness neither forgets nor declares an act (or person) blameless; he is right, too, to suggest that forgiveness troubles subject boundaries, even as it reassures. We return not (only) to, but before and so beyond ourselves. Forgiveness does not imply that the forgiven person was never wrong in the first place. It suggests, rather, that that which was or might have been blamed is still blame*worthy*, but that blame, nonetheless, no longer attaches to it or that blame attaches but that the effects or results of that blame no longer hold. Atonement would be unnecessary if none merited blame. Forgiveness makes the wrong irredeemable by way of restitution or compensation but is itself a less predictable, yet more effective, mode of redemption.

This importantly distinguishes forgiveness from the resolution of guilt. Covering South Africa's hearings before the Truth and Reconciliation Commission, Antjie Krog writes, "I . . . know better than to ask my Jewish colleague whether anyone was forgiven on the basis of reparation [by the Germans]. Is contrition in the form of reparation, then, just as futile as denial?"[32] Without being so presumptuous as to claim to answer the question, I will at least toss out a suspicion: reparation may well be vital for justice, but paying off a debt is not precisely contrition; it does not seek absolution. Guilt, as Nietzsche noted, may well derive from an economic model, "the contractual relationship between *creditor* and *debtor*."[33] He chastises "previous genealogists of morality" for their failure to consider "that the central moral concept 'guilt' had its origins in the very material concept 'debt.'"[34] (Our sense of guilt as "bad conscience" is an internalization, he argues, of the pain proper to punishment.[35]) To be forgiven, on the contrary, does not erase but may indeed increase my sense of indebtedness—and my gratitude, the proper response to grace. I am not forgiven for what I can, or do, pay off. To be in need of forgiveness is not be indebted, nor is it even to be accused. It is to be in need of return, to want to be back in good graces, to want to be re-related, to be in need of some possibility not offered by condemnation, to be in need of possibility itself.

Forgiveness must, therefore, operate outside the law (since it acknowledges both that an act merits a penalty and that it will nonetheless not be thus penalized). Like grace, it must always come as a bonus rather than as merited; in or as an act of absolution, it ceases to renew the perpetual present of condemnation. And as Blanchot indicates, that bonus, like the redemptive desire of the previous chapter, must also call the neatly bounded self into question; opening the subject together with time. If the desire of the undistracted is eternity in the present moment, the grace of forgiveness is eternity in the open future.

If the rule of law is always death, or the threat of death, always penalty, we may include forgiveness on the side of affirming life outside rules. Foucault writes, apropos of Nietzsche, "Rules are empty in themselves, violent and unfinalized; they are impersonal and can be bent to any purpose."[36] Law universalizes rule, presumably, and renders it unbendable (there is no opting out of the law as there is opting out of the rules of the game by ceasing to play),[37] but it too must be impersonal, and it too must remain in touch with violence. Forgiveness operates outside this order; it can act as a corrective to law, but not from within—it directs itself precisely to persons. Still, this corrective is both vital and widespread; it is only thus that we can *live* with the law (only thus is the world sustained in existence).

Conducive Conditions

> There would be no gift at all if not the gift of what does not have, under duress and beyond duress, in answer to the entreaty which strips and flays me and destroys my ability to answer, outside the world, where there is nothing save the attraction and the pressure of the other.
> —Maurice Blanchot, *The Writing of the Disaster*

Because it lacks law's predictability, forgiveness cannot (successfully) be demanded, even if we sometimes want to say—knowing ourselves not quite right about it—that it has been earned. "Forgiveness," as Berel Lang notes, "is . . . a moral bonus, a gratuity—something that cannot be assumed beforehand but that by a combination of conscience and circumstance may, if we are fortunate in what we do (perhaps also in what we don't do), become part of the moral setting in which we act."[38] Yet just as one cannot quite shake the feeling that a person who has lived well and carefully and kindly; who has meditated, contemplated, prayed and *tried*, might somehow be more deserving of grace than one who is self-indulgent and thoughtless, so too we find not quite avoidable the sense that the truly contrite (perhaps precisely those who suspect themselves unforgivable) may somehow deserve, not the guiltlessness that justice would declare, but forgiveness from those they so regret having wronged. I want to hold at once to two propositions in tension (though not contradiction) with one another: first, that this feeling that some acts and some people are more forgivable than others is grounded in the realities of forgiveness; and, at the same time, that forgiveness cannot be merited, earned. Anyone might be forgiven or refused forgiveness; if we were so innocent as to merit forgiveness we would have no need of it. Outside the sacramental setting, the openness begun by dialogue is not guaranteed (in this, perhaps, lies that "power to determine," though what is "determined" is openness, indeterminacy). The sense of merit corresponds not to law but to likelihood: in significant part, to the likelihood that the offensive act or one resembling it will or will not be repeated. That is, that the future will not recreate the past or freeze the present.

Unless forgiveness is sought at the time of the deed itself (which, except in the case of wholly accidental wrongdoing, seems unlikely; we tend to regret our misdeeds only when the pleasure of the act has worn off), the wronged party must not only register but remember the offense—if I gather my courage and humble my pride and ask forgiveness for something I've done, only to find that the person I'm asking hasn't the slightest recollection of what I'm talking about, I may feel a bit relieved, but almost certainly a bit let down as well, and not exactly forgiven.

So in the mundane as in the divine sense, some form of memory is a precondition for forgiveness. Wolfson presents the contrast elegantly. "Forgiveness," he writes, "is the presence of the sign, inscription, the cutting of the covenant upon the rock; forgetfulness the absence of the sign, erasure, the depositing of the trace beneath the rock. . . . In forgiving one gives before, participating in the dialogue that releases the tension of the moment; by forgetting we remain submerged in the oblivion of the past, the silent speech of senseless chatter, the emptiness that is full."[39]

Forgiveness, as Wolfson indicates, is only falsely linked to forgetfulness: "I do not think that forgiveness is consequent to forgetfulness; on the contrary, it seems reasonable to assume that the two are mutually exclusive, for if a matter is forgotten, there is no need for it to be forgiven."[40] No need, and also no chance. To forgive requires that we remember (we are held to be infinitely forgivable in the perfection of divine memory), while to be forgiven is much helped by our remembering (and it is correspondingly difficult, though possible, to forgive someone who has no memory of having acted wrongly).

The popular phrase "forgive and forget," I suspect, is based upon a misperception of memory as somehow constant, unaltered except by its loss; and upon the belief that the past thus remembered is also constant save in the measure of its distance. This seems to me wholly to misperceive the way in which the future is freed. Forgiveness is a change in the *meaning* of memory, a transfiguration rather than a dismissal of the past. It is in many ways less about the past (though it must begin as the past's alteration) than it is about the future, which is likewise transfigured by it (a transfiguration effected in large measure by that of the past).[41] The pairing forgive and forget may be based, too, upon our experience with those transgressions that we find ourselves unable to forgive, where the best we can do is to refuse the persistence of memory. Perhaps not every human relation can be modeled on divine openness, however potent the appeal of such an ideal might be. Harold Kushner argues that forgiveness declares: "I refuse to give you the power to define me as a victim. . . . I don't hate you; I reject you."[42] This is indeed a *kind* of future freeing—it opens up new possibilities for me, a future unburdened by memories and anxieties associated with the person who has wronged me. But it does not open transformative possibilities in that *between*, the between of you and me; rather, it forestalls them. To say "I'm over it"—still more, to say "I reject you"—is not to say "I forgive you." It is, on the contrary, to insist that no possibility can lie before *us*, however usefully it might open new options for *me*.

Before we can remember—so that we can remember—we must pay attention, which is not merely to suggest that we must observe but that we must be attentive: we must have some measure of openness (the opposite of rejection), of the capacity to allow in or to feel with. A certain inattentiveness, I suspect, may be a very grave moral or premoral flaw, so grave that even the added grace of forgiveness may be hard put to overcome it (though, again, it does not suffice to render forgiveness impossible). It is true that we do not *need* to know, or care, that we did something wrong in order to be forgiven. Lang notes that we may even forgive those who are not able, because they are not available, to benefit from the forgiveness[43] (one can forgive even the dead, without any belief that they can know or respond). But if we do not know what we did, then that forgiveness cannot be transfigurative or redemptive for us, and in the case of significant transgression it is likely to make forgiveness much more difficult for the one who grants it.[44] The offender may fail by somehow not registering an offense, but also in a more complicated and profoundly disturbing failure of the understanding, such as Hannah Arendt attributes to Adolf Eichmann, or the Truth and Reconciliation Commission to many of those who enforced the brutality of apartheid: the failure or incapacity to be aware of doing harm. We must be listening,

FORGIVENESS

whether the call is the voice of another human being and the infinite demand of responsivity it places upon us, or the call to return and the infinite possibility of life that it opens before us.

It is in this sense that "they know not what they do" (Luke 23:34) becomes a hindrance to forgiveness rather than an argument for innocence—when they know not because they were too inattentive to notice, or too unconcerned to remember. Among those we are least readily able to forgive are not only those who refuse to repent or even regret but those who simply do not remember or even notice what they have done—those whose wrongdoing has failed to make any impression, or at least any lasting impression, upon themselves. Memory in one who did harm suggests that the injured party is not alone in being marked by the wrong, and this mark—this sense of regret or even just discomfort—is a potential impetus to transfiguration. Krog writes of a devastating moment in the TRC hearings in which a torture victim finds his suffering not denied but wholly forgotten by his torturer: "But for [former prisoner Gary] Kruser it is too much for flesh and feelings: that this experience, which has nearly destroyed his life, made not the slightest imprint on [former police captain Jeffrey] Benzien's memory."[45] Appalled as we are by the initial offenses of which Kruser tells in his testimony, we are perhaps more appalled still that the agent who committed them cared so little that they made upon him no lasting impression. If Kruser cannot forgive, in this instance, we are unlikely to find his inability difficult to understand.

But again, such forgiveness is not impossible. To forgive those who do not remember, as to forgive those no longer available, is still a transformation of a relation, though in the former case to one with whom I may not continue close relations, or in the latter to another whom I hold in memory rather than to another who confronts me in dialogue or exchange. Even these open new possibilities, if only in my ways of responding and continuing to respond to that person's (past) actions, my ways of understanding myself as shaped by them or functioning in relation to them. Thus, too, the influence of those acts on my own living is altered. (This may well, of course, alter other relations and connections involved in that living. "My own" is not intended to imply isolation.) It is not clear that the unavailable forgiven benefit here; rather, the obvious transformation accrues to the one who forgives. I suspect that we would be less *likely* to forgive such persons if, living and present, they had simply forgotten. Those not haunted by memories are unlikely to seek, or to receive unsought, forgiveness from the injured who remember. But there is no guarantee in remembering, either.

FROM TRAUMA TO REVELATION

It is helpful to the one who would forgive if, beyond simply remembering, the wrongdoer feels guilt, or shame, or unhappiness regarding the injury—this too not (or not only) because we may feel that these affects are themselves a sort of punishment (such that a form of *justice* has been done by the paying of a psychological penalty) but rather because they argue for the possibility of a *transformation*; they give the transgressor a reason to make the future different from the past. While it is possible to forgive those who hold themselves blameless, it is at least extraordinarily difficult; the range of possible transformations is most likely to be limited to the severance of the connection. Here Kushner's "I reject you" is easier, and likely to feel affectively "safer," than actual forgiveness. Even forgiveness will take up its transformations differently when addressed to the unrepentant than in other cases. That is, I am unlikely, in forgiving an unrepentant person, fully to reopen an interactive space between us, more likely to alter the meaning of my memories (which are, of course, a part of that space between) without structuring my life to include this particular other's continued interactive presence (or at least to keep that interaction inside narrow limits). But these are only probabilities—many more options are possible. And this is divine forgiveness as present in every act of human forgiveness: the very existence of options. The open uncertainty that is the future—the temporal dimension that manifests the eternal divine forgiveness—is the condition of possibility of human forgiveness, which is also to say that all forgiveness is divine: it gives us (back) the future.

Dialogue

> Sin is a matter of a certain kind of deafness, not whether this should have been done instead of that.
> —Stephen H. Webb, "The Rhetoric of Ethics as Excess: A Christian Theological Response to Emmanuel Levinas"

> Giving means opening out, means forging our tomorrows from the best in us gathered for others.
> —Edmond Jabès, *The Book of Questions*

Rather than simply being an attempt to follow or enter into the law, the purpose of sacramental confession may be a Leibnizian one: not simply to be forgiven as some rather calculated consequence of a causal process, but to open oneself to the space of possible forgiveness, with its

FORGIVENESS

necessary difficulty and mutuality. Dialogue makes this openness necessary; the sacramental imperative to confess introduces, of course, the chance element of human error, but it guarantees both being heard and the input of a second voice. (In fact, some thinkers, including Peter Lombard, have held that confession to a lay person will do if no priest is available, emphasizing the dialogical element even further.[46]) In dialogue the transformation of the past and the transfiguration of trauma into memory (of which more below) become possible, such that the future becomes true future, and not just the past once again. That is: the damnable moment can cease its iteration.

Dialogical forgiveness may not be easy. We might think that we can more readily forgive where we most easily understand (where the offense could most easily be our own), but part of the importance of dialogue, with its multiplicity of voices and ears, is to bring us to the awareness that no one can fully occupy another position. Nancy writes: "A discourse must indicate its source, its point of utterance, its condition of possibility, and its shifter [*embrayeur*]. But I will never be able to speak from where you listen, nor will you be able to listen from where I speak—nor will I ever be able to listen from where I speak."[47] While we might suspect that if we perfectly understood another person we would necessarily forgive, it might as easily be true that we would find forgiveness impossible, that we actually grant one another leeway for all of the possibilities we cannot know; that we interpret generously, with the potential for forgiveness already built in.[48] Or perhaps with perfect communication forgiveness would become meaningless, as—to take up too briefly Derrida's consideration—we forgive only what might be, what is potentially, unforgivable.[49] For forgiveness to matter, there must be or must have been some possibility that it would not be granted. Even if we argue that divine forgiveness is never withheld, it can certainly go unaccepted. (We can refuse the very ignorance of the future that brought Nietzsche such joy.[50]) To dwell in the possibility of forgiveness, we must be open, responsive, but without ever knowing what will arrive, without *knowing* even ourselves entirely, still less one another. To allow the future, we must make space in which to hear, always knowing we hear imperfectly, always listening more, rather than trying to predict the conversation or impose upon it a predetermined form. When we heed the call to return, we go back to the future, not to an easy comfort that we already know.

The imperative here is to listen and to see and to feel, to open oneself to the invariably elusive other. This sense of responsibility has to do with the barest level of what is shared, perhaps something as simple as the *possibility* of sharing, the capacity to attend, the ability to respond. Thus it is not merely a formal, ethical, or legal acknowledgment of what we share, though law too presupposes commonality. (As Arendt notes, "the law presupposes precisely that we have a common humanity with those whom we accuse and judge and condemn."[51]) We must, as Nelle Moreton has it, hear the other to speech.[52] Forgiveness, in opening the future, creates something unpredictable and hence uncommandable. In accepting or affirming the openness of the future, therefore, we do not obey (rules, or even the summoning voice)—we *respond*.[53]

The pathological incapacity for responsiveness is famously vivid in what Arendt calls the "banality of evil" in her analysis of Eichmann. In some obvious sense, Eichmann may recall every act he has performed in his official capacity—indeed, he proudly writes his memoirs. Yet in another sense he has never known what he is doing. He does not remember the evil of what he has done, the profundity of the horror he has caused, because they failed to register for him at all, because nothing in him is open to the call of another's pain. (Precisely this, as I previously suggested, makes him spectacularly difficult to forgive, though never in some ultimate sense unforgivable; that is, we could not insist that none of his victims forgive him.)

What all of this suggests is that both eternal, theological damnation and its temporal counterpart in condemnation echo that strange moment of original sin: always preferring the self, they sustain the impermeable imperviousness to the outside wrought in that first forgetting, directing only hate (or anger) beyond the self. They continue to turn away, oblivious and self-absorbed, from the relational possibilities of desire shared—or cutting-across and breaking. The forgiveness of the damned mends the split within them, their own separation, not merely from a God as other than themselves, but from themselves as sacred, from their own forgivability entangled in their own capacity for forgiveness. The coming of atonement is built into humanity, and forgiveness arrives, only arrives, without staying. It is already given as the promise of a novel arriving. Temporal forgiveness splits the two moments of forgiving and being forgiven, but for both—whether we grant forgiveness or receive it—a transfigured past opens a once foreclosed future.

Memory, in true Socratic fashion, is dialogical, and to forgive we must remember, must share across in the transformation of time.[54] The closing off is reopened in dialogue. Again, the insistence upon the sacramental role of confession to a priest, so often criticized (a silent and personal conversation with God presenting an evidently preferable alternative), may reflect some psychological insight, some awareness of just this dialogical character. More particularly, forgiveness requires that stories be told and heard. Among creatures, these are not only, not even primarily, the stories of those seeking forgiveness, which slide with dangerous though hardly necessary ease into self-justification or self-pity (though, we must remember, they may also be difficult and transformative confessions).[55] The most urgent narratives may be told by those *from* whom forgiveness is sought. The most urgent task of one who would be forgiven is listening, whether to the story of one injured or to the call to divine return. To understand the urgency of this telling, we need to look more closely at forgiveness as the inverse of trauma.

Trauma

> That is why to speak of loss, of pure loss and in pure loss, seems even though speech is never secure, still too facile.
> —Maurice Blanchot, *The Writing of the Disaster*

I have already argued that forgiveness, given or received, does not let go of the past by forgetting it but rather allows the past to release its hold upon the future by transfiguring what is remembered. This release is the reverse of traumatic temporality. To make sense of this claim, a somewhat longer digression into the elements of memory and narrative in trauma may be germane.

In psychoanalytic theory, trauma bears an odd relation to consciousness, which psychoanalysis holds to be the locus of temporality (that is, the unconscious mind is not structured in terms of time; thus a repressed long-ago experience, though consciously forgotten, may retain all the power it had when fresh). A traumatic "experience" never properly enters into time. Rather, exceeding the capacity of consciousness to register and organize—to cope via the simple act of being aware—trauma enters straight into the unconscious, and hence straight into the atemporality of repetition. In the classic version of trauma, the event that might have been experienced is repressed from conscious awareness entirely; we might also (if loosely) speak of "lesser" forms of trauma, in which the event is perceived but its affective force is too great to register. Ernst van Alphen writes, "the cause of trauma is precisely the impossibility of experiencing, and subsequently memorizing, an event."[56] And the very notion of a "traumatic memory" may therefore be misconceived:

FROM TRAUMA TO REVELATION

Traumatic events in the past have a persistent presence, which explains why that presence is usually discussed in terms of memory—as traumatic memory. Yet . . . the concept of traumatic memory is in fact a misnomer, if not a contradiction. Traumatic memories remain present for the subject with particular vividness and/or totally resist integration. In both cases, they cannot become narratives, either because the traumatizing events are mechanically reenacted as drama rather than synthetically narrated by the memorizing agent who "masters" them, or because they remain "outside" the subject.[57]

The time of trauma is that of a particular repetition, the time of the amplified moment: an endless present (which was, however, never presented) reasserting itself into all other presents—and, unless brought into time as memory, asserting itself as the future, foreclosing the open possibility inherent in the latter, and thus, again, making always more of the absent present. It is also, as the notion of reintegration suggests, a time of fragmentation, of affect and experience unintegrated into the psyche. Thus it creates a wholeness, a suffocating, totalizing foreclosure of time, by refusing integration, keeping outside of memory the trauma that is this repetition's very cause. One fragmentation is maintained at the cost of another.

Freud argues that the contrary to this damning repetition is memory, brought about in the technique at the heart of classic psychoanalysis: dialogue. Trauma repeats because its energy, its anxiety and pain, must somehow be "mastered," made manageable, but without memory it eludes that mastery, slips out from under it every time.[58] Only remembering allows the possibility of "working through."[59]

Trauma thus has a very peculiar present or presence. It tends to present itself, psychoanalysis argues, symptomatically, in repetitions ranging from dreams to tics to interpersonal relational patterns. As a rule, it is, in any case, presented in the body, which becomes without physiological explanation paralyzed, pained, insensitive—incapable or reluctant in its response to the world. But what is presented symptomatically is not "traumatic experience." It is precisely the absence of such an experience, the inexperienceable quality of it, and consequently the absence of memory. Traumatic "memory" might more accurately be described as a strange forgetfulness in which the body itself cannot forget, cannot let go, but must recreate the past. Only memory can redeem this lost time;

memory, though no guarantee, is the only way out of the repetition of trauma. We have to find our way back into the openness of time.

What brings the trauma into the present—not "again" so much as, in some odd sense, for the "first" time—is, if not the psychoanalytic session or other intentional dialogue, a sensation or event that somehow resonates with that absent memory. Jonathan Lear writes that this second, evocative experience is not precisely traumatic either:

> On [Freud's] model, neither of the two experiences is traumatic in and of itself. The earlier experience need not have been traumatic when it occurred, because it was registered but not understood. The later experience, for its part, can be innocent itself—as, for instance, the experience of mild sexual arousal in a situation that triggers a reminiscence of the earlier occasion. What becomes explosive is the cocktail of both those experiences.[60]

A presence nudges up against the particular absence of memory, its echo lending just a bit of presence of its own—in trauma as in the redemptive elusion of original sin. This temporal transformation is at the same time a transformation of form, of *language*. Bal writes, "Reenactments of traumatic experience take the form of drama, not narrative, and are thereby dependent on the time frame of the 'parts' scripted in the drama."[61]

The transformation from drama to narrative, from reenacting to telling, depends upon something crucial: a listener. "This other is often a therapist, but can be whoever functions as the 'second person' before or to whom the traumatized subject can bear witness, and thus integrate narratively what was until then an assailing specter. In other words, a second person is needed for the first person to come into his or her self in the present, able to bear the past."[62] One has to tell the story, to another.[63] Forgiveness is a story told again for the first time.

Memory is not purely reproductive even at its clearest and most simple; to construct a narrative from the symptoms of a forgotten drama is a dicey and delicate undertaking. Small wonder that the arguments over recovered versus constructed memories, especially regarding childhood traumas, have been so intense and even bitter. This is due not only to the remembering adult's chronological distance from childhood but to the necessarily dialogical quality of the narrative (of knowing, too, and of memory), which so easily draws out the tendency of the listener to fill in, extrapolate, help out with the telling.

FROM TRAUMA TO REVELATION

Let us grant the real risks a listener runs here, and even acknowledge that just as surely, sometimes, the listener's contributions are a bit too directly constructive. Even so, to begin to surpass trauma is to remember it, and to remember it is to make a narrative of it rather than a drama, and to make a narrative is to speak it to someone—to speak it but also to have one's speaking heard, to encounter and to participate in the creation of a receptive space in which time can become open. Trauma still in its traumatic form cannot be spoken or heard; it can be seen, but almost always the viewer lacks the knowledge to interpret the dramatic presentation. Like the bodies of the mad in Foucault's *Madness and Civilization*, those of the traumatized "speak" a highly somatic language unintelligible to reason.[64] "Healing" begins when that private language is rendered articulate. The mended self is open in time, the healed future open to difference—to other possibilities for experience, to other subjects who may forgive or be forgiven.

The gradual release from trauma as such—its release into consciousness, even if this is not immediately a release of whatever pain or sorrow may come along with it—is, in common with forgiveness, the gradual freeing of the future. What is released is the grip of repetition, its ability to form the future indefinitely in the shape of the absent past. But if no one hears the story the traumatized tell, the strangely atemporal "memory" may allow the past to retain much of its grip. The right to tell and the need to hear are both elements of transformative, redemptive memory.

This, too, is the importance of narrative in forgiveness, even when what is forgiven is not, in this classical psychoanalytic sense, a trauma. The sense is a dual one: the epistemological significance of telling and of being heard in the necessarily shared construction and the vital reconstruction of experience, and the transformative significance of the genre shift from the dramatic repetition of the traumatic scene to the unfolding, open-ended narrative of the future.

The first point I would emphasize in justifying this extended digression, the link to the questions of forgiveness, is the importance not only of speaking, which is so often emphasized, but of hearing. Indeed, to speak and not to be heard—to be persistently disbelieved or simply ignored—is more likely to give one a sense of ungroundedness or irreality than of understanding. And among the most important kinds of hearing, surely, is that which draws forth speech.

The dialogical quality is inseparable from the necessity of memory: memory, to say it once more, is never quite solitary. It is essential, as I

FORGIVENESS

have claimed, to forgiveness. To tell one's hurt and have it heard in some instances makes forgiveness possible: we can remake the meaning of the memories together. To tell one's wrongdoing and have it heard may go some way toward being forgiven, too.[65] Dialogically acknowledging my culpability, confessing, I put into play my memory and my regret, the material for the possibility that you, if I am fortunate in my conditions, may be able to meet with possibilities of your own. When repentance becomes dialogical, putting into play the desire to be forgiven, divine desire, as suggested by the analysis of original sin, is that which does not turn away—it draws toward. Open possibility, futurity, or eternity is for anyone who re-turns it. The trauma of sin is damnation, the repetition of separation. What the promise of forgiveness reveals is that damnation is the refusal at once of living eternity and of open time.

In dialogical confession, central to sacramental penance, bringing to language has long been considered vital. As Virginia Burrus notes:

> the pragmatic theorizing of Augustine's contemporary (and sometime rival) John Cassian suggests to Foucault that the willed submission of thoughts to the power of words is indispensable for the process of conversion toward which confession always aims. This is the case first because verbalization allows for discernment: evil thoughts—that is, the kinds of thoughts that *need* confessing—can be conveniently identified by their resistance to linguistic expression. Yet that formulation is already somewhat misleading, for confessional language does not simply represent pre-existing thoughts but collaborates continuously, and indeed vigilantly, in their strategically reluctant production.[66]

Often conceived as forced admission, confession might be understood more fundamentally as the requirement to speak, at once to reveal and to construct what was. As dialogue, it is at once essential and disruptive to memory, as Burrus further notes: "Confession, when it happens, breaks (upon) us, disrupting the very certainty of our yearnings. (So too does forgiveness.) Its aim may be framed as the nostalgic recovery of a fantasized wholeness yet it manifests as an abysmal and salvific brokenness."[67] Indeed, she understands confession as "a sustained state of contrition, repentance, conversion. Not a catharsis but an ongoing responsiveness—a painfully unrelieved openness. Confession performatively constitutes the matrix of the infinite responsibility of which Levinas writes. It does not produce independently verifiable truth but offers testimony to the desire to *make truth*."[68]

The point of speaking is only in part a consequence of what is said; to speak at all, to transform to narrative, may matter more. The conversation, the chance and the need for responsiveness, is *opened*, and the future created with it. As Burrus adds of Augustine's very famous, not altogether penitential confessions, "Augustine's confession of his lowly status enacts not only his own 'turning' but also God's 'turning.'"[69] Turned toward one another, speaking and listening to the call of the word, human and divine open the space of the sacred, the possible, the yet to come, which was always given as the very fact of possibility.

We might note that the failure of the initial event to register connects trauma to the banality of evil. The shared characteristic is exactly that of not (quite) being experienced—in the case of trauma, an event is not experienced because the ability of consciousness to register the "experience" is exceeded; in the case of banal evil, a regret or sorrow that would seem appropriate to the rest of us is not experienced because the capacity of otherness, of *humanity* outside oneself, to register in one's consciousness is absent. In both cases the offense—the symptom or the evil, the restriction on possibility and on response—is likely to go on repeating. In forgiving, we either trust that the offense will not be repeated or insist that it will not carry the same meaning. This is why we find repeat offenders so hard to forgive (in justice as well as in mercy); repetition seems to reinforce itself, and the more often a similar act occurs the less likely appears a future without it.

The damned, living in the time of trauma, have damned themselves in refusing to forgive or to speak with; they are both those who must forgive what they hate and those who, by that act, could become the forgiven; they are evil and traumatized at once. They refuse the double openness of time and word.

Trauma occurs in the absence of knowledge; one who seeks to be forgiven must know what she has done—the odds of releasing the future and making it different from the past are otherwise poor. One who seeks to forgive must know what offense she is forgiving—and may need to say it or to hear it spoken, share the memory to know the material for transformation. While trauma demands the absence of memory, forgiveness functions only where we do not forget. Memory, for both forgiver and forgiven, is the transfiguration of the past and the opening of the future, the way out of the eternal dullness of repetition that forms the life of the damned. The release from repetition is the key to freedom, the release of the future from the sameness of the past. By retelling the story, by shifting emphasis, by including and excluding new elements, forgiveness changes the ability of the past to form the future in its own image; by remembering and then transforming memory, it breaks open the future.

This transfiguration releases time from either linear inevitability or same-again repetition; it is closest, I think, to the time of revelation, in which a transformative change of meaning alters our understanding of the past and opens our sense of the future.

The Opening of the Future: Revelatory Time

> Praise this world to the angel. . . . He will stand astonished.
> —Rainer Maria Rilke, Ninth *Duino Elegy*

Elizabeth Grosz writes, in "Thinking the New: Of Futures Yet Unthought": "In seeking an open-ended future, one is . . . required . . . to acknowledge the capacity of any future eruption, any event, any reading, to rewrite, resignify, reframe the present."[70] The possibility of an open future, its ability to reframe, to rewrite, extends also to the past. A new past emerges in forgiveness; the old is subject not to forgetfulness as a simple lapse or loss but to an active "forgetting," to the retelling of the story to make new chapters possible. The past is revealed as what it was, yet newly known, made new by the possibility of novelty.

Damnation may appear to be the persistence of memory, but in fact it is structurally closer to the persistence of trauma in memory's absence, the repetition that *cannot* let go. Forgiving, requiring the gratuitous risk of a gesture in which we do not keep ourselves safely, carefully to ourselves, in which we cease to predict the future by gambling upon it instead, taking the chance of allowing chance's reentry, is also risk. Bataille links this openness to the spirituality that fascinates him: "I can't imagine a *spiritual* way of life that isn't . . . dependent on chance."[71] To be forgiven opens the future not by *losing* the past but by *changing* it, changing its meaning and thus loosening its grip on the future; to be divinely forgiven is to be given the future, the spirituality of chance.

Again, forgetfulness might seem, like forgiveness, to release the grip of the past. Only the latter, however, is transfigurative; the former is more likely to be no more than the repetition of the past by those who cannot remember it (a high probability, as Santayana famously pointed out). The future can be a repetition of those pieces of the past that remain insistent, psychically or historically. It can hold condemnation, the constant renewal of separation, the refusal of forgiveness in the reassurance of sameness. Or it can hold forgiveness, the transformation of the past into the openness of the sacred, the inviting, the seductive and frightening.

Forgetfulness fragments, loses pieces. Memory re-collects. We associate re-membering with wholeness (in opposition to dismembering or fragmenting). But perhaps in fact forgetfulness is also a false wholeness; perhaps it is sometimes the spaces that we forget. Memory is not stable, not totalizing; it is not only incomplete but never, in such senses, whole. Memory, too, opens the future.

In its curious temporality, forgiveness shares the temporal character with which Peter Manchester characterizes Christian revelation, which he calls "a radical and retroactive transformation of understanding."[72] Such revelation (within Christianity paradigmatically that of Christ risen) is for him the starting point of Christianity, a beginning that is itself memory, the resurrection casting the time of the historical disciples into a new light. Citing both Augustine and Kierkegaard, Manchester argues for the time of Christian revelation as "a disclosure space, as a field in which horizons can be opened, manifestation and occultation embodied, configuration and transfiguration of events presented, and not merely as a metric space supporting location and order in sequence."[73] Revelation, in this model, is not the sudden disclosure of some new thing at some particular time but the transfiguration of time—in this founding instance even of temporality—as it is: the emergence of old things as quite other than they were (and yet as they were already). "The temporal structure of Christian revelation is not however innovation, the insertion of novelty, but transfiguration, which is above all a mode of recovery and continuation."[74] In this transformation of the temporal by eternity, "Christian temporal experience is one of outliving the endings of the world,"[75] a set of endings beginning with the death of God.

Wolfson likewise notes in Kabbala the revelatory element of forgiveness, a revelation that nonetheless retains mystery: "Significantly the return to origin is marked by the uncovering of that which is hidden.... inasmuch as the disclosure is always of that which is concealed, the uncovered withholds its own presence in the moment of its uncovering. What is revealed, therefore, is an absence that is present only as that which shows itself as concealed."[76] In such return, the traumatic absence meets a more salvific absence of presence; without insisting too strongly (and thus falsely) on the parallel, we still read here an echo of the necessarily hidden future.

FORGIVENESS

As the time of damnation parallels that of trauma in refusing to release the potential openness of the future from the rigidly structuring grip of the past, the time of forgiveness parallels that of revelation. Both revelation and forgiveness retell "new" stories about the "same" material, and so make it not the same at all. In forgiving, I do not deny that someone has acted badly toward me, but I transform the meaning of that action so that its harm is no longer constitutive of our relation. In being forgiven, I am granted that same openness, that the past need not create the present and the future in its own image.

This openness of the future through the alteration of the meaning of the past—releasing the future from repetition by recharacterizing the past as forgiven, by remembering that transformation is possible—is forgiven time as well. For Augustinian and Kierkegaardian readings of Christianity, Manchester writes, "in a distinctive way the *future is in the first place*."[77] As he goes on to note, "The striking thing in the position is that eternity itself is modulated by the future, 'maintains its relations with time' in such a way that the future becomes its phenomenon."[78] Eternity and futurity alike are openings of time. Manchester analyzes temporally the theological virtues of faith (a foundational mode of relation to the past), hope (the mode not of reaching to the future but of grasping the promise inherent in the present), and love, adding, "It is love to which the future belongs, and the reverse, the future belongs to love. The question that opens to the future is, what is worthy of love? What in the present situation, entered in faith, understood with hope, elicits and confers the wholehearted self-gift that is love?"[79]

We need not love those we forgive, but forgiveness and love share generosity's risk taking (humanity is sure to sin eventually). Original sin, a primal or preprimal forgetfulness, separates me, makes me myself unto myself and closes me within myself. But prior even to this is forgiveness. Damnation affirms, indeed violently reaffirms, this separation into an eternity of repetition; its fragmenting repetition is also a closing off, a closure of the open multiplicity of the future as chance, and even the open multiplicity of the past, the potential for multiple stories, for new tellings. Leibnizian damnation is a malign Nietzscheanism, an eternal return of the same without the yes-saying upon which Nietzsche insists as the ethical import of that return. (This *yes*, we recall, is also what makes of the eternal return an opening to infinite difference: if I say yes to every return, I say yes to every alternate possibility into which each moment fragments in the temporally infinite reconfigurations of finite matter.) It is an eternity of refusal—and so, if we allow eternity the meaning of vibrant openness, the refusal of eternity. It is an eternity of unforgiveness, the persistent refusal to hear the call. Forgiveness opens the future by its transformative illumination of the past—it is a revelation and a construction at once. As damnation consists in a persistent repetition of the past dragging its condemnation into the future, forgiveness, by its nonforgetful transformation of the past, makes it possible for the future not to be a repetition of past condemnation. And this possibility is always, divinely, already given to us.

This might seem to separate original from subsequent sin; primal forgetfulness must seem quite contrary to damnation as the persistent return of the present. But in fact both participate in the damaging atemporality of trauma, eluding memory with its capacity not only to recognize but to transform. Sin separates, whether originally or recurrently; forgiveness mends and yet, by mending, opens—opens the self to something other than separation (perhaps even to intimacy) and the future to the grace of chance. Yet divinely the space was open all along (only our capacity for response is transfigured). We must confess—that is, enter into dialogue—to begin to hear the voice calling for return, the voice that precedes the turning away.

If forgiveness is transformative, that is precisely because it does *not* forget—it takes up the hurtful, the evil, the potentially unforgivable and transforms its meaning, thus transforming the future along with the past. Thus forgiveness takes on the character of the affirmation behind the positive formulation of the Nietzschean eternal return—not a yes to a few favorite things, but a yes so strong it takes up everything and says, this is worth it. It refuses resentment. Redemption, the fundamental consequence of forgiveness, is entangled in memory, but memory *not* as repetition: rather memory as transfigured and as essential to transfiguration.

If the damned are kept so by their hatred of God, we can easily see that they are bound by their refusal of futurity and of eternity: by their grim, furious hate, which holds on only to the past as irredeemable. Inverting the common conception that heavenly perfection must be boring, the Leibnizian view makes of damnation the ultimate boredom, perpetual sameness in the absence of pleasure.[80] Only the willed openness to self-loss, this willingness to take the chance that forgiving must be, is enough of a *yes* to allow us to live. (I shall go further, in the next chapter, and argue that love predicated on finitude, on mortality, requires at the beginning that we forget our own forgetfulness—that we assume ourselves able, always, to love as to forgive.)

FORGIVENESS

This ability can never be a requirement; forgiveness without its gratuitous character has only its legalistic sense, whether economic (as of a debt), sociopolitical (as in amnesty), or even theological (penance as restitution). We can require of ourselves and others that we be just but not that we be merciful, not without losing the character of mercy—that is, not without bringing it back under justice. The fullness of forgiveness here requires our own divinity, our own willingness to forgo the predictability of damnation. If it is divine to forgive, if forgiveness is divinity within us and calling to us, it cannot be legislated; we cannot set up rules for the divine, for the sacred, for the eternal. Nor does forgiveness fix a future; it guarantees nothing and is not accomplished, not completed; it provides not an ending to the story but instead a new way of telling it.

The fragments of memory mend together into a new narrative to break open the future, mend and break again, constantly retelling and making retelling possible. Its time is that of the promise, the revelation of the future in its openness instead of the traumatic, damning closure of repetition. Forgiveness addresses a break: between human beings and across human and divine, addressing a relational space in which stories are told. It must, therefore, be more personal than legislatable, a trait, as we shall see, that it shares with love. Like love, too, it surprises us with its revelation of what already was enfolded in the possibility of what might yet be.

4

POPPIES AND ROSEMARY
Love

189. Which are the two great commandments that contain the whole law of God? The two great commandments that contain the whole law of God are: first, Thou shalt love the Lord thy God with thy whole heart, and with thy whole soul, and with thy whole mind, and with thy whole strength; second, Thou shalt love thy neighbor as thyself. And one of them, a doctor of the Law, putting him to the test, asked him, "Master, which is the great commandment in the Law?" Jesus said to him, " 'Thou shalt love the Lord thy God with thy whole heart, and with thy whole soul, and with thy whole mind.' This is the greatest and the first commandment. And the second is like it, 'Thou shalt love thy neighbor as thyself.' On these two commandments depend the whole Law and the Prophets." (Matthew 22:35–40)
　　—A Catechism of Christian Doctrine, Revised Edition of the
　　Baltimore Catechism, Part 2, Lesson 15

Curious Commandments

　　I perceive that the distinction between lover and loveable is beyond the wall of the coincidence of unity and otherness.
　　　—Nicholas Cusanus, *The Vision of God*

　　There's rosemary, that's for remembrance. Pray, love, remember.
　　　—William Shakespeare, *Hamlet*

The commandment to love, referred to in this chapter's catechismic query and response, is given in several New Testament gospels,[1] largely repeating Leviticus 19:18 ("You shall love your neighbor as yourself"). Yet love seems even less readily commanded than does forgiveness, and in fact the passages cited here don't legislate in a conventional sense. Eckhart writes of Luke's version ("Love God above all and your neighbor as yourself"): "This is a commandment from God. But I say that it is not only a commandment but that God has given us this as a

LOVE

gift and has promised to give us it."² This commandment comes as forgiveness does: with the force not of penalty but of promise, more gift than order to give, more twist in time than causal chain.

"Love," in the imperative, is less an order than a substitution for orders, for regulations, for laws—which is not to say that it countermands them, as then it would simply be another order. The *Catechism* suggests, rather, that if one has managed to keep these commandments to love, then all other commandment keeping will follow: "all the other Commandments are given either to help us to keep these two, or to direct us how to shun what is opposed to them."³ But of course the only reason one *would* manage to keep them would be if one loved already. This sort of twist, this already-there demand/gift of love, is central to this chapter. Love can be an imperative only if it is already present, can be a promise only if it is already kept. Love's promise is not one we make after careful consideration of relevant data, but a promise in which we find ourselves already. "I was astonished to find that already I loved you, not a phantom surrogate for you,"⁴ writes Augustine to God, precisely in his discussion of memory, and this amazement is perhaps characteristic of love, which comes as a discovery of what already is, however gradually it may have crept up on us. *How in the world did I get here?* one wonders in love, and somehow one never remembers. Love's promise, which is in large measure a promise not to forget, is given as something remembered.

Like the promise of forgiveness, that of love is elusive: it promises only itself. It is a promise of memory against loss, a promise that sustains the possibility of the (shared) future yet also twists out of time; a promise that the lover finds has been made, without subjective intentionality, in some strange "already" whenever one loves (a promise we do not remember making, a commandment we find ourselves obeying already), a promise that forgets the mortality implicit in it; finally, a promise that is "kept" simply by its remaking, by the once more of what was made before the knowing of it. The eternity of love, that is, is an eternity of implication: promise (with its futurity), joyous affirmation (of the amplified present and its infinite splitting), and memory (of a past that is bigger than information could contain). Memory is promised to the future to allow the present its never-sufficient intensity.

Obsessive memory and deep forgetfulness play off of one another here. What is it, then, that we have to forget, and what must we remember, in order to love? The answer is by now an unsurprising one: in order to promise, love forgets the law, especially as the law is death (disintegration and decomposition and loss, of lover or love or beloved or all of them), and it forgets forgetfulness itself. This particular forgetfulness of forgetting tangles us up with remembering again.

As the strangeness of the commandment to love already suggests, love in most of its versions is far from the precise and formal letter of the law. While it sometimes appears to follow ethical laws—often we do, after all, treat well those we love, or at any rate we try to do so—Blanchot notes in *The Unavowable Community* that "Love may be a stumbling block for ethics, unless love simply puts ethics into question by imitating it."[5] And in fact love is just as often contrary to most ethical formulations, precisely in its particularity (of which more below) as well as in its anarchism and its greed.[6]

We already know that rule-defying desire is far more readily and steamily portrayed than any sort of legitimated eroticism. (Indeed, the very term seems curiously contradictory. As Mark Jordan notes, "In many ways, the theology of Christian marriage has tried to promote sex without eroticism."[7]) Myths that lead to marriage tend to end there, as if acceptance into the legal and social order precluded further flights of desire or of imagination, as if it were impossible to marry *and* to burn. Of course, real marriages and real eroticism may in reality coexist, even if they remain discursively elusive—but one suspects that eros emerges in these relationships as the return of the anarchical, the resurgence of desire with its disordering tendencies within order, of greedy unrest within peaceable coexistence. Love promises something not other but more than desire, seeming in the promise to stabilize this destabilizing force, since we think of the promise as a kind of guarantee, and thus an imposition of order. But in fact this time-turning promise does not grant fixity at all, any more than the open promise of forgiveness does; time, in fact, is taken out of order.

Love's disordering tendency also appears as the instability of identity. Memory's recurrence to what one loves is both unitive (joining together lover and beloved) and famously obsessive, holding the beloved greedily, near-constantly, in memory. Yet, as Roland Barthes points out, we must sometimes forget, lest we die "of excess, exhaustion, and tension of memory."[8] We must, that is, also remember ourselves.

Neither the intermittently remembered I nor the obsessively recollected You ever quite has or holds onto love, which is always moving toward and across, always between particular subjects yet always problematizing those subjects too. Luce Irigaray argues for a love that, moving between and opening spaces, yet importantly retains a space to which a subject might return (though never quite returning, never the same subject unaltered, never to quite the same place, never to stay).⁹ To complicate this further, we are not preestablished subjects who, from a securely identifiable position, go out and love, or even befriend; all of this construction, of the "I's" and the "we's" in relation, is in flux, made in the outgoing and the flowing back and the cutting across. To play Irigaray's intuition off of Barthes', we might say: I must forget that I love, sometimes, to return to my self, in order that I might be a self who can love. Or, to put it differently, I can only love incompletely, and perhaps inadequately. But I *can* love, and we still must wonder how, and what in the world it means; we must wonder how such an improbable commandment might be fulfilled.

It is a commandment with several variations. According to John 14:34–35 (roughly repeated at 15:12 and 15:17), the disciples are to love other persons, not as each loves himself, but as Christ loves them. "I give you a new commandment: love one another. As I have loved you, so you also should love one another." It is as if this love were too much simply to receive and contain, and so must overflow those who receive it into love of others, so that those others are loved with a love that has flowed through multiple bodies, multiple selves.

Earlier in this gospel, Christ tells his disciples: "I have told you this so that my joy might be in you and your joy might be complete. This is my commandment: love one another as I love you" (John 13:11–12). Here too joy is linked to love as both are linked to a sharing that cuts across boundaries: "that my joy might be in you." When Nancy writes of love, his words echo this boundary-crossing property of joy: "Thus there is, strictly speaking, neither giver nor receiver—and there is no appropriation, either. There is gift, abandonment without resistance—to something like possession, but 'possession' here means mutual abandonment."¹⁰ I am given myself only by giving that self over; I "possess" the one I love only by abandoning my self-possession, and so, yet again, I am not there to possess. I am not there, either, as the one to whom the law, or the commandment, might apply.

In fact, we attribute to love a paradoxical pair of relations to the loving and remembering subject. First is the commonplace that love makes whole a previously partial, fragmentary, or even damaged self, whether this wholeness comes "again" or "for the first time." In this view love, whatever it is, restores me to myself, gives me (back) to myself, somehow more fully myself than before.¹¹ The second, equally common, notion is that love is particularly and profoundly disruptive of selfhood, that it takes me out of myself. Of course, neither restoration nor rupture will be in any way simple. We forget ourselves in what may be still more profound forgetting, which entangles our sense of self as interior with that of another sensed self outside of us. We find that we have already been promised.

Thus, even in vague and popular notions, love entails both making whole and disintegrating: "at once the promise of completion," writes Nancy, rendering this vagueness more precise, "but a promise always disappearing—and the threat of decomposition, always imminent."[12] The possibility of completion, with its sense of finality or finitude (finishedness), is never itself completed (never other than possible: "they lived happily ever after" does not complete, but only gestures toward, a life); that of decomposition, fragmentation into everlasting oblivion, is always deferred. Love thus suspends itself, neither unitive fusion nor utter disintegration, but constantly moving or reaching toward both; it suspends not only the couple (to take the simplest case) but each subject implicated in the relation; it suspends the relation itself, which is rather more choreographic than sculptural. That is: the couple or other grouping is never completed, never fused, never stabilized in a consistent relational space; the subjects, as we have said, never return to themselves the same, but never lastingly disappear into some thirdness, let alone oneness, of loving, either.

That is: we are "completed" in being taken out of our incomplete isolation (a completion never realized, never fulfilled for the self that seeks it); we are fragmented into the absence of ourselves (without ever losing ourselves altogether, always with a place for return, though an altered one). The promise is fulfilled by being deferred; it is kept only by keeping it (as) a promise. This must mean, too, that love is never identical with a complete or totalizing sort of satisfaction.

"The promise does not anticipate or assure the future," says Nancy: "it is possible that one day I will no longer love you, and this possibility cannot be taken away from love—it belongs to it. It is against this possibility, but also *with* it, that the promise is made, the word given. Love is its own promised eternity, its own eternity unveiled as law."[13] Yet this law, as we quickly see, is neither determination nor death. The promise, though it points toward the future, is not about the future alone, any more than forgiveness is solely about the past it transforms. Love is the promise both of endurance and of *eternity*—a promise impossible for any person to *keep*. As Nancy also notes, love is *not* the combination of promising and keeping the promise: "When the promise is kept, it is not the

LOVE

keeping, but it is still the promise that makes love. Love does not fulfill itself, it always arrives in the promise and as the promise. It is thus that it touches and that it traverses."[14] It remains at once imminent, even immanent, and yet deferred.

Law and Sacrifice

> The world will start from nothing in order to dissolve in the All. Likewise any law.
> —Edmond Jabès, *The Book of Questions*

What cannot be kept cannot quite come under law, with its necessary stability, either. Yet Nancy writes: "The promise neither describes nor prescribes nor performs. It does nothing and thus is always vain. But it lets a law appear, the law of the given word: that this must be."[15] As we have begun to see, this law in its insistence ("this must be") nonetheless works against the law that prescribes and proscribes, that forces; it works, instead, to open, to give the gift not only of the possible (as forgiveness does), but of the security that we find in being remembered, of a safe space from which to risk ourselves. The "this" that must be is a space of possibility and shared joy, made and held by memory. What must be is at once clear (that love shall be) and unspecific (as possibility must be). It is a law as pledge working against law as death. The death penalty demanded by law (in exchange for transgression) is transfigured by the generosity of love (into an inexchangeable gift).

Here I would recur to a passage from Blanchot cited in the discussion of original sin: "The law reveals itself for what it is: less the command that has death as its sanction, than death itself wearing the face of the law," he writes in *The Step Not Beyond*. "The law kills. Death is always the horizon of the law: if you do this, you will die."[16] *The law kills* takes up, of course, Paul's contrast between the law's inflexible justice and the life-giving spirit, between strict adherence to the letter of the law (that is, to the law *as* law) and nuanced attention to the spirit of the law (that is, to the law as mitigated by mercy, by grace, by love).[17] Natural and formal law are linked in death, which is not only a legal penalty for sin but a law of nature, the fate of mortals.[18] But the Pauline relation of law to death is more complex still. The law may be death, but death frees us from the law, too: for example, a woman is bound by law to keep her marriage vows, but not after the death of her husband (Rom. 6:23). Still more subtly and more dramatically, the death of Christ breaks an older law: "In the same way, my brothers, you also were put to death to the law through the body of Christ, so that you might belong to another, to the one who was raised from the dead in order that we might bear fruit for God. . . . But now we are released from the law, dead to what held us captive, so that we may serve in the newness of the spirit and not under the obsolete letter" (Rom. 7:6). We are dead to the law of death. This "obsolete" law bound death to sin as more than penalty: "What then can we say, that the law is sin? Of course not! Yet I did not know sin except through the law, and I did not know what it is to covet except that the law said, 'You shall not covet.' But sin, finding an opportunity in the commandment, produced in me every kind of covetousness. Apart from the law sin is dead" (Rom. 7:7–8).

Law, that is, is responsible for sin not simply because there is always a bit of pleasure in doing what one ought not to, but also because the law gives us ideas; it would not have occurred to me, suggests Paul, to covet had covetousness not been forbidden. The boundary makes its own crossing possible. The penalty for this crossing is death, but Christ, undoing death (by double-crossing into resurrection), undoes too the necessity that legislatively links consequence to action: that is, he breaks the law. Or, at any rate, he reveals that it has an outside.

Blanchot complicates this notion too:

> The law cannot transgress itself, since it exists only in regard to its transgression-infraction and through the rupture that this transgression-infraction believes it produces, while the infraction only justifies, renders just what it breaks or defies. The circle of the law is this: there must be a crossing in order for there to be a limit, but only the limit, in as much as uncrossable, summons to cross, affirms the desire (the false step) that has always already, through an unforeseeable movement, crossed the line. The prohibition constitutes itself only by the desire that would desire only in view of the prohibition.[19]

Desire has already crossed the line of the law, allied itself with life; yet it can only exist in this complex entanglement with the law that kills.

For Paul, what has held us captive to law in the first place is the mortal consequence of original sin (desire turned away from the infinite and directed toward the finite, drawing us into finitude, into death). If death begins in original sin, it takes another death to establish mercy: standing in for humanity, Christ is *justly* sacrificed—except that this standing in is impossible for justice. That is, though the law is impersonal, it is nonetheless precise in its application. It does not concern itself with the person to whom it is applied, yet it must pick out just *that* one. Its precision is numerical (in the sense of identifying exactly a particular one) rather than human. In its mortal substitution, the sacrifice of the crucifixion again undermines the law with which it seems to accord.

That the law can only be applied impersonally, even if it must apply to the person of the transgressor, means that it cannot matter to the law who crosses it. Blanchot writes, "The law says 'in spite of you,' familiarity that indicates no one. Grace says, 'without you, without you there for anything and in your own absence,' but this familiarity which seems to designate only the lack of anyone, restores the intimacy and the singularity of the relation."[20] Without simplistically identifying grace with love, we may legitimately predicate an intimate singularity of both. *There in your own absence*: "not the failure of love in a singular case, but the fulfillment of all veritable love which would consist in realizing itself exclusively according to the mode of loss."[21]

The precision of love is not legal but personal. It is not only that I love this particular one (love emphasizes the irreplaceable singularity of the beloved) but also that *I* love; it is not enough to me that the beloved be remembered in general, or held as something valuable in the memory of others. Just as much as I enter into love, so too it comes to and through *me*. The self is as vital as its abandoning; if I love you, I must hold too to the space of my memory where you are held. Sometimes, I must remember myself.

The impossible substitution of one death (or one defendant) for many belongs not to law but to love (trading price for gift once more); the fourth gospel famously declares that "God so loved the world that he gave his only son" (John 3:16). Paul emphasizes the extreme improbability of this loving act: "only with difficulty does one die for a just person. . . . But God proves his love for us in that while we were still sinners Christ died for us" (Rom. 5:6–8).

This might read cynically as a substitution nonetheless, if we argue that a God unwilling to die is willing to send a son in his stead. If, however, we take the Trinity seriously, Christ is sent not in God's place but as at once God's son and God's self, which is also to say as the message of divinity in—or even as—human flesh. Thus the giving of the Son is also the gift of the Father, the giving both of what is most loved and of the loving self.[22] At the same time, the death of the incarnate Son stands in for all human dying—and so hints to us that the precise separations we conceive, between father and son but also between human and divine, are not so exact as we might have believed.[23] Love flows through multiple bodies.

As we've already noted in contemplating forgiveness, the law alone, justice by itself, is unbearable: inhuman, but not divine either, something more nearly infernal, something that sentences God to death. Luckily, the application of law in its ultimate penalty, mortality, is here turned around upon itself by an excess of love.[24] Death becomes love's ultimate proof ("No one has greater love than this, to lay down one's life for one's friends"; John 15:13), but love becomes death's ultimate undoing ("he who loves death makes the law vain in making it lovable"[25]). This is not a love of death against life (the sort of ascetic turn that Nietzsche so vigorously condemns[26]), but a love of the transient even as it passes, a love "proper" to the very law it undoes. This is the emergence of eros in the impersonal, the persistence of the possible in the open space of the promise. The sacrificed God returns, twisting the line of mortal time in resurrection, promising memory and demanding it, and thus, once more, sharing with forgiveness the possibility of a salvific transformation of temporality.

Do This in Memory of Me

> The lover's anxiety . . . is the fear of a mourning which has already occurred, at the very origin of love, from the moment when I was first "ravished." Someone would have to be able to tell me: "Don't be anxious any more—you've already lost him/her."
> —Roland Barthes, *A Lover's Discourse: Fragments*

In the ritual commemoration of this not-quite-legal sacrifice (a sacrifice in which even the legislators appear a bit anxious[27]), we find, curiously enough, a story about love as promise, a story at once peculiar and exemplary: the workings of the promise of love appear with unusual clarity in and around the Eucharist, in which "mourning . . . has already occurred," and keeps recurring, mutually, with joy.

Christ, before dying and thus before rising to open time again to the possibilities of eternity, will promise to be reciprocally present for anyone who will remember him. In all the canonical versions of the tale, he calls upon memory at the last supper with his disciples, and he links this memory to flesh. Luke recounts the promise thus:

> Then he took a cup, gave thanks, and said, "Take this and share it among yourselves; for I tell you [that] from this time on I shall not

drink of the fruit of the vine until the kingdom of God comes." Then he took the bread, said the blessing, broke it, and gave it to them, saying, "This is my body, which will be given for you; do this in memory of me." And likewise the cup after they had eaten, saying, "This cup is the new covenant in my blood, which will be shed for you." (22:17–20)

Paul presents a similar version.[28] Matthew and Mark, though they do not evoke memory quite as explicitly, do also connect the food transfigured into flesh with a curious temporality. The former writes: "I tell you, from now on I shall not drink this fruit of the vine until the day when I drink it with you new in the kingdom of my Father" (Matt. 26:26–29). And the latter, similarly: "Amen, I say to you, I shall not drink again the fruit of the vine until the day when I drink it new in the kingdom of God" (Mark 14:22–25).

Performing the proto-act of transubstantiation, Christ offers himself, in the flesh, as flesh, to those who love him: take and eat, this is my flesh; take this, all of you, and drink from it: this is the cup of my blood. In this corporeal exchange, eternal memory is (has always been) made, and is always remade, in the flesh.

In every one of these accounts, temporality is strangely turned. Where memory is evoked, it is a future memory in the imperative: I am going to do something which I will ask you to remember and to call upon as a re-created past (made once more present) in the future. Or, where futurity is invoked: This is the end, until everything is new; this is the end, until the beginning. A dual promise is at work here, one given and one elicited, but the promise is not to do anything other than remember, and thus to renew itself.

In the fourth gospel (in which we find a rather different account of this last supper), a complex crossing of identities is evoked, together with futurity:

> Whoever loves me will keep my word, and my Father will love him, and we will come to him and make our dwelling with him. Whoever does not love me does not keep my words; yet the word you hear is not mine but that of the Father who sent me. I have told you this while I am with you. The Advocate, the holy Spirit that the Father will send in my name—he will teach you everything and remind you of all that [I] told you. (John 14:23–26)

POPPIES AND ROSEMARY

Christ twists time, here as in Paul and in the synoptic gospels, in making a promise for a beginning after (what one would have every reason to think) the end, foretold but not yet come: a promise for a future teaching of a message already given, part of which message is simply that it will come again. It is a promise of recollection before the passage of the remembered. As Denys Turner notes, the Eucharistic temporality embraces both the presence and the absence of Christ:

> In fact, Christ is absent in the Eucharist along two dimensions of time: he is absent in respect of his historical existence pre-mortem and he is absent as he will be for us in the beatific vision in heaven. If, therefore, the Eucharist makes Christ present by signifying, it does so only on a double condition of the absence of what is signified: the Eucharist is time past and time future insofar as they can be present in the present, as it were in a kind of "nostalgia for the future."[29]

The Eucharist is no simple present or re-presentation, but is complex with all the complications of memory.[30] In it, waiting in hope is sustained with mourning in memory,[31] and in the present is love. Absence is always coming, always has come, but even in absence memory holds to the place of the beloved within the self; flesh is taken into flesh, and the sacrament remade.

Communion, communication, and the transformation by memory of finitude all figure here. It is at this later-reiterated final meal that Christ enjoins his disciples (those who love him, those whom he loves) to remember. It is here that he calls upon memory: whenever you do this, do it in memory of me. Preparing to die, he prepares the defiance of death: not only the initial resurrection with its transfiguration of temporality, but innumerable resurrections or reappearances of the flesh, millennia rather than days later on. He makes a promise of memory after his own death.

In this (perhaps central)[32] act of memory there is something fairly astonishing, regardless of the metaphysical considerations that make transubstantiation the source of significant doctrinal headache.[33] That there is a sharing of transformative memory is true regardless of whether we are buying into a metaphysics distinguishing essence from substance or from accident, taking the Lutheran route of belief in consubstantiation,[34] or arguing for transignification,[35] in which the transformation of the bread and wine is said to be in the significance that they hold for the assembled congregation.³⁶ The extraordinary act of memory occurs even without *any* dogma of transfiguration or transformation. As Elizabeth Anscombe points out:

> There is the now old dispute between Catholics and Protestants whether we eat what only symbolizes, or really is, the flesh of the savior. . . . Because of this dispute, it appeared as if only the Catholic belief were extravagant—the Protestants having the perfectly reasonable procedure of only *symbolically* eating Christ's flesh and drinking his blood! The staggering strangeness of doing such a thing even only symbolically slipped out of notice in the dispute about transubstantiation.³⁷

However conceived, the re-incarnation or re-membrance of the body of Christ in the form of bread and wine is supposed to occur within the context of the ritual re-enactment of the last supper—the miracle that makes possible the "doing this," sharing of bread that is flesh, that is performed in memory. Loss, however, also precedes recollection, and all four gospels feature death scenes.

At death, according to two of our sources, Christ cries out in abandonment: *Eli, Eli, lama sabachthani?*—"My God, my God, why have you forsaken me?" (Matt. 27:46, Mark 15:34). But God replies to him no more than Elijah, and the sense of abandonment stays. This final cry is not the confident exclamation that one might expect from a god, still less the expression of calm acceptance that one would anticipate from God's son, a son who has already, though expressing his wish to live, turned over his fate to the father's will.³⁸ It is an outcry of despair in the turning away of one from whom love is expected, to whom it is given: *Why have you abandoned me?* In despair, into emptiness—forgotten, abandoned—Christ dies. But more, given the sliding boundaries of persons (risking, of course, Patripassianism³⁹), perhaps he cries out too against having abandoned himself. Or if, as Hans Urs von Balthasar has it, the son is the self-giving of the Father,⁴⁰ perhaps he cries out against the possibility that the gift will be more rejected than truly received. That is: that he has given himself out into nothing, that no safe harbor has been held for him in memory.

Love, after all, is not merely pretty, and it casts us into the terrifying possibility that, having abandoned ourselves, we will be left with nothing, not even us, that no safe space has been held for our return. It includes always within it the possibility of mourning, for the self as well as for the one loved.

The despair of abandonment sets into relief the shock of the resurrection: though foretold, it remains unexpected, unexpectable, the sense of loss having overwhelmed any awareness—as it would seem, even, to overwhelm any chance—of future possibility.

There are other accounts. According to Luke, the final words are more resigned: *Into your hands I commend my spirit* (Luke 23:46). Here the surrender of will is emphasized, but also the surrender, the handing over, of self. The fourth gospel suggests death as completion: *It is finished* (John 19:30). This initially unsurprising and elegant statement is, however, strangely placed in the gospel with perhaps the most developed resurrection stories; it is not finished at all. If anything, as I have elsewhere suggested,[41] this gospel fascinates with Christ's manifestations of incompletion. To be completed here seems not to be whole, integrally or hermetically closed off, but to enter into a curious time in which life can follow on death, in which completion is not a neat wrapping up or an end but an always, all of time. ("And the end and the beginning were always there," as Eliot puts it, "Before the beginning and after the end / And all is always now."[42]) The promise of completion is always deferred, or, perhaps, completion is not what we thought, not a finishedness making finitude, not a cutting off or a closure. Rather, *it is completed*, it is perfected, in entering into the openness not only of futurity but of eternity, in the time twist that allows life to succeed death. The promise of completion is "complete" only in the making, kept only by its remaking. But this opening into eternity also means that every now opens onto the infinite, shatters into uncountable pieces and possibilities. Though his bones remain unbroken (John 19:36), the vessel of God (or the vessel that is God) shatters time—carrying, as I shall argue in Chapter 6, the flesh itself into eternity.

Of course, it is central to these stories that, within the entanglements of the Trinity, Christ lives in the perfection of divine memory. But the father's forgetfulness (even if only seeming) in these stories is important, too, a reminder of the inseparable intermingling of forgetfulness with memory. A warning, maybe, not to foreclose mourning from love, not to forget that the Eucharistic presence marks an absence, too.[43] Nancy writes: "What 'the God of love' means is that love alone abandons. What is not love can reject, desert, forget, dismiss, discharge, but love alone can abandon, and it is by the possibility of abandonment that one knows the possibility, inverted or lost, of love."[44] What the flicker of absence in

LOVE

the doctrinal Real Presence means is that for humanity, too, it is, it must be, possible that some day I will not love you, and this gives meaning to my promise that, nonetheless, I will.

It is to the imperfect human memories of his disciples that Christ commends his flesh. It is the body that rises, still damaged: Christ bears beyond death the wounds of the flesh.[45] It is in love that the body returns, and it bears its wounds with it. If, as I have elsewhere suggested, identity is made in wounds and scars, made in the spaces of absence and the imperfect seams of their mending,[46] Christ becomes himself in this act of love, is completed in this disruption—a love he carries past death to his return to life, carrying the marks still with him, the traces of a literally opened self. The body remembers, and among the moments it remembers most vividly are those of its own breaking. We carry in our flesh the memories of our loves and our lovers, and like our scars these memories play a part in our self-construction. Love gives us ourselves, perhaps, but not as wholes, not unbroken; if some part of us was missing, this makes a strange completion. Love remains, rather, as a promise of completion and fragmentation both.

We are accustomed to hearing that the crucifixion is an act of love or evidence thereof, but this characterization seems still more conspicuously true of the resurrection and its commemorative feast, both of which are returns to the world for the sake of those loved. These returns alter, in turn, the meaning of time. Here it seems the reappearance in and of the flesh is meant, in part at least, as reassurance—I really will recur to you, *I will not forget*. Eucharistic return is the reappearance of memory, with its paradoxical and paradoxically corporeal combination of absence and presence.

The donation of Christ eucharistically literalizes the giving of self in love, and it tells us something of the timing of that gift. The Christ risen in the resurrection stories dies, or is taken away, doubly: after his brief return to those who love him, he is gone from their lives again. This time, however, he seems to be gone from the world without the process of dying. We might say that the clarity of the distinction between life and death is muddled here, or we might more optimistically read this mysterious moment as life's strange triumph in loss. Christ returns not to stay but to promise return (to promise again)—and the love is not simply in the returning but in the promise, not a love beyond death but a love through death, an always not, or not only, of steady endurance but of infinite return, the repetition of remembrance. Absence returns with presence. Wherever you look, this return suggests, I am already there—

but your looking is what has brought me, and you sought me wondering if I might be gone (every search and remembrance is undertaken on the chance of absence). We find love only in the possibility of abandonment, the risk of mourning, both already in the memory of the promise.

The body brought back in the Eucharistic rite is neither dismembered (it is said to be whole in every fragment of the host[47]) nor ever, quite, forgotten (in some places one can witness still the perpetual adoration of the sacrament,[48] meant to guarantee as nearly as the limits of human attention allow the constancy of memory of Christ's body). Yet it is torn as well as whole; not only flesh but blood is presented at the Eucharist. It is absent until called, and present in its absence.

Christ returns himself to the world and promises a return, something more or other than loss, to those he loves. But *his* memory alone will not suffice, as the exhortation to memory in turn ("do this in memory of me") indicates. That is: those who are loved must love as well, and in love by the dual act of memory reinstantiate the always absent/present God. The command "do this in memory of me" is also the command to love—but of course love cannot be commanded and must have been already, in a foresworn oath and foregone conclusion. No one, that is, will follow this injunction to the memory of the incarnate God without having loved him first, without finding him in memory already.

Thus we find an interesting sense of love's shift in the space between lovers. The God which is also love is given but cannot be received except as a regiving: I give myself to you, but you can only receive me by loving me, by remaking me in the space of your memory, holding onto the promise to love—that is, to remember to promise again.

The exhortation "do this in memory of me" emphasizes the point that the receipt of love can never be passive. To forget is not to have the lover turn away, but to turn oneself away, distractedly, and so to cease to bring love back. Memory in turn forgets death, both to grasp the miracle of return and to make love bearable.

But we do well to remember the moment of abandonment and the sense of being forgotten. Hard to reconcile with the notion of a call between persons of a divine Trinity, the *Why have you forsaken me?* is nonetheless human and divine at once.[49] Whatever faith this call may indicate, it is certainly not a matter of belief, nor an unshakeable certainty. It seems, rather, to be an ineluctable need to call out, to try to be heard: a need also to listen, and ask to be called; a need to call toward, and hope to be heeded.

Memory, yet again, is dialogical. The memory eucharistically invoked is an act of impossible faith, trust in a near-unbelievable love—a love that consents to death and in that consent defies it. Nothing can break the law of death, but, like forgiveness, love tells us that there is an outside to the law—a promise of the future with is openness; of the eternal with its intensity; of the return with its multiplicity.

But none of this renders death any less intolerable, makes any less likely the outcry—My God (my love, my friend), why have you abandoned me? The God who returns is neither broken nor whole, but open, wounded; we are reminded that the God in this story is vulnerable to humanity, to desire as well as to hate. And we are reminded that human divinity must also be vulnerable to desire. Remember: in this act, bring me back, renew each time my body.

And yet, of course, one must be absent to be remembered; love's vow in this story is predicated upon death. "[T]here is probably no amorous discourse," says Blanchot, "if not the language of love in its absence, 'lived' in loss, in decline—that is, in death."[50] The command at the last supper refers to the future tense, but only by calling upon a love that was and is already present, foreseeing an imminent loss: here is the act you can later perform, here is the way to re-call me, when absence has come around again. The loss itself is not lost; that is why memory has to be reperformed. (That is: we cannot remember once and have done with it.) But loss is now conjoined to reclamation. If you do not forget, death is cheated of the final say; if you do not forget, or if you do not only forget (but also remember, at least sometimes), you will not be forgotten. More exactly: in order to love, you forget the law of death and forgetfulness. The Christ who calls out to the agony of death, of being forgotten, knows the worth of remembering. *Do this in memory of me*—and I shall remember you as well, more than intermittently. Eucharistic reenactment invokes a double promise: a promise extracted (remember) but only in virtue of a vow already made (I will already have remembered you).

Death is the Mother of Beauty

> We love each other like poppy and recollection
> —Paul Celan, "Corona"

> Death is the mother of beauty; hence from her,
> Alone, shall come fulfillment to our dreams
> And our desires.
> —Wallace Stevens, "Sunday Morning"

"Death is the mother of beauty," writes Wallace Stevens, meaning not that only what is dead is beautiful (or, as the verse suggests, desirable), nor even that we should turn our love, Goth-style, toward morbidity, but that desire, or longing, is linked to passing and loss. He goes on to write, in the next verse of "Sunday Morning":

> Is there no change of death in paradise?
> Does ripe fruit never fall? Or do the boughs
> Hang always heavy in that perfect sky,
> Unchanging, yet so like our perishing earth,
> With rivers like our own that seek for seas
> They never find, the same receding shores
> That never touch with inarticulate pang?[51]

We love one another both in and against our mortality; all love shares the divinity of being promised before death. Given an added edge—Stevens's "inarticulate pang"—and urgency by the passage of time and the ever-increasing risk of losing the beloved, love nonetheless declares itself "forever" and often even means it, forgets loss and passage, forgets the fallibility of the lover's mortal memory (both in order to love and in order to believe in the chance of being loved). In the founding, generally inexplicit promise of the future and of the eternal that love makes, it is necessary to forget that we forget, necessary to presume ourselves perfect in our fidelity.

Love's sense of loss comes not from the absence of possession but from the impossibility of staying. The two are not entirely unrelated; often we wish to possess so that we will not lose, not face absence. In a brief essay, "On Transience," Freud argues that "Transience value is scarcity value in time. Limitation in the possibility of an enjoyment raises the value of the enjoyment."[52] In seeming contradiction, however, we may resist loving what passes, or we may hate the passage of what we love. Freud argues that we find here an effort proleptically to resist mourning. He urges against this resistance, noting how invariably mourning comes to an end: "When it has renounced everything that has been lost, then it has consumed itself, and our libido is once more free (in so far as we are still young and active) to replace the lost objects by fresh ones equally or still more precious."[53] The essay is devoted primarily to love as directed to abstractions and to nonhuman objects, and it seems to work rather better there; love across human beings, or in the realm of the sacred, may be less amenable to the cheerful realism of knowing that there are always others available for loving, a replaceability that comes a bit too near to "indicating no one."

LOVE

Still, the sense that we resist the built-in mourning of loving the transient seems important for love more broadly. We resist mourning, but we feel too the added edge and urgency it gives to our connections and our desires. Eros has been called "bittersweet" at least since Sappho apparently coined the term,[54] and surely the inherence of mourning—the reaction to the (ever-present possibility of the) loss of what is loved, which feels like a loss of self,[55] to the dual impossibility of satisfaction and staying—is no small part of this sense. Contrary to Freud, I suspect that we already resist mourning if we see it in advance as bearable and passing, if we already anticipate the ease of replacement. That is: to tell ourselves that mourning is followed by replacement is already to refuse to mourn. I would agree instead with Nancy, who writes: "But mourning is without limits and without representation. It is tears and ashes. It is: to recuperate nothing, to represent nothing. And thus it is also: to be born to this un-represented of the dead, of death."[56] Love carries mourning in its knowledge of mortality, its memory of absence. This inherent mourning must be not repressed or limited but taken up, or it may be fatal to loving at all—as in the case of the friends who prompted Freud's writing of his transience essay, who refused to see any beauty at all in any of the things that pass.

Memory is not invariably the force of love, return, and gathering; forgetting conversely is not only about death, descent, and disintegration. The persistence of memory can be its own kind of brokenness, but fragmentation has its forms of redemption, as well. It is not incidental that in our myths love is so often entangled with loss. "A great love carries with it a mourning for love," writes the poet Edmond Jabès.[57] At the center of the most satisfying love, the most gratified desire, there is still not only an absence but a loss, a craving for the impossible: not only for eternity but for everlastingness, of the beloved, and the lover, and of love; not only for the hopeful legislation of the promise but for the mortal guarantee of law. There is slippage in and into the sacred; as Burrus writes: "God appears (and also disappears) in the movement of love between and beyond persons, in the slide from the personal to the impersonal, from the self to the loss of self, from the discontinuous individual to the continuity of all existence."[58] The impersonal, the lost self, the continuously disindividuated, is no simple destruction of the self nor simply the impersonality of law; again, we find the doubleness of being ourselves while outside ourselves, too.

In the passage from which I've been quoting in this chapter, Blanchot makes some startling connections among love, desire, and death, writing of "this death that desire, far from turning itself away from it, gives itself as its ultimate aim, desiring until death, in order that death, even as death of desire, is still the desired death, that which carries desire, as desire freezes death."[59] The law still sets its limits; the only way to surpass them is to take them up into the mixing of memory and desire, to, as Bataille has it, assenting "to life up to the point of death."[60]

The experience of full assent is joy. In the midst of considerations of longing and mourning, of mortality, we must also remember that the sharing of joy is in some important measure constitutive of the relational space of love; joy shares us. Nancy calls joy "a serenity without rest." Though he is writing here primarily of a specifically sexual sense of joy, his sense of joy and joyous eroticism opens widely:

> To joy is not to be satisfied—it is to be filled, overflowed. It is to be cut across without even being able to hold onto what "to joy" makes happen. To joy cannot contain *itself*. . . . The joy of joying does not come back to anyone, neither to me nor to you, for in each case it opens the other. In the one and the other, and in the one by the other, joy offers being itself, it makes being felt, shared.[61]

Joy and sharing, in this version, are caught up in one another; joy carries within it an irresistible desire for sharing, and it is what shares. We "hold" joy in memory, promise to share joy and to find joy in sharing and in being shared. It is in joy that we say *yes*, affirming life even as life passes, affirming the life that passes while at the same time holding one another as safe as human memory can; we affirm the love of those we may yet mourn, or who may yet mourn us, or who may, all swearing notwithstanding, forget.

In all human love is the madness, as Augustine has it, of "loving one who was mortal as though that one were never to die."[62] We love so intensely that loss becomes devastating, and yet we love so intensely in part because loss is always possible. The beloved, perceived as necessary to one's own existence, as necessary as the "law" of the promise, is in fact contingent—is one who might not be.[63] Joy's affirmation is not simply an acceptance of what cannot not be.

This affirmation at once bursts the moment through to the eternal (an affirmation of this now, always: not again horizontally but cutting straight out of time vertically)—and opens time to possibility (an affirmation of all possibilities opening from now). This is, again, the possibility caught up in eternal recurrence. But we have already noted that in time, too, there is the possible—as futurity. And love, as promise, promises mnemonic fidelity; it too promises the future, not only in openness but in recollection. Love both requires passage and resists it. Divine love and divine forgiveness open an infinite possibility. But so, in their unique and momentary ways, do ours: a moment of joy opens onto the infinite, the promise of love holds open time, opens eternity in joy and the future in the promise. Even in the presence of joy is the mourning of absence, but, crucially, the joy is thereby *complicated*—not diminished.

Conceived sometimes as an infinitely extended line into the future, this promise of the possible may also be understood as the vertically infinite possibility of eternity, of divine infinity or eternal return as it cuts through, saying: everything else, too, may open from here; so long as this ever was, everything else may be. In this sense, the self-sacrifice of God is the reopening of possibility, the refusal of the mortal insistence that possibility end—the law's insistence that possibility be foreclosed. In this sense, the absolute risk of the self, the openness to being forgotten or abandoned, gains everything.

To love, we forget how little is allowed.

When Is Memory?

> It's a poor sort of memory that works only backward.
> —Lewis Carroll, *Through the Looking Glass*

> Only what disappears will have called for us.
> —Edmond Jabès, *The Book of Questions*

Love's memory is never uncomplicated; it comes before the passage of the remembered, based upon the forgetfulness of the future as death—I remember the other (obsessively, even) because I love; I love the other although and because we die, because I want to hold what I love safe in the face of mortality and because some part of what I love is caught up in passage and movement and change. Because I vow to remember forever, I have to forget that we die in order to swear to remember by having sworn in an immemorial somewhen. I must deny the limits, the mortal inattentiveness, of my own memory, and others' too. And I must continue to follow the commandment that gets its force from the obedience I had already given it.

Loss, annihilation, and even mortality are implicated within love, which at the same time defies them. The work of love is to forget forgetfulness itself; it is to swear to go on remembering, to hold within the

POPPIES AND ROSEMARY

space of re-collection, however it changes and shifts, to bring back the beloved in each return to myself.

Forgetting is lethal, but there is nothing simple about Lethe as the flow of death:

> The Ancients had already sensed that Lethe is not merely the other side of Aletheia, its shadow, the negative force from which the knowledge that remembers would deliver us. Lethe is also the companion of Eros, the awakening proper to sleep, the distance from which one cannot take one's distance since it comes in all that moves away; a movement, therefore, without a trace, effacing itself in every trace.[64]

It is death itself to be forgotten; love's memory is the only force stronger than death, greater than forgetting, memory as the force of resurrection—a coming again as always arriving. But memory, like eros, requires forgetting. We are astonished to find ourselves already loving, already doing the remembering love promises to do. We forget how we might have gotten to this.

So the incompleteable subjects of love find themselves motivated in some measure by a future loss (necessitated by the mortality of lover and beloved) already forgotten in the promise of memory. Love is a foresworn promise to remember, to rejoice in this union founded in the face of its own passage. Before we leave ourselves, we swear, we shall remember one another. (And thus we face the risk of abandonment too, and the risk of self-loss.) As long as *I am, you are* re-collected, unforgotten, present even in your absence, generous even in your loss. In the end, we begin: before we love, or at the founding instant, we have promised that we will not forget.

This demand is self-evidently impossible. It demands that we return, always *and* eternally, to a promise to remember that we don't remember making. It demands that we vow to remember, and, in order to vow, that we forget. We can only swear before ourselves. Love is thus founded at once on the futurity of the promise and on the death it overcomes, the death of the other, which gives me myself in intolerable isolation, the death of my self, which gives me continuity with the other through my own loss, the passage of all onto which it would hold. Love colludes with both memory and fragmentation in both integrating and fracturing the subject.

LOVE

We both recollect and redeem imperfectly, incompletely, constrained by mortal memory. But this, too, is enough, this brief entry into time of the eternal. And not enough, not nearly enough. "*Once* I lived, like the Gods," says Hölderlin, "and no more is needed."[65] This seems right: once, one moment absolutely affirmed, one shared joy, suffices to eternity. And this is not right at all, not sufficient at all; this is not satiation, not satisfaction, not fullness or fulfillment or completion. *Not enough*[66]—love is famous for always asking more.

At once mourning and rejoicing across the gulf of discontinuity,[67] love remembers a continuity that cannot have happened, not yet, not to separate persons. "Do this in memory of me," says Christ, before his absence can call upon that doing, and these words are remembered in each reiteration of that commemorative rite. In order to have sworn already, we must forget that we have not yet perfectly joined, that we cannot join. We cannot even always, from inside the passage of time, remember. But we swear to remember, nonetheless, each to hold the other safe in recollection.

The gratification of the desire for total merging could only be the end of me.[68] To become wholly disindividuated is death, and it is not death but life (at its most emphatic) that love desires. I desire the impossible, to be myself as a loving subject and to be outside of being and time in joy. Desire at its most impossible enwraps in obsessive memory the body of the beloved, bringing it back, disrupting time with the eternal. We lose ourselves in love, and we are completed in disintegration.

Love is, then, as Nancy says, a promise, kept not by fulfillment but by remaking, in the manner of memory. I would add that it is a promise to remember in the face of death and forgetfulness, and thus a promise that folds time, bringing memory into the future, promising return. It is a promise as well to share joy without denying mourning, and thus a promise to cut through time, a promise of the eternal. "So life could come and go," says Hélène Cixous, meditating on the notion of taking leave, and taking leaves, and love: it could "come back from going."[69] We will forget, and wander in our attention and our recollection, but we can, remembering, promising to hold in memory, take leave from merely going away; we can turn toward, and draw into, and—faithful if never quite constant in memory—love.

5

DISMEMBERED DIVINITY
Saints' Relics

216. How can we honor the saints? We can honor the saints: first, by imitating their holy lives; second, by praying to them; third, by showing respect to their relics and images. . . .
219. Why do we honor relics? We honor relics because they are the bodies of the saints or objects connected with the saints or with Our Lord.
—*A Catechism of Christian Doctrine*, Revised Edition of the Baltimore Catechism, Part 2, Lesson No. 17

The Making of Saints and the Rules of Relics

Break my body, hold my bones—hold my bones.
—The Pixies, "Break My Body"

In this chapter I want to talk about the relics of saints, about their paradoxical play between fragmentation and wholeness, vitality and mortality, sacrality and profanity, and about the kinds of memory at work in the display and understanding of these bodily bits, the kinds of temporality thus evoked. Relics, while no longer central to the structure of churches or most habits of worship, retain a persistent fascination. They literalize the body's fragmentation, but they suggest a peculiar persistence of wholeness, too (a persistence upon which the next chapter will pick up as well). As Patricia Cox Miller notes of hagiographic texts, relics maintain "their subjects in a tensive perch between transcendence and materiality," while they still "constantly strain after inferences to wholeness or spiritual completeness."[1] Both the flesh and the text of the saint's life function in this curious space.

SAINTS' RELICS

The kinds of memory that relics evoke affect, even in some measure help to construct, the identity of those in their presence, yet they undercut the certainties of those identities too. My own suspicion is that relics—in some sense, and to our senses, one of the most direct possible encounters with sainthood—tell us (once again) something unsettling about identity itself. They tell us something about remembering and about breaking apart, and they emphasize the enduring importance of the somatic.

It seems to me that there are three kinds of memory evoked by relics, at least by those I've viewed—kinds I have loosely labeled historical, communal, and sacred. These categories are based both in the abstraction of theory and in many visits to the sites of relics and reliquaries, primarily within the United States. My very limited experience with Christian relics in other places (Catholic relics in Europe, Orthodox in the Middle East) suggests that they intend chiefly the last of these. A deep sense of history or community may well be present, but these are not evoked with such deliberation or intentionality as at the American sites. Given this "fieldwork" of visits to a number of American reliquary sites, there will be a fair amount of description in and around the theory. My examples here are drawn from a few of the sites I visited for research purposes, in a series of trips on which I was accompanied by various friends, both for the pleasure of their company and to elicit their responses; the theory is drawn from a wider range of such trips, as well, of course, as from the usual practice of reading and what is called thinking.

I will begin here not in the late antique cults of the saints but in the realm of more recent memory, with just a little about the late Pope John Paul II, specifically about his unprecedented rate of canonization—that is, the designation of a given person as a saint—and about the possible relevance of saints, and more exactly of saints' bodies, to our sense of the sacred. John Paul II canonized about five hundred new saints, thus exceeding the saintly output of the entire previous half millennium. The standards for canonization were formalized under Pope John XV in the eleventh century, and the Congregation for the Causes of Saints, which applies those standards, was established in 1588. (Saints were designated prior to this time, of course, but by less formal means.) Between 1588 and 1978, when John Paul II took office for his very long (twenty-seven-year) reign after the very short (thirty-three-day) reign of John Paul I, a *total* of 296 new saints were canonized.[2]

Before 1978, there were only about three thousand Catholic saints altogether. The previous canonization record, so far as I've been able to determine, was held by Paul VI, who between 1963 and 1978 canonized some eighty-four new saints. It seems clear that John Paul II was dedicated to the making of saints, rather than simply happening to find them everywhere because humanity had gotten so remarkably good, and it seems at least possible that this dedication will continue. (John Paul II's successor, Benedict XVI, canonized several new saints within a few months of taking office and accelerated the canonization process for his predecessor.)

One reason for so thinking is that John Paul II made canonization much easier. His 1983 streamlining of the canonization process included the removal of the devil's advocate (the member of the Congregation for the Causes of Saints whose role it was to present arguments against canonization). Cardinal José Martins notes, "This reform of John Paul II came as a response to a desire expressed by the Second Vatican Council to see on the altars saints who are contemporaries—persons with whom every Christian can easily identify because they lived in the same cultural setting, with problems similar to those which all of us have to face every day."[3] This demands, in part, that the sainted not have been deceased for so many years that their lives have become foreign to us. The reasoning behind this desire is that people will be drawn to a church that allows them these means of identification, a church in which the sacred does not seem distant and strange and wholly superhuman. The post–Vatican II church has encouraged attention to the saints: "we are urged by the Second Vatican Council to ask the saints for help by interceding for our needs before God.[4] Part of the ongoing recovery of a more integrated Catholic theology . . . has included a turn to the saints as sources for theological reflection."[5]

As this implies, the upsurge in sanctification is in some measure an effort to retain and recruit members to the Catholic church. Many of the newly canonized have belonged to countries where Catholicism remains strong but is not unthreatened by evangelical Protestantism. The abstractions of Trinitarian theology, the intricacies of dual-nature Christology, the nuances of Mary's immaculate conception are not very gripping for most people, however much they may fascinate and delight the theogeeks among us. The papal hope is that saints have some of the mass appeal of evangelism and can help the Catholic church retain or even increase its popularity. Christianity may technically worship the consubstantial God who is one coeternal being in three distinct persons, but it's not hard to notice that, of those persons, the Holy Spirit receives the least devotional attention, almost certainly by virtue of being the hardest

SAINTS' RELICS

to picture as a person—no matter how fond one is of doves, they simply lack the drawing power of more anthropomorphic depictions. People like people.

The saints don't need to be anthropomorphized, because they're *anthropos* in the first place. They get what it's like to be human and can plead our case with the abstractions. While it is always doctrinally delicate to aspire to be God,[6] we can easily, the thinking goes, aspire to be saints, in the recognition that the (necessarily postmortem) success of this aspiration depends not only upon our own best behavior but upon a special grace. But is this kind of identification, a simple "we are (or can be) similar to one another," enough? Does it really give us a sense of the role of saints? The question of that role is certainly too large to be answered here, but I want to look at the small part played in it by relics and to suggest that the simplicity of identification by similarity is too simple after all, too simple to help us in understanding either identity or the complex character of relics.

That is: like John Paul II, I think that, if we consider seriously the idea of sainthood, and in particular the idea of saints' relics, it must affect our sense of identity. However, while he seems to have understood the saints' effect upon identity to be the perception of similarities between the potential church member and the one canonized, thus strengthening the possibility of identification with the Catholic church, I mean seriousness as a more abstract, less dogmatic consideration and take the effect upon identity to be a kind of troubling. In these broken bits we find not only the persistence of memory and of corporeality (the latter in a church always made a bit uncomfortable by it) but once more an opening of ourselves, now still more explicitly through the flesh.

A few details about relics themselves may be in order, both for clarity and to start to suggest that there is something about them that threatens to slip out of order, an unsettledness to their canonical place. Relics would seem to be a rather minor aspect of sainthood, yet their importance in cults of the saints, even now, seems fairly significant. Relics are saints' bodies or, much more commonly, pieces of saints' bodies, or items associated with the saints by bodily contact. The bodies themselves provide first-class relics, which may be major or minor. A major relic is a whole limb or head or the part of the body specifically implicated in martyrdom, such as a piece of skin with an arrow hole through it. The rest are minor.[7] Usually these are, in terms of size, very minor indeed (some barely visible), with bone chips being among the most common. Other relics are not bodily pieces but items that have directly touched the body of the saint. If the association with the saint's body occurred when the saint was alive, the relic is second-class—as, for instance, the spring from St. Frances X. Cabrini's dentures, proudly displayed at the gift shop of her namesake church in Manhattan. Items that have only touched the body of the dead saint are third-class relics, and they alone may legitimately be sold; the tiny fabric swatches often attached to holy cards and medals are in this category.[8]

An obvious problem with most relics (excepting the very rare cases of whole bodies and the whole lot of third-class relics) is their relation to the canonical prohibition against the desecration—which includes the division—of corpses. As Carolyn Walker Bynum notes, "Some theologians in Paris in the 1280s argued that division of the cadaver was heinous cooperation with the forces of putrefaction because it severed a corpse that still retained its integrity and shape."[9] If it is forbidden to divide a corpse, how can the veneration of various pieces of corpses, their division from the whole body, and their transportation to various sites be permitted, even encouraged? (Until relatively recently, a first-class relic was required for the building of an altar.) Finding no answer in my reading to the question of how a corpse might be divided by those most invested in its sanctity, I finally asked a friend of mine who has the advantage of being a Jesuit priest. Somewhat surprisingly, he explained that the issue is one of intent. If the intent is reverence, then division is not desecration—indeed, he recounted with some relish the (possibly apocryphal) tale that the cult around St. Thomas Aquinas had grown so strong so quickly that upon his death, without waiting for the official seal of canonization, his followers boiled the abundant flesh from his bones so that they might more quickly venerate the latter as relics. The emphasis on intent is startling in a religious tradition so emphatically focused on form, and it is correspondingly unsurprising that considerable squabbling about the practice persisted for centuries after its origin.

Technically, relics are not objects of *worship*, though they may be *venerated*. This means that relics are to be respected as something beyond the ordinary or profane, but not to be treated as if they were gods or in some way divine. As Augustine notes in the *City of God*: "we Christians do not assign to the martyrs temples, priests, ceremonies and sacrifices. They are not gods for us; their God is our God."[10] Sacrifice may be offered *at* the martyrs' tombs, he notes, but not *to* them; the sacrifices are made to the God worshipped alike by the martyrs and those offering sacrifice.

Of course, and relatedly, technically relics cannot be responsible for miracles, either. To believe that they are would be some version of paganism, from which some significant part of the cult of relics is derived, even on the admission of the most dogmatic authorities.[11] Relics aren't supposed to be magic; they are just supposed to *remind* us of God's presence to human beings. They are efficacious, that is, *as* mnemonic: these fragments are meant to work on (perhaps through?) our memories. Augustine writes, "even now miracles are being performed in Christ's name either by his sacrament, or by the prayers or the memorials of his saints." He lists many such miracles, beginning with the curing of blindness in Milan, where "A great crowd had gathered to see the bodies of the martyrs Protasius and Gervasisus, and the miracle took place before all those witnesses."[12] The relics of St. Stephen, Christianity's first martyr, seem to have been especially efficacious in this regard. Some cures and even restorations to life, he declares, are effected by placing upon the ill, or upon the dead, garments that have been brought to reliquary sites.[13]

The insistence that relics are not themselves efficacious accords awkwardly, though not quite impossibly, with the usual requirement that miracles must be performed for a saint to be canonized and that some of these miracles must be posthumous—potentially very close to miracles wrought by relics—to "count."[14] The key point, of course, is agency: the relic is held to be the site, not the source, of power. Again, though, it is not clear how carefully most who venerate saints maintain this distinction. As Miller puts the matter apropos the descriptions of saints' bodies in hagiographic texts, "saintly presence does (not quite) incarnate divinity."[15] What relics make vivid is the startling independence of this (not quite) incarnation from the corporeal integrity of the saint, the presence in pieces necessarily evoking the absence of other pieces.

According to Thomas Aquinas, God works or may work miracles *in the presence of* relics, "and this apparently supposes that the relic is not the cause of the miracle, but rather the occasion or condition for it."[16] Similarly, "the Council of Trent stated that relics were agencies, '. . . *through which* . . .' God worked prodigies. (Session XXV)."[17] The language of these declarations is ambiguous, perhaps calculatedly so. That a relic may be the condition for a miracle does give the relic a kind of necessity, though this stops short of agency. Certainly the laity have not infrequently regarded relics as quite directly efficacious or even magical, even if this power is acquired through a special closeness to or blessing from God;[18] less certainly, but quite possibly, they have not been alone in so doing.

Nor does practice support the theory that these bits of bodies are not themselves powerful. While methods of display vary, quite often kneelers[19] face reliquaries and in some cases even contain them, so that to observe the relics one is constrained not only into a kneeling posture but

DISMEMBERED DIVINITY

into kneeling with bowed head, a traditional position of worship. What's more, the reliquary historically *precedes* the monstrance—the often ornate container for the wafers of bread transubstantiated into the body of Christ. That is, the "body of Christ" in the form of these wafers is encased, displayed, and revered in a manner based on the display and veneration of saints' relics, not the other way around.[20] If relics are not, in fact, supposed to be objects of worship, this move is particularly strange (even if aesthetically comprehensible).

The somehow sacred quality of relics, the sense that they are not simply objects in a reductive materialist sense, is further evidenced by the fact, alluded to above, that for quite some time canon law declared that no church could be consecrated unless its altar contained the first-class relic of at least one saint.[21] Though this was the general custom starting in at least the late eighth century,[22] it was not general church law until formalized by Pope Clement VIII in 1596[23]—and it did not cease to be practice until after Vatican II in the 1960s. This practice, too, indicates relics' unusual status. Not gods, they nonetheless seem to have some difficult to define direct participation in divinity; sites of sacred workings, they bring this sacredness to other sites. Given that, according to a later section of the canon law, no corpse may be buried beneath an altar, it is clear that some sense of vitality remains linked to these bodily fragments. That is, a relic *must* be present, and a dead body *may not* be present, and it seems unlikely that merely having the dead body in parts (itself generally forbidden) suffices to make the difference.

Here too we find a curious relation between life in all its corporeality and the law of death. The fragmented body as relics retains or sustains vitality without the characteristics of living things (such as the capacities to sense, move, or ingest) but also without the finality and closure of death. The memories associated with relics are not simply remembrances of things past but also folds and even breaks in the present. They tell us that the body, too, has the capacity to disrupt linear time, or to remind us that there is more to time than linearity.

Fullness in Parts

> The afterlife [*survivance*] no longer means death and the return of the specter, but the surviving of an excess of life which resists annihilation.
> —Jacques Derrida, glossing Lou-Andreas Salome, *Archive Fever*

Bynum tells us that "the saints sometimes opposed their own fragmentation, although without it the central cultic practice of relic veneration could not have existed at all. Moreover, when fragmented, the saints frequently remained incorrupt in their parts."[24] Note the paradox of this, another kind of living within death: if corruption is a form of division, and the saints are incorrupt even when divided (i.e., corrupt), then neither division nor unity matters, or at least neither can hold to its usual meaning—to be incorrupt in parts is at once meaningful and contradictory. This intriguing play between fragmentation and wholeness is more dramatic still when we recognize that the saintly life is understood as somehow more full, more intensely alive, than most: in even a piece of the body, there is an overabundant fullness of life.

Gregory of Nyssa, in his unusual discussion of the soul and resurrection with his sister Macrina, offers a theory that makes some sense of this curious claim. Taking on, some thirteen hundred years before Descartes, an early version of the mind-body problem,[25] Gregory and Macrina discuss the relation of soul to body with a particular interest in what becomes of that relation at death and resurrection. Our bodies, according to this dialogue, are composite, "composed from the blending of . . . atoms." At death, "when that framework is dissolved, and has returned to its kindred elements," one might expect the soul either to dissolve likewise or to leave the body. The soul, however, is immaterial, "intelligent and undimensional"; it is a "vivifying influence exerted by a law which it is beyond the human understanding to comprehend."[26]

Descartes will use the same claims to argue that the body, because it disintegrates, is mortal, while the soul, being nonspatial and hence indivisible, cannot disintegrate and so carries on after bodily death.[27] In Gregory's dialogue, however, Macrina argues:

> the intelligent and undimensional . . . is neither contracted nor diffused (contraction and diffusion being a property of body only); but by virtue of a nature which is formless and bodiless it is present with the body equally in the contraction and in the diffusion of its atoms, and is no more narrowed by the compression which attends the uniting of the atoms than it is abandoned by them when they wander off to their kindred, however wide the interval is held to be which we observe between alien atoms.[28]

And she adds:

> In locality, in peculiar qualities, these elemental atoms are held to be far removed from each other; but an undimensional nature finds it no labour to cling to what is locally divided, seeing that even

DISMEMBERED DIVINITY

now it is possible for the mind at once to contemplate the heavens above us and to extend its busy scrutiny beyond the horizon, nor is its contemplative power at all distracted by these excursions into distances so great. There is nothing, then, to hinder the soul's presence in the body's atoms, whether fused in union or decomposed in dissolution.[29]

Gregory is particularly interested in this claim as an argument favoring bodily resurrection, when the intelligent soul, knowing its own, reassembles the body's component parts. It may equally provide material for thinking of bodily pieces as something other than mere lifeless matter, some ground for the odd idea that the pieces of saints' bodies, bodies of those who were unusually close to the divine with its full force of life, retain some unusual version of liveliness even when dead and divided.

Comparisons to the Eucharist are irresistible. To expand upon a point from the previous chapter, we are told by the *Catholic Encyclopedia*, "Christ is present wholly and entirely in each particle of the . . . Host and in each drop of the collective contents of the Chalice."[30] Further on, the *Encyclopedia* discusses "the multilocation of Christ in heaven and upon thousands of altars throughout the world. Since in the natural order of events each body is restricted to one position in space (*unilocatio*), . . . multilocation without further question belongs to the supernatural order. . . . There is, moreover, the *discontinuous* multilocation, whereby Christ is present not only in one Host, but in numberless separate Hosts, whether in the ciborium or upon all the altars throughout the world."[31]

The parallel, of course, is inexact. The multilocation of the divided saint's body is no mystery. However, the multilocation of the vitality indirectly, but significantly, attributed to these fragments does remain mysterious (is the virtue of the saint in each piece?), echoing, if not exactly imitating, the "bilocation"—existence in two places at once—attributed to some ancient saints as a miracle. This is a vitality placed in the body yet not restricted to a single location: the sites of the body are multiplied, as are the workings of divinity, the attributed miracles, through them.

The parallel is also inexact in the obvious sense that relics are venerated in a tradition which holds that the saints are not gods (*vide supra*) and Christ is. The saint's body must "allude to the larger context of Christic power without in effect replacing it or claiming identification with it. As Rowan Williams has explained, 'only in Christ is the flesh fully and lastingly saturated with the indwelling divine power.'"[32] But the parallel remains revealing, in that despite the emphasis on spiritual presence it is the body, material and vital, that manifests whatever presence there may be. Here, too, we find that curious insistence on life. We might see the lives of the saints as overflowing from each fragment, manifesting a fullness of life that does not demand wholeness but multiplies its sites in fragmentation. Instead of an ordinary life in time, indeed, even within such a mundane biography, life burns on instead of out, manifesting, as Blanchot writes: "Instead of finality, the burn of life which cannot burn out. From this fever all ending is excluded, all coming to a finish in a presence."[33] What is present is almost overmuch, yet it evokes just as strongly an absence—it is only a part, and so often a small one, and a part at that of someone who has, as we euphemistically say, left us. To understand how this evocation happens, how the infinite and eternal are present/absent in the absent presence of living flesh, we turn now to more specific discussion of the kinds of memory that a relic may invoke.

History

> The body maintains, in life as in death, through its strength or weakness, the sanction of every truth and error, as it sustains, in an inverse manner, the origin—descent.
> —Michel Foucault, "Nietzsche, Genealogy, History"

The first version of memory appealed to, the historical, is, at first surprisingly, most evident in the relatively new saints—those whose histories are shortest. Many of these saints are displayed, in (almost) whole or in part, in chapels with small museums (the emphasis of the latter is generally biographical) and gift shops attached. The relic of an ancient saint is usually *only* a fragment, without the whole of the body present, nearby, or even known in its whereabouts, while the fragments of contemporary saints are often more tightly collected, with only a few smaller bits dispersed. This dispersal is important, though, especially because it is often concealed. These fragments have the quality of metonymy, the piece standing in for the whole with all of its power, the pieces in their scatteredness nonetheless each possessing the full power of the sanctified. Indeed, some sources suggest that each fragment takes on the full life presence of the saint,[34] a variant, perhaps, on Gregory's claims for the persistent ensoulment of the flesh.

DISMEMBERED DIVINITY

With more recent saints (especially those from the nineteenth century onward), though there are certainly exceptions, the availability of most of the body and the relatively full history or biography changes the sense and display of the fragments as well. Consider as an example the modern reliquary of Elizabeth Ann Seton, the first American ever canonized, at her chapel in Emmitsburg, Maryland. A bone fragment from her body is displayed, rather discreetly (one must kneel before the altar to see the chip in the intersection of a cross), next to the carefully marked and quite concealed remains of her entire body.

In contrast, the bodies and histories of the older saints are misted over by time and myth, by the seductiveness of faith.[35] The artifactual quality of the bodily fragment is enhanced and emphasized by this layered, intricate, and at least slightly mythical kind of historical quality, offering us a different sense of history, less concrete and data-filled than that provided by the biographical museum. The ancient fragment *evokes* the rest of the body, here absent; thus too it evokes a story, a history, which is only ever evocative, which has holes in it and has not been wholly and neatly set down. The bone chip displayed before the hidden-present body in Seton's case is part of a different context of memory. We have records; we have correspondence; we have no great need to reconstruct either the life or the body in our thoughts and our imaginations and our hopes or wishes that it were so. The life (or, to be sure, one carefully presented take on the life) is documented; the body is present (if hidden). In the very display of these bodies, a certain discomfort with corporeality is suggested: among newer saints, we see very sanitized, small pieces that can barely be thought of as bodily (though it remains centrally important that they are indeed corporeal), with larger, more conspicuously somatic remains concealed and indicated by polite signs. Or we see curious facades of wholeness—bodies concealed, as I shall note, even when they seem to be fully displayed. An arm or heart, such as those of St. Teresa famously displayed at Alba de Torres, is seldom set forth.

And this I think may be part of the strange sense of irreligiosity one often, though not inevitably, perceives in the more modern contexts. It is not just the lack of grandeur, which is so difficult for us, perhaps especially in the United States (where austerity and kitsch often seem to be our only options). It is more importantly the minimizing of evocation, of those sudden and disturbing openings of mystery. In the display of medieval arts at the Cloisters (a medieval branch of New York's Metropolitan Museum of Art), the reliquaries somehow have more dignity than most later versions. Even the most ornate (they range from fairly simple crystal containers to wholly rococo combinations of metal and jewels) seem to evade the tackiness that always threatens the more contemporary displays. Undoubtedly this is in some measure an effect of age. But maybe it is also because these come from an era with a stronger public sense of the sacred, of something that is really worth precious metals and precious time. History is evocative, certainly—we are no doubt all familiar with the sense of awe in the presence of an object that has strong associations with events or even cultures long vanished. But what such an object evokes, we tend to feel, is something *potentially* definite or at least more definable, even if it is not at present known to us, even if we will never know it. The evocation of the sacred, as I shall later suggest, is still more unsettling than that of history, not only unfixed but also implicitly unfixable. The placement of the relic and the saint in history may, ideally, do both: that is, it may both evoke history in its aporetic complexity and remind us of the disruptiveness of the sacred. Often, however, we seem to prefer the false security of a known and settled narrative (false if only because neither history nor biography is ever so linear or simple).

The presentation of Mother Seton's relics seems designed to appeal not to the open, incomplete sense of history but to a relatively simple and straightforward sense, where memory is understood as the reproduction of a clear narrative line, as if the relics were illustrations in a history textbook; historical biography, rather than hagiography, is the mnemonic sense at Emmitsburg. This is true too at the shrine of Mother Frances Xavier Cabrini in Manhattan, where the saint reposes in a glass coffin (like Snow White, the viewer unavoidably notices) beneath the chapel altar near the high school bearing her name.

The Cabrini altar is surrounded by edifying mosaics of Mother Cabrini's history—her work in education, or with immigrants, or with the poor. Pamphlets outside the chapel and books in the gift shop summarize her life, with an emphasis on her work with the poor and in education. She is presented as an exemplar of virtue, someone in whom we can see the best of ourselves—someone with whom we might identify—and someone we might, striving to further that identification, imitate. But a closer look opens stranger possibilities.

As I've said, Mother Seton's body is entirely hidden, except for that minuscule chip. Mother Cabrini's, seemingly all on display, is in fact far more odd. Her hands, for example, are conspicuously artificial as they lie folded above her garments. Whether they are simply replicas or are built, like the body of Bishop John Neumann (of whom more below) of wax

DISMEMBERED DIVINITY

around her bones, they are not her flesh, nor is it likely that a viewer would take them to be. Neither is her head, which, as it happens, is no mere death mask: the head itself is in Rome, though no person or source has been able to tell me what it's doing there, nor do the pamphlets provide any explanation. (I might note that many people with whom I've discussed this have been happy to engage in creative, though ultimately unconvincing, speculation on the matter.) Again, though the unknowing viewer might assume that a real skull is present, the face is not likely to be mistaken for either living or preserved flesh. The rest of the body is covered by the robes of her habit.

As my friend Virginia, who accompanied me to the chapel, points out, what is most intriguing here is what is actually illusory, the spectacle of wholeness, the body itself laid peacefully before the devout with its dismembered character utterly suppressed. One wonders whether the spectators could not be trusted to invoke that wholeness for themselves, or whether the visceral fact of the partible body was held to be too disturbing.[36] This illusion of wholeness reminds us of the Lacanian mirror stage so important in the formation of a sense of identity: in the mirror, a young child sees (which is also to say that she constructs) a single, unified being she takes to be herself, giving her a unified sense of an "I."[37] Later in life, others reflect us back to ourselves still more effectively. It seems that to have a sense of self is to have a sense of wholeness; fragmentation is, from our very beginning, so difficult to deal with that we dwell in the illusion of self-unity. We forget that we are not perfectly collected; we persistently re-collect ourselves in an illusion.

The wholeness of the relic-body is illusory, but more: it's fake. The fragment *evokes*; the wax model instead *re-creates*, but it lies. Trying to mimic wholeness and fullness of presence, it inadvertently emphasizes instead the absence of flesh, as if it tries and fails to evade the complex doctrinal considerations of part and whole, corruption and incorruptibility, life and location. In Philadelphia, another glass coffin displays the similarly reconstructed body of Bishop John Neumann. My somewhat skeptical friend Colette, an artist, points out that the short, vividly colored figure looks rather more like a comic book character than one generally expects of a saint. His body is in fact a colored wax model, but the wax forms a kind of reliquary as well, being shaped around and so encasing his bones. Again, we must wonder if his skeletal or mummified remains would simply have been too unsettling for worshippers and viewers. A small museum off to the side of the chapel, full of the bishop's personal documents and artifacts, both hints at and forcibly downplays some of the peculiar violence of saintly bodies, a consideration to which I'll return later.

The seamlessness of history, like the wholeness of these bodies, is only seeming. We know that histories are multiple, with stories intersecting and disconnecting; we know that they are aporetic, even in the simple and obvious sense of including (and excluding) unknown events and persons. The placement of saints, and thus of the unsettling fact of sainthood, in history necessarily evokes this incompleteness and disruption: first, by telling us that the storyline includes the sacred, which is an ill fit with more linear historical narratives (not least because it disrupts linear time); second, by the very existence of relics, which scatter the body in numerous places, and thus place it in numerous narratives, retaining a sense of vitality—confusing our neat distinction between whole and divided. Yet it sometimes seems that these disruptions are *too* disruptive for contemporary understanding, and so they are minimized—by wrapping bones in pseudo-flesh, by hiding bodies, by handing out biographies that purport to tell us all we need to know—in ways that curiously, and by all evidence unintentionally, serve to call attention back to the disruption. Fragmentation sneaks in, although the body on display attempts, in the illusion of full revelation, to conceal it. This kind of display is in contrast not only to the fragment displayed and marked as such, but also to the relics hidden within reliquaries of metal, wood, or crystal, or within wrappings of velvet. In the latter, the fragmentation is not concealed; there is no feigning of a body that is not there, only the hidden presence of a part, the open absence of the whole. History too, the saintly fragment reminds us, has sacred spaces, indefinable openings where the line of time is cut through by divinity. And the displayed body, precisely by what is not whole in it after all, tells us the same.

The consideration of history must lead us as well into that of community. Nancy notes that community, with its sense of constant becoming, is the place of history:

> history—if we can remove this word from its metaphysical, and therefore historical, determination—does not belong primarily to time, nor to succession, nor to causality, but to community, or to being-in-common. This is so because community itself is something historical. Which means that it is not substance, nor a subject; it is not a common being, which could be the goal or culmination of a progressive process. It is rather a being-in-common that only *happens* or that is happening, an event, more than a *"being."*[38]

DISMEMBERED DIVINITY

Thus we will not be surprised to see overlap in the ways in which history and community open spaces, or pull on our memories, neither one settling down into the straightforward presence of a simple object.

Community

> In place of such a communion, there is communication. Which is to say, in very precise terms, that finitude itself is nothing; it is neither a ground, nor an essence, nor a substance. But it appears, it presents itself, it exposes itself, and thus it exists as communication.
> —Jean-Luc Nancy, "The Inoperative Community"

"In the communion of saints," write James Keating and David McCarthy, "human limitations give way to the bounty of life in Christ."[39] The phrasing "communion of saints" is a Catholic commonplace that emphasizes, obviously, the communal element in sainthood—but less obviously, perhaps, the loss of identifying "limitations" as well. The Neumann shrine suggests, even more than history, this second kind of memory, the invocation of community. Neumann's presence as a member of the community is strong here, where his rebuilt body lies in a church run by the Redemptorist order to which he belonged. I overheard Redemptorist priests leading visitors through the museum and chapel, using "us" as a casual inclusive clearly taking in the late bishop as well. At Neumann's much less ornate reliquary in the Baltimore suburb of Elkridge, the display is fairly austere, but it too evokes community. In Elkridge the relic, a large bone chip or perhaps a tooth, is not at an altar, even a side altar, but set into a niche at the back of the church. There is a statue of Neumann next to it, a table with two chairs in the niche, and nothing more. The base of the statue tells his dates of service there. Neumann is commemorated not for his subsequent achievements but as "our pastor," however brief his stay in that capacity may have been. It is interesting, if perhaps obvious, to note that the absence of the tooth (or bone chip) is nowhere made evident in the recreated body at the Philadelphia reliquary, an omission sustaining the illusion of wholeness.

Nearby, at Baltimore's Holy Rosary Church, Fr. Ronald Pytel—the parish priest whose healed heart condition was one of the miracles behind the canonization of St. Maria Faustina Kowalska in 2000—officiated at evening mass the day I visited. One sensed strong attachment between him and the congregants of the Polish-American church, who crowded around him to talk before the ceremony.

SAINTS' RELICS

The display of relics at Holy Rosary is more old-world ornate than Seton's, though slightly less so than at Faustina's national shrine in Stockbridge, Massachusetts. The sense of community at Holy Rosary was even stronger than at the national shrine, though the latter has a minor seminary on the grounds; stronger too than at Mother Seton's shrine in Emmitsburg, despite the presence of an order of nuns there. The relic at Holy Rosary (which appears to be another bone fragment) is small but splendidly displayed in a kneeler looking onto a side niche. In the niche is Faustina's signature image, one she envisioned and then painted: Christ beaming as streams of light flow from his robed side, symbolizing the blood and water emerging from the wound in his side at the crucifixion. The image is inscribed with the phrase, "Jesus, I trust in you," which accompanied her vision and is present in most depictions of it. Here, as at many other reliquary sites, a napkin is provided next to the glass-covered relic, so that the devout who kiss the glass may wipe away their smudges.

The relics of Maria Faustina seem integrated into the parish and echo the parishoners' proud participation in her canonization. There's a sense that one of us made good, even if Faustina wasn't precisely one of them. Sanctity has in some way emerged *here*, and it intensifies, for those whose identity is also here, a sense of belonging to the body of the church: of being a part in something whole. The attempted recreation of whole bodies, such as Mother Cabrini's, reminds us of disintegration; the incorporation of bodily fragments, through the complexities of commemoration, into the communal body of a parish church re-collects partiality into a reminder of wholeness. Patrick Geary suggests that in fact the theft of relics, often justified by the claim that, after all, a saint could "decide" where her or his relics end up, displays a sense of the relation of saint to community: "Thus the formal tradition of *furta sacra* provided an appropriate memory of how and why a particular community came to be graced with the presence of a powerful new patron. It demonstrated the saint's love of the community and his concern with its problems while simultaneously showing the lengths to which the community was willing to go in order to bring the saint to live with its human members."[40] Thus, the sense of belonging with or to a community may be so strong that it is held to remain powerful even in fragments. Geary's phrasing, "to live with," is revealing; here again we sense the curious lingering vitality attributed to the saintly fragment.

The communal sense was also emphasized by the friendly Carmelite father who spoke to me at the National Shrine of Our Lady of Mt.

DISMEMBERED DIVINITY

Carmel in New York's Hudson Valley, where a number of relics of Therese of Lisieux and of St. Patrick, along with those of several lesser-known Irish saints, are on display at the back of the church. Here the relics of Therese are revered in large measure because of her membership in the Carmelite order, while those of Patrick and other Irish saints are explained by the fact that the particular Carmelite order in residence here had its origin in Ireland.

At the Jesuit novitiate in Syracuse, New York, an assortment of several dozen minor relics, hung together in a wall-mounted display case, includes those of many Jesuit saints. The priest who showed them to me displayed as well a sense of community not only with the novices in residence (who, unperturbed by my presence, set up for mass around me) but also with the saints. Over the course of our conversation, it became clear that this was not because they were people just like him, but because they were seminarians, or priests, or educators: that is, they worked within the tradition in which he had placed himself. The relics occupy a case with the presentation crucifixes that priests receive when they take Holy Orders, objects of aspiration at the height of the community. Such a community is founded not on personal similarities but on the sharing of both memory, including the strength of communal tradition, and futurity, including the desire to become someday a part of the communal memory.

The communal sense seems strongest where there is already a sense that "this is one of us" or "this is one of ours." At Stockbridge there is some sense of community through the seminary, and at Emmitsburg through the convent, but in each it feels as if the communities were planned and formed around the saints (as in fact they were), as opposed to the emergence of the communal within (or among). True community is always a space of "compearance," to use Nancy's term, of appearing-with and appearing-to the others among whom my identity takes form. A healed priest or a well-liked bishop can be part of a community; when sanctity emerges in connection with them, it is *already* part of the community, not a kernel around which the community is subsequently and somewhat artificially formed. Community is a matter of co-emergence, self with and among others; if a saint is part of a community, the community itself is transformed—not necessarily sanctified, but made a place shared by sanctity, by the memory of a transfigurative event.

Relics have long evoked a communal history. Brown notes: "In his sermon *de laude sanctorum* Victricius deliberately presented the installation of . . . relics as an event heavy with paradox: the splinters of bone and drops of blood were mysteriously joined to an immense invisible unity that embraced the cult sites of the entire Mediterranean. It was a moment for the distant congregation . . . to linger on the ideal of a 'perfect and total concord.' "[41]

Nor is this concord restricted to interpersonal relations. Keating and McCarthy note: "Saints point not to 'individual perfection' but to perfect communion, not to self-sufficiency but to relations that extend our vulnerability and interdependence. . . . The stories told about the saints portray human goodness, but they also point to a fullness of the human good that no individual saint can sustain. The saint is open to God."[42]

Unreflectively, we associate community with a sort of enclosure and security. In fact, though, the appearance-within of mortal beings, the fact of compearance, makes of us something constantly unsettled, drawn together not by resemblance but by the combination of natality—the emergence of ourselves as new, but also the emergence of novelty constantly among us—and memory. Both sacred and communal are in fact sites of constant emergence, and so of constant change, disruption, and mnemonic shift. The saints are open to God: their broken-open bodies remind us of God in the flesh and of the constant disruptive emergence of the sacred, of saintly openness, within our gatherings together. They open the community itself to the tug of memory, and to the memory of fragmentation.

The Sacred

> God is encountered in the hagiographical texts in the moment when the beloved body traverses the boundary between life and death, in the saint's last, rejoicing breaths, in the disciple's lingering embrace of a corpse that already slips beyond the grasp of transient particularity—dissolving into finest dust, mingling with desert sand, participating again in the capacious potentiality of the cosmos.
> —Virginia Burrus, *The Sex Lives of Saints*

A closer look at the evocation of the sacred will help to make more sense of this. Note, for instance, those relics of Therese, at the shrine where several dozen more relics are also displayed. The priest here reminded me that Therese, the "little flower," wanted to rain roses upon the world—to shower it with blessings, as he translated the metaphor for me—and her relics are displayed in an ornate reliquary in which each small bodily piece forms the center of a golden rose. But the fact remains that the best-displayed of these is a neatly labeled "fragment of undecomposed flesh," a chunk of body plucked from a corpse and preserved under glass. The philosopher friends who accompanied me on this visit were rather perturbed by this relic, creating scenarios of saint-makers poking about the exhumed corpse with magnifying glasses and tweezers. The undecomposed flesh (flesh that does not disintegrate can be a point in favor of canonization, its preservation counting as a miracle) is necessarily a vivid reminder of decomposition, of falling apart. It is a fragment of life (as we commonly recognize it) persisting in the presence of death—persisting, and so reminding us of the persistence of *possibility* that we associate with life. Its very wholeness, its freedom from corruption, is already partial—the body may not have (entirely) decomposed, but even so it comes to us in fragments; it is not quite composed, either.

This flesh also evokes the complexity of Christian attitudes toward the body, reminding us of the contrast between those attitudes more prevalent in medieval and in contemporary (and most particularly North American) versions of Christianity. Suffering, the willingness to suffer, and woundedness—we might more provocatively say mutilation—have long been celebrated as imitations of and identifications with Christ, but this celebration is much diminished as Christianity becomes progressively more staid and less somatic. The body's breakable nature, the fact that it can be torn open and even broken apart, is vital; that we can be opened to the outside is fundamental to any sense of the divine or sacred, even to any sense of the communal or historical, though it is not often so literalized in the body (except, of course, in the images of the crucifixion and of many of the more gruesome forms of martyrdom). It is true that sainthood, as we have already seen, likewise celebrates the persistence of wholeness, not so much against fragmentation as in its mutual persistence with the fragmentary. Larger, more complete parts are more venerable. Flesh that retains its composition manifests its sanctity. But it takes partibility to make this evident to us, to make it matter; and it is in *parts* that this lingering "wholeness" is shown. Moreover, these parts have, as I have already started to indicate, an effect of breaking-open, detotalizing.

This gets at what seems to me the most identifiably "religious" sense of memory evoked. I would argue that in this context the bodily fragment, broken from a seeming whole, also has the effect of breaking open, making openings in our memories, opening holes in the seeming whole. Here is the sense of the evocative, the role of the memory of an "origin" that is no origin at all, of the oneness before the self that evokes at the same time an equally prior forgetting. All we ever have are pieces.

We might see the illusory wholeness we find in the mirror as a small-scale effort to refind (yet again) the all-relational oneness that comes "before" and "after" us, a oneness impossible to find because it must be destructive of the individual seeking self, still more because the notion of one, without many, eludes any sense making. The saintly fragment, powerful with all the power of the "whole" living body, and that to excess (so vital that its force miraculously overflows every fragment), presents us with an image of this impossible unitive state: a wholeness in the very fact of fragmentation, a wholeness somehow greater for being, like the transubstantiated host, multiply present; it presents us too with the self's loss of its own oneness in the very "finding" of an ante-origin somehow deeply "true" of itself. The whole does not replace the broken but rather complicates it; each broken bit folds up that whole within it.

The sense of the sacred—of a memory that opens onto openness itself, of the astonishment of the eternal in the profane world—was most nearly evoked, among the relics I visited within the United States, at the National Shrine of Divine Mercy in Stockbridge, though here too the senses of community and history nearly overwhelmed it (despite the fact that both were less pronounced than at some other sites). There is something of an old-world feel to the place; a mass was in progress when I arrived, in English but delivered with a heavy Eastern or Central European accent. Faustina was a Pole living in the United States, and a cynic might suggest that there was some nationalism in John Paul II's enthusiastic push for her canonization—a push so enthusiastic that the image of her vision can be found at almost every reliquary gift shop in the country, even those dedicated to other saints, and so determined that the pope entrusted the entire world to divine mercy (as depicted in her vision) during a visit to Poland in 2002.[43]

Faustina's relics are clearly hagiographic, and the details of her life given in materials available at the shrine dwell on her prayer-filled journal and the painting she created of her famous vision, rather than filling out the rest of the biography with greater detail. Memory here opens onto hushed spaces, rather than filling in narrative gaps.

Something similar is true at the shrine of St. Jude, in Baltimore, perhaps because of the antiquity of the saint. The evocation of memory here is more clearly of the sacred type, with relics placed in an elaborate side shrine and set into the side of a pillar-type reliquary before the lectern. Some historical accounting is available, but what we find in the literature at the site is chiefly a celebration of Jude's role as the patron of desperate causes. These sites tell us that relics can remind us of the sacred, in two specific, slightly unorthodox ways: by being fragments and by being bodies, both observed *as* sacred, as reminding us of an opening onto what is at once interior and exceeding. There is something *mysterious* about them, not simply the unknown in the absence of information. In the presence of these fragments and the absences they evoke, "we realize," as Andrew Louth writes, "the true character of mystery: mystery not just as the focus for our questioning and investigation, but mystery as that which *questions us*."[44] Everything has its beginning in a question. The mystery is in the play between fragment and whole, death and vitality, but only wholeness is emphasized in most of these public presentations. (There is, then, a tendency to demystify, to refuse the question.) I want, therefore, to end this chapter with a contrary emphasis on fragmentation, a further exploration of its significance here, an emphasis on what it does to memory and to the ways we live time.

Fragmentation in Denial

> Self in self steeped and pashed—quite
> Disremembering, dismembering all now.
>   —Gerard Manley Hopkins, "Spelt From Sibyl's Leaves"

As Therese's flesh reminds us most directly, perhaps because it is flesh and not dry bone, fragmentation is inherently violent. We find a less direct reminder in Bishop Neumann's museum: alongside the historical artifacts and the documentation of his progress to canonization are objects, such as an iron belt and a knotted whip, used by the bishop upon himself for penitential purposes, casting a curiously medieval light on this nineteenth-century saint. Here there is a sense of a curious ease, or at any rate an easy familiarity, with violence. Fragments, too, are never simply violent or even simple reminders of violence. Rather, they serve—without denying the violence it takes to shatter something—to open up the *spaces* that a seamless whole cannot offer.

They remind us that, beyond its social value and its political practices, the religion in which they have their shifting place is about evocation and excess; it is about the possibility of the sacred, which tantalizes us—not simply here in but as a part of the profane world, about ecstatic possibilities that shatter our very sense of self and throw us and the divine mutually open to one another, threatening the distinction. Relics literalize our fragmentation by breaking the very element of us that seems most clearly whole and yet self-evidently divisible, the somatic. They evoke

SAINTS' RELICS

Gregory's sense of the perpetual ensouledness of bodies, even in bits. They remind us not only of what we may stand to gain but of the loss inherent even in joy. Here, too, we are reminded not to repress mourning.

As I've indicated, many modern reliquaries and relic displays seem to try to reassure us with illusions of wholeness or carefully normalized life stories. Fragments are so disembodied as to be neutralized, or else wholeness, always in some measure illusory, is presented as genuine. But this pretense of wholeness, or denial of fragmentation, misses something vital. The relic, a piece of the dead body endowed with more fullness of life than most of the living, "reminds" us in the tug on our memories of the powerful sense of some moment outside our selves and our time. That is, relics evoke an experience of self lost (and regained, and transfigured) in the finding of something felt elusively in the flesh, heard elusively in the silences, stutters, and overflows of language. This experience belongs (in any of a range of ways) to bodies (even third-class relics must have touched, at least, the corpse).

There are intriguing connections between bodies and fragmentation. Descartes, as we have noted, held divisibility to be the chief characteristic distinguishing body from mind. For him, this was proof of the soul's immortality: since mind or soul cannot be divided, it must continue on its own when the dead body disintegrates into its component elements. But he, of course, does not retain the complex theological faith in the paradox of wholeness in division, or at any rate he doesn't seem to—it can sometimes be hard to be quite sure what Descartes is up to. Gregory's vision of the soul's persistence, as we've seen, works better for the paradoxical vitality of relics, where flesh is evocative and excessive and sacred, in its movements and stillnesses and pain and joy; and here, in the relics of saints, in the unity and the fragmentation of its parts.

The sense of joyous open space is also, in a deeply corporeal way, the experience of the earliest saints, the martyrs. Brown writes: "The explicit image of the martyr was of a person who enjoyed the repose of Paradise and whose body was even now touched by the final rest of the resurrection. Yet behind the now-tranquil face of the martyr there lay potent memories of a process by which a body shattered by drawn-out pain had once been enabled by God's power to retain its integrity."[45] Noting a crucial connection, he states: "At the root of every miracle of healing at a martyr's shrine of late antiquity there lay a miracle of pain. . . . For the sufferings of the martyrs were miracles in themselves."[46] There is life in these bodily fragments of the dead, each with the fullness of life of the

DISMEMBERED DIVINITY

whole, but it is their death that makes life so miraculous. There is joy in this shattering pain of the flesh, but it is pain that makes the joy so transformative. This is what safe, wholesome versions of religiosity repress—the miraculous character of pain, of breakage, of the openness that comes only in fragments.

And thus, in turn, fragmentation evokes wholeness. To be myself alone is to be closed off, and I am an individual only to the extent that my boundaries are secure. No one is quite impenetrable, however, and this potential openness is part of what it means to be human. The very fact of existing in history and in community, where I "find myself" outside myself in exposition, tells us that our boundaries fluctuate; existence in the sacred reminds us, as well, that they break.

That is, all three senses of memory I've listed threaten self-containment. To place myself in history is to be only imperfectly closed off: even if we simplify our sense of time, I am *now* insofar as my "now" is grounded by its past and reaches, of course, out into its future possibilities. To see myself in the line of history is also to see myself as, at least in temporal terms, not being self-contained, belonging in some small way to a much longer story; more precisely and more complicatedly, to many stories. Likewise, to identify myself as part of a community is to be only imperfectly closed off: I *am* insofar as I am *with*; I am transformed by what has emerged in the community with me. But to lose myself in the sacred is to be least securely closed of all, to be open to the terrifying joy of the infinite—and that, I think, is where quicker and less-discriminate saint making, and the ways we have of observing it, risk going wrong.

To make more sense of my argument, I return to Faustina's vision. Visions have long made church authorities uneasy, and for good reason. Politically, they present problems for a hierarchical structure, seeming to grant a direct and perhaps authoritative access to the divine and so threatening the right of ecclesiastical officials to establish truth in dogma. Theologically, they trouble those who wish to be certain that a vision received is indeed divine and not, in old terms, demonic or, in new, a mark of imminent psychosis. Faustina's, as any viewer will note, is as untroubling as a vision can get. Christ smiles and reassures, and his trustworthiness is emphasized. Even the blood and water streaming from his side—surely a vision of violence if there ever was one—are reenvisioned as streams of soothing light.

But it's important to realize that, however lovely the vision may be—and it is potentially lovely[47]—it is a vision violent at base, of a deliberately broken body, a body wounded as it was just before death, streaming vital fluids. In a way, Catherine of Siena's medieval vision of drinking that fluid, which she extrapolated to the self-imposed mortification of drinking pus from the sores of lepers, comes across as rather more honest than this gentle, happy, light-streaming and trustworthy image. I don't mean to deny possibilities of transfiguration. But I *do* mean to emphasize the corporeal, and with what I think is good reason. The relics so reverently placed in these containers intended to be works of beauty, whether or not they succeed in that intent, are not points (or streams) of light. They are pieces of bodies, and their real material presence is part of a tradition of real material presences in Christianity—a tradition always in tension with the element of canonical Platonism in Christianity that would edge away from the body (which is also to say that the tension within the tradition has existed from very near the beginning). The miracles attributed to the presences of relics have their part in a long tradition—Jesus may heal bodies by body, through touch, or even by using spit to make mud[48]—but the urge to pull away from the flesh sets in quickly.

As we have noted, the claim that Christ's body was illusory, or in some other way inessential, is one of the earliest Christian heresies. Despite the tensions of a persistently and increasingly disincarnate tradition, Christianity remains at base, in important addition to its Jewish roots and its assimilation of Platonism and Aristotelianism, a faith about the body, a faith in an incarnation and a carnal resurrection. Bynum points out the deep paradoxes in medieval Christian corporeality: "prurient fascination with torture and division in a culture that not only articulated opposition to these practices, but also found innumerable euphemisms for them—these aspects of the thirteenth century are profoundly contradictory. Yet, underneath them all lies a deep conviction that the person *is* his or her body."[49] These descriptions are, after all, not so distant from us today. But the body in this earlier understanding is ensouled throughout, not dead matter, matter from which the soul is inherently and essentially distinct. Perhaps this is why the power of relics has invariably been invested not in the senses that don't necessarily require real material presence—such as sight or hearing, which can be given their sensed objects by artificial means (photographs, audio recordings)—but in touch: one body brought into contact with another. Even when the fragments are guarded by glass, lips are pressed as near to them as possible. (One must wonder, though, if present-day fastidiousness mightn't stop short of actual contact were the glass not there. The illusion of touch, or perhaps the comforting thought that that we *would* touch, were it only hygienic, is easier and more "safe" than the risk of corporeal contact.)

DISMEMBERED DIVINITY

In the end, the flesh resists sanitizing into perfect safety. We are reminded here of two things: of fragmentation and disruption against smoothly complacent wholeness, and of the body and its power against the focus on the spirit. (Although my own religious emphasis has always been rather more aesthetic than ethical, I do think there are real ethical and political implications here regarding the care of bodies.) Relics remind us of the paradoxical faith that embraces both: the wholeness of the broken, the ensoulment of the flesh.

The saints whose relics are displayed are, to a degree that becomes a qualitative difference, more broken than most and more whole, more frangible, more deeply somatic and more powerful against the weakness and weariness that embodiment means for most of us, more full, more vital. And yet this is a difference of degree, suggesting the divinity of the human condition more broadly. It's not just that they remind us of the whole paradoxically within the broken, the intact within the corrupt. Jill Harries argues rightly that relics show us the triumph of life even in death;[50] they show us, too, that the relation is not such a simple negation as we casually think. What makes relics both bizarre and effective is that they remind us of a key point in religious experience: the full force of the closeness of the canonized to the divine, in which mere proximity gives way to mutual disruption and the nearness of God itself becomes shattering. Openness is not wholeness, and sanctity is not easy, and the saints are not just really nice. That is: the value of saints' relics, unlike the value of parts of their life stories, is not in the ethical example they set, useful as it may be to have such examples; it is in the vivid and paradoxical reminders of the sacred in the flesh, its literalized openness to a God whose flesh is likewise, exemplarily, torn.

The experience of encountering a saintly relic, rather like the experience of the sacred more generally (perhaps even like that of living a saintly life, whatever that might mean) is at once the wholeness associated with life—indeed, a *fullness* of life—and the loss of self that going beyond the ethical requires.[51] The obtaining and display of relics, or their inclusion under altar-stones, requires that we break what is otherwise canon law; they have always been just a little out of place in the order of the church into which they are nonetheless, and not always marginally, incorporated. Despite papal efforts to bring them into line, I would argue, their very nature as bodily fragments full of life will keep them a bit out of order. The suggestion that they remind us of God rather than being themselves sites of the sacred may actually point to a semantic

SAINTS' RELICS

distinction; perhaps the sacred *is* this sense of reminder and remainder, the opening of memory beyond the subject, an outside of self nonetheless within the flesh. As we move from consideration of the special case of relics to the curious doctrine of general resurrection, this consideration of our corporeality becomes more fundamental still.

6

ETERNAL FLESH
The Resurrection of the Body

176. What is meant by "the resurrection of the body"? By "the resurrection of the body" is meant that at the end of the world the bodies of all men will rise from the earth and be united again to their souls, never more to be separated. *Behold, I tell you a mystery. We shall all indeed rise again. (I Corinthians 15:51)*
—*A Catechism of Christian Doctrine,* Revised Edition of the Baltimore Catechism, Part 1, Lesson 14

The When of Eternal Flesh

Beauty is momentary in the mind—
The fitful tracing of a portal;
But in the flesh it is immortal.

The body dies; the body's beauty lives.
—Wallace Stevens, "Peter Quince at the Clavier"

In this last question and answer we find, with typical catechismic succinctness, one of the most intriguingly odd of Christian notions: once we correct for the lingering gender bias, we are faced with the notion that human "immortality" is something somatic, or, to put it differently, that human corporeality is something immortal. Here we seem to find no fragmentation at all—indeed, integrity (or "entirety") is one of the signs of the resurrected flesh. But I will argue that we find once more a particular fragmenting of the experience of time, a fragmenting that gives eternity to life. The role of memory here is likewise odd, particularly if

THE RESURRECTION OF THE BODY

we attend to Augustine, for whom it must loop back, back to the Edenic corporeality that the resurrected body takes up, restores, and yet exceeds. In this chapter I want to look particularly at the ways in which we, corporeally, live the eternal even as we live extended through time; I also want, therefore, to emphasize the corporeality of lived eternity.

More exactly, I want to emphasize the recurrent, breaking, or suspended times of the body, in which we may recognize the capacity of the body to be (as those early monists insisted) more than mere matter, yet wholly material; to be, as flesh, more than linear and brief in temporal occupation. Looking at both function and sensation in the living body, we find more than a time that endures: we find a time cut through and transformed by an eternity we can evoke, if not understand,[1] in memory.

What I would like to do here, to phrase it differently, is to take the "eternal" of eternal life seriously, take it as a nontime that already cuts through our time, or within which our temporality is already enfolded: the outside edge of time that we touch, barely, where staying is impossible. I want to suggest that eternal life in the body tells us more about eternal life as well as about bodies. Nancy quotes Hölderlin as declaring, "Even in a limited existence, man can know an infinite life, and the limited representation of divinity, stemming for him from this existence, can itself also be infinite." And Nancy goes on to add: "Even in a limited existence, man can know an infinite life: this is living on, this is exceeding. Infinite life neither *succeeds* nor brims over *life*. . . . The infinite brims over inwards."[2] In the body as it lives, within the limits bounded (imprecisely) by the skin, are the traces of the infinite, the eternal, brimmed over into the flesh.

Since, in thinking the resurrection of the body as the materiality of eternal life, I read eternity as a quality and fullness of corporeal life in time and not as indefinite endurance, I would read the "end of the world" (the "time" in or at which the resurrection of the body happens) as language's struggle with the unsayability in the world of the atemporality that disrupts it; "end" is perhaps no worse a metaphor than "outside." Somatic eternity is not the endurance of the body but the transfigurative rhythm and rupture of time and the fullness of life, in and through the flesh.

The resurrection of the body is declared doctrine in Augustine's *Enchiridion*, where he writes, "Now, as to the resurrection of the body, . . . that the bodies of all men—both those who have been born and those who shall be born, both those who have died and those who shall die—shall be raised again, no Christian ought to have the shadow of a

133

doubt."[3] Tertullian is likewise emphatic, opening his work "The Resurrection of the Flesh" by declaring: "The resurrection of the dead is the Christian's trust. By it we are believers." He emphasizes that this is not a resurrection of discorporate souls: "I wish to impress this on your attention, with a view to your knowing, that whatever God has at all proposed or promised to man, is due not to the soul simply, but to the flesh also." The resurrection of the body appears explicitly in the Apostles' Creed ("I believe in . . . the resurrection of the body"), as well as in the Athanasian ("At his coming all people shall rise bodily"), and in the Nicene Creed by traditional interpretation ("We look for the resurrection of the dead").

Dogmatically, risen bodies are said to be characterized by "identity, entirety, and immortality."[4] That is, the risen bodies of good and bad alike are their own (which does not mean that they are firmly bounded in impenetrable solitude, but rather that the kind of body-identity exchange that forms a comic subgenre of Hollywood films is not an option). They are whole (by now, we are alert to the potential complications here; the idea seems to be to prevent multiple body bits from running about, each proclaiming itself a person, and it also has to do with the reintegration of loss, as we shall see). Finally, they do not die again (which might mean something other than to say that they endure), having acquired a glorious incorruptibility that nonetheless does not seem to preclude change, such as motion.

As with many of the counterintuitive claims of Christianity, there is, I think, something more here than at first reading meets the mind's eye. I recently suggested that one might read the resurrected body of Christ in the fourth gospel as hinting at eternal life, not in the sense of endurance, but in the sense I've been using here, in which life laid out horizontally in time is also vertically intensified in eternity—that we might read the stories of Christ's corporeality as stories of eternity's breakthrough into time, as an invocation of eternal life.[5] The Christian idea of the resurrected human body is generally, if somewhat vaguely, modeled upon that of the resurrected body of Christ, so it seems legitimate to ask if spirited human flesh might likewise be read as eternal.

Traditionally and doctrinally, the resurrection of the body is regarded not as a bizarre improbability but as natural—more precisely, as a restoration of a natural order disrupted by death. It is in this sense that it returns us back before original sin. This now-disrupted order is that of prelapsarian nature, the nature of the body prior to its separation either from the human will or from the divine. Augustine writes, "Therefore, if

THE RESURRECTION OF THE BODY

Adam had not sinned, he would not have been divested of his body, but would have been clothed upon with immortality and incorruption, that 'mortality might have been swallowed up of life.'"[6] Contrary yet again to Augustine's reputation for hostility to the body, we find here the notion that, in fact, the perfect human state is one in which we are never "divested of" corporeality. Perfect humans are bodily. Gregory of Nyssa makes a similarly strong claim; corporeal resurrection, modeled on Christ's, restores us to our proper essence.[7]

The resurrection of the body, then, is viewed (like forgiveness, with its mending of rifts) as a restoration to some kind of *integrity*, a return to a prelapsarian absence of separation. Original sin, as I've read it here, is separation from divinity and from immortality, both cause and effect of the will's self-separation from its oneness with the divine will. Augustine connects this split clearly to the separation of the body from its animating spirit: "When, indeed, Adam sinned by not obeying God, then his body—although it was a natural and mortal body—lost the grace whereby it used in every part of it to be obedient to the soul."[8] The separation of flesh from life, from will, and from God is the separation mended by corporeal resurrection. We have to suspect, though, that matters are more complex than simple mending would suggest, that the fragmentary persists within the whole.

Despite Christological debates, those views of eternity that might allow us to see it as perpendicular to and intersecting with time have been, on the whole, singularly uninterested in embodiment. Whether simply indifferent or downright hostile, they tend to see the body as either a burden or a distraction from a higher truth. As I've noted, Neoplatonism, generally speaking, is often understood as turning away from the lowest, most multiple reality of bodies to the contemplation of an immaterial One. But even if this were true of most of its versions, Augustine would be arguably an exception.[9] So too would Gregory, for whom, as we have seen, the soul not only reintegrates, but disintegrates with, the body.

Matter is conserved, as material or as energy, but its configurations pass, alter, are lost over time. Time passes, or is passage. Spirit—in the sense of life, *anima*, or animation—seems to pass even more quickly, leaving the purely material corpse behind, for a time, until that time too passes, until the material disintegrates and reconfigures. Yet, again, I want to suggest that perhaps something intersects this rapidly passing time, this often unbearable mortality of animate matter, material spirit, flesh—some form of eternity. Eternity, I want to say, belongs not to disincarnate souls or to the perpetual reconfigurations of matter but to the flesh of bodies, even in—and indeed in a way particularly belonging to—their passing. Nancy and Lacoue-Labarthe write of the "touch me not" story, in which the newly risen Christ tells Mary Magdalene not to touch him because in fact he is not yet risen:[10] "It's an ordeal, a joy, and a disappearance all at once. And the glorious body that disturbs you shines here with a glory so poor that it is neither recognized nor named as such."[11] This, I want to suggest, might be true of all glorious (i.e., resurrected) bodies: they may appear entirely ordinary, in fact. They may be unrecognizable as glorious. They may exist in simultaneous struggle and joy. They may, it will come by now as no surprise to hear, be ours, and now, even as they pass.

Here we are reminded again of the mutability that we recognized in Chapter 3 as the possibility of the future. In book 12 of the *Confessions*, Augustine hints intriguingly at passing or slipping as something rather like materiality itself. Struggling with the opening books of Genesis, he wonders what it could mean to be "without form," as these books claim of that which was prior to God's creation of the world. The preformed world, he declares: "was not absolute nothingness. It was a kind of formlessness without any definition."[12] He recognizes, with some frustration, that his efforts to envision formlessness simply result in mental images of ill-defined and rapidly multiplying forms: "I concentrated attention on the bodies themselves and gave a more critical examination to the mutability by which they cease to be what they were and begin to be what they were not.... For the mutability of changeable things is itself capable of receiving all forms into which mutable things can be changed. But what is this mutability? Surely not mind? Surely not body?"[13] Neither abstract spirit nor unspirited matter, this mutability is the capacity of the corporeal for change, for motion, for passage—but also for the very existence of material things, or formed matter.

Mutable *things*, we recall, are not eternal,[14] yet there is, beyond time, mutability as well as changelessness: "It is true that the formlessness, which is next to nothing, cannot suffer temporal successiveness. It is true that the source from which something is made can by a certain mode of speaking bear the name of the thing which is made from it. Hence the kind of formlessness from which heaven and earth were made can be called 'heaven and earth.'"[15] Formlessness, which is *the very possibility of passage*, the between of forms, is prior, precedent not in time, but in "priority ... of origin,"[16] a kind of priority we might call ontological (were it not potentially unwise to attribute being to this pure possibility); the kind of priority of the "first time" of which Deleuze speaks.

THE RESURRECTION OF THE BODY

Deleuze is intriguingly Neoplatonic in his sense of time's synthesis as an "origin" of time occurring, somehow, in some other sort of time, a sort with distinct echoes of eternity. He writes in *Difference and Repetition*:

> Although it is originary, the first synthesis of time is no less intra-temporal. It constitutes time as a present, but a present which passes. Time does not escape the present, but the present does not stop moving by leaps and bounds which encroach upon one another. This is the paradox of the present: to constitute time while passing in the time constituted. We cannot avoid the necessary conclusion—that there must be another time in which the first synthesis of time can occur.[17]

There must be another time. Matter is cut through, interleaved, with the eternal; it lives (it is living) not only in the progression of time but in time's strangeness, in recurrence and suspension, its shattering and its outside-within. The strange moments at the intersections and enfoldings of time with eternity are also the times that tell us that there is more to spirited matter than a mechanism gradually grinding down. Despite the physicality of both forgiveness and love, and the veneration of bodily relics, we retain a curious tendency to assume that spirit, if it means anything, is other than flesh (which is related to the point that we have a hard time, still, thinking eternity as somatic). But as Merleau-Ponty argues in *The Visible and the Invisible*, "We must not think the flesh starting from substances, from body and spirit—for then it would be the union of contradictories—but we must think it, as we have said, as an element, as the concrete emblem of a general manner of being."[18] And when we think body beyond mechanistic matter, when we think flesh, we cannot think of time as only linear. "[P]ast and present are *Ineinander*," Merleau-Ponty writes, "each enveloping-enveloped—and that itself is the flesh."[19] This is true too of the eternal and the temporal: we live in a time interwoven with eternity; we live in a time bearing its own redemption, in which futurity along with memory is wrapped up with the passing present. And we live this time as flesh, finding there what Wolfson calls "the redemptive capacity of time, or, to be more specific, . . . the redemptive capacity of the moment in which time is redeemed by time. In this moment opposites coincide."[20]

Sempiternal endurance, the extended living that we usually mean by "immortality," is an appealing notion in all but the most appalling circumstances, but it doesn't keep us from loss. In a sense, it *guarantees* time's infinite loss as present slips irretrievably into no longer, even if it goes on slipping forever. Eternity gives us this sense of immortal flesh not as flesh that lasts forever (even unagingly, like that of, say, vampires) but as time's own redemption, its own transfiguration of this slippage, in rhythm and in rupture. I won't claim that this keeps us from loss either—we do well to retain our sense of the mutual inherence of absence in presence, mourning in joy. But it redeems or, a little more exactly, transfigures loss, in a more complex sense than the repeated slippage of endurance.

Endurance, we might say, renders every moment replaceable: there will always be more. (We may be reminded of Freud's odd urging that we not object to transience.) Eternity, however, takes its moments disruptively out of place—and nothing replaces them. Each moment, arriving in time or extended into eternity, is its own newness. Nancy writes of this constant natality: "Presence is what is born, and does not cease being born. Of it and to it there is birth, and only birth. This is the presence of whoever, for whomever *comes*."[21] There is only birth.

Here we find an intriguing theological parallel with Eckhart's Christ, who is always being born in the human soul, always arriving as new divinity within, thus troubling the boundaries of interiority, and profanity, and time. "If someone were to ask me: . . . why did God, the All-Highest, take on our flesh?—then I would reply: in order that God may be born in the soul and the soul be born in God. That is why the whole of Scripture was written and why God created the whole world and all the orders of angels."[22] In this double birth, "all time must fall away,"[23] drawn together into "the Now of eternity in which the soul knows all things new and fresh and present in God."[24] The world is arriving before us, born to presence in us, as we are constantly arriving into the world, eternally, even as it slips and we slip in it.

The moment of arrival is not deferred to the future, as what is only going to come, but neither is it only a constantly slipping away. It is, rather, constantly new and never finished. Nancy adds: "Experience is just this, being born to the presence of a sense, a presence itself nascent, and only nascent. Such is the destitution, such the freedom of experience."[25] The present is only just coming before it is irreplaceably gone; the eternal does not hold onto presence but exceeds it. The God mortally sacrificed is the God always just being born.

It is difficult to conceive of this nonending newness in the flesh. After all, bodies endure even as they change. Endurance is even necessary for the concept of a changing body to make sense; otherwise we have simply a succession of novel bodies, generating all manner of (admittedly interesting) conceptual problems. The "resurrection of the body" is classically thought in terms of endurance: the mortal flesh, risen again after its exanimation and disintegration, is transfigured into a glorified flesh that can endure, not only for a while but everlastingly. Even in arguments about Christ's incarnation, the mutable, changing, and passing character of the body has long given theorists pause. Aside from wondering, in the manner of Anselm, how a perfect God could change (that is, become otherwise, thus necessarily other or less than perfect), they have also wondered how a timeless God, eternal in the Augustinian sense, can in any sense be said to be bodily, to take a form that seems exemplarily temporal.[26] One approach to such a puzzle, perhaps, is to suggest as I have that no body is in fact lived solely within time.

I am not claiming that the body has some part outside time,[27] but rather that time has an outside, and that this outside can come to us (as does time) corporeally. That is, once again, *this* world is blessed, and this body, too, is redeemed in time.

Time Returned: Somatic Rhythms

> The majesty! what did she mean?
> Breathe, arch and original Breath.
> Is it love in her of the being as her lover had been?
> Breathe, body of lovely Death.
> —Gerard Manley Hopkins, "The Wreck of the *Deutschland*"

Perhaps the most evident way in which the living body is distinguished from the corpse is by rhythms, most conspicuously those of the breath and blood. At the moment of separation that is birth (there is only birth, constantly differentiating), we draw breath and are rejoined to a long tradition of divine participation in the flesh. The tradition goes back philosophically as well as scripturally. Plotinus writes: "We have not been cut away; we are not separate . . . ; we breathe and hold our ground because the Supreme does not give and pass but gives on for ever, so long as it remains what it is."[28]

In the second of the origin myths in Genesis, animation is the sharing of divine breath: "At the time when the Lord God made the earth and the heavens . . . the Lord God formed man out of the clay of the ground and blew into his nostrils the breath of life, and so man became a living being."[29]

The association of breath with life, the fact that we breathe while we live and not otherwise, is experientially obvious well before it is scientifically clarified. The Hebrew Bible has any number of references connecting life to breath. In Job, we find an intriguing development: not only is the divine breath the beginning of life, but it is breathing-with that sustains this life. Elihu, "son of Barachel the Buzite" (32:6) declares, "For the spirit of God has made me, the breath of the almighty keeps me alive" (33:4). Indeed, "If [God] were to take back his spirit to himself, withdraw to himself his breath, all flesh would perish together, and man would return to the dust" (34:14). Ezekiel even grants to divine breath the power to restore a life already lost: "Thus says the Lord God: From the four winds come, O spirit, and breathe into these slain that they may come to life" (37:9). All of these, like the very terminological ambiguity between breath and spirit,[30] suggest a participation in divinity as a condition of life. Moreover, they suggest that this participation is a matter of sharing breath, and that prelapsarian nonseparation, in the flesh, is a matter of being somatically in sync.

John Paul II, in his *Urbi et Orbi* address for Christmas 2000, declared with surprising gracefulness, "That divine breath is the origin of the unique dignity of every human being, of humanity's boundless yearning for the infinite." Linking our bodies' self-sustaining intake to breathing-with the divine, we find as well the desire for that divinity, the yearning for eternity—*I drew in my breath and now pant after you.*[31]

And not only do I desire breath, particularly and intensely if I find myself without it; desire also alters my breath, quickening, catching, even suspending it. It imposes a new rhythm, a reminder of my openness to the outside, my susceptibility to its influences. Burrus elegantly weaves together the related senses of this respiration:

> Inspire: write and be read! Expire: let go of the self! In the midst, in between such daunting imperatives, our lives transpire. Heavy breathing, shallow breaths, suspenseful breathlessness: so we might measure the soulful, sensual embodiment of what Christians have traditionally named the "Spirit of God." More modestly, we might also note the persistent vitality of mortal creatures who continue . . . to hope, to desire, to strive . . . to keep on breathing, for a little while longer. Such improbable aspirations![32]

In the rhythm of breathing, exchanging oxygen for carbon dioxide, inside for out, we mark something other than a simple linear time. Naively, we might conceive of rhythm stretched out across just such a time line. That is, the time of rhythm seems, initially, to line up, to occupy the same before, during, and after of linear time as it passes, time that we cannot interpret as eternal. But only a little thought already tells us that rhythm, definitionally, recurs, returns again to the accent, the upbeat, the one. And as pioneering modern dancer Martha Graham, herself a careful observer of time and of rhythms, noted, "one" is never first; we never begin at a beginning but are always starting over. Marking out rhythms, we count "and one . . ." whenever we begin (again). The rhythmic phrase is not a cut-out segment of the time line, but a recurring loop, back to the one count and forward again, spiraling around and cutting spirally across the line of time, around time and through it, sometimes meditatively suspending us, sometimes propelling us urgently and dynamically on. Every "origin" in a rhythm is a beginning again, in the middle without a first, a new recurrence. With every inhalation, we breathe eternal breath, as if prior to separation, as if already restored.

Deleuze emphasizes the complexity of this constant renewal. It is a mistake, he suggests, to see rhythmic periods as simply identical replications:

> a period exists only in so far as it is determined by a tonic accent, commanded by intensities. Yet we would be mistaken about the function of accents if we said that they were reproduced at equal intervals. On the contrary, tonic and intensive values act by creating inequalities or incommensurabilities between metrically equivalent periods or spaces. They create distinctive points, privileged instants which always indicate a poly-rhythm. . . . A bare, material repetition (repetition of the Same) appears only in constituting itself in disguising itself.[33]

Thus, without a first, each measure is new, and part of its newness is a new relation to those preceding and following it. Each accent, each indrawn breath, each heartbeat is singular, yet given its intensity by its place in a return.[34]

For Deleuze, at least, difference—the difference of each new measure, the difference of inside and out, including the unincludable, always breaking outside of time, is inherent in and fundamental to the rhythm of repetition. He declares:

> The clothed and living, vertical repetition which includes difference should be regarded as the cause, of which the bare, material and horizontal repetition (from which a difference is merely drawn off) is only an effect: . . . every time, the material repetition results from the more profound repetition which unfolds in depth and

produces it as an effect, like an external envelope or a detachable shell which loses all meaning and all capacity to reproduce itself once it is no longer animated by the other repetition which is its cause."[35]

As we draw rhythmic breath, our hearts beat, their tempo varied by our interactions with the rest of the flesh of the world (and the divine): "God becomes our bodies, as our bodies relax, breathe and bleed into the Sacred Body of all bodies."[36] Rhythm is recurrent, the same again and never the same. Nancy writes: "Time's system is not the skipped beat; rather, time skips, and skips itself: suspension, pulsation, continuity broken off and started up again on its very disjunction, thus the same (the same time) and never the same (*never* the same time)."[37] In both rhythm and its rupture—in the desire for the return, for the *and*, for the again and for time's own break out of time, out of passage (the desire that says *now, always*)—we find an eternal yes.

Just as stories tell us that the divine breath is shared, so too we hear of a shared beating of the sacred heart. The heart of the incarnate god beats iconographically between inside and out, becomes visible through the wounded side of the dying Christ—the same wounded side into which Thomas puts his hand in search of proof (John 20:27–28). A long history of fascination with the sacred heart includes numerous tales of identification and exchange, Christ taking all or part of his own heart and placing it in the chest of a devoted believer, for whom heartbeat as well as breath then sustains the divinity of her life.[38] Like the stories of shared breath, these suggest to us that what animates is what is divine in us, divine and rhythmic both. As it beats with the ease of sleep, the unconscious pace of the everyday, in the relaxed tempo of sitting, walking, I am seldom aware of my heart, which calls attention to itself in fear and in desire, tangibly first, as if trying to push through my chest to join with the body's outside; visibly next, vibrating my breastbone, pulsing in my throat, my abdomen; audibly even, manifesting its beat in my ears as if distinct from me. As inward, it seems, as it is possible to be, my heart still draws attention like an outside object, its intensity and its sudden shocked stutter reminding me of the rhythms of contraction and expansion, drawing in and reaching out, which I usually ignore.

Derrida writes: "The heart is not only the insensitive figure of the centre or of secret interiority; it is the sensible heart, the rhythm, respiration, and beating of the blood."[39] I consciously or attentively sense the beating of my heart, as I do the flow of my breath, only intermittently,

THE RESURRECTION OF THE BODY

but it is always sensible, awaiting my attention to its rhythms, rhythms readily and often obviously altered by my interactions with the world, where desire and fear and hope can quicken its beat or increase the volume or cause (at least the sensation of) a syncopated skip in its expansion and contraction.

Rhythm not only sustains us, it draws us in, kinetically, muscularly. Whether or not we are instantly inclined to movement in response to music, or able to move along with it, we find it difficult to walk or otherwise move against a strong beat. Nietzsche goes further, arguing that rhythm draws not only human bodies but gods; the original intent of poetry, he argues, was to ensnare divine attention.[40] This seductive power of rhythms, drawing us out of self and into beauty, has been noted at least since Plotinus wrote in the second century: "The musician we may think of as being exceedingly quick to beauty, drawn in a very rapture to it: . . . he answers at once to the outer stimulus: as the timid are sensitive to noise so he to tones and the beauty they convey; all that offends against unison or harmony in melodies and rhythms repels him; he longs for measure and shapely pattern."[41]

What draws us to beauty, what draws our language into memory, into poetry, and draws our bodies into participation, is what we have created to seduce the gods. (One can't help wondering, too, if this accounts for some measure of the fabled seductiveness of musicians generally.) We might read here simply a slightly outrageous anthropocentric projection, but we might do better (better at least in the sense of more interestingly) to consider seriously the possibilities of this overlap. We are drawn, bodily, by what draws the gods, into what draws divinity, into another structuring of time. The divine in us, the breath of life and the beating of blood, is not in the line of time but in the enfolding and returning structures of rhythm. Somatic return is not limited to short-cycling rhythms. Memory, too—even in the simplest sense—spirals around (loops back) and cuts through time, presenting the absent past or leaving us absent-mindedly dwelling, for a moment, elsewhere than in the present. Platonic and Neoplatonic memory, Augustinian memory—any understanding of memory under Plato's influence—is no mere storehouse, full of ideas and events placed therein after the establishment of the subject. Rather, in these more complex versions, memory spirals back before the self, in what Deleuze calls the repetition before the instant (perhaps, even, nontemporally prior to time).[42] Perhaps, then, in resurrection the body remembers, repeats, slips out of its self-separation, before original sin. Perhaps the resurrection of the flesh is its living at the intensity of eternity: a potent integration in which the self shatters.

Importantly, memory is not simply intellectual but somatic, too, often intensely so. Muscle memory runs surprisingly deep and lastingly—hence the cliché that one never forgets how to ride a bicycle. So too for the memory of a particular sensation—though scent is famous in this respect (evidently for neurological reasons), sudden familiar images, musical phrases, the taste of a madeleine in tea, kinaesthetic sensations of particular movements or positions, or tactile memories of arousing touch can also be affectively strong and can immerse us with startling thoroughness in a recurrence of our corporeal pasts. (This, negatively, can be the reawakening of trauma, but it can recall us to joy as well.)

Memory does not persist—like rhythm (or like its own absence in trauma) it returns, summoned by desire or by another recurrence, a similar sensation. In memory, time overlaps, contracting in folding forward into the slipping present, opening the present to time beyond itself. The fact of passing, of past-ness, is present whenever the past is present again; memory redeems loss, but does not undo it. Here too we find eternity not in endurance but in the structuring of passage itself, its inclusion of the chance of recurrence.

In bodily memory and somatic rhythm, we as flesh are always starting again, always new, or, perhaps, always rejoining, never for the first time. If sin is indeed separation, then it is surpassed, redeemed in rejointure. And our bodies already hint at their own immanent redemption, their participation in the divine breath, the pulsing of the heart. *This* is my blood, too, or perhaps: this is *my* blood, released and returned in the sacrality of every body remembered. And perhaps, too, what breaks through in the rhythm of our breathing is indeed that original breath. We are sustained by these rhythms of breath and blood, but they already hint at something more than sustaining or carrying forth—at a return, at a before even of the beginning. At time redeemed.

The Rhythm of Sensation and the Rupture of Time

> The experience of the body in its extreme states (sex, sickness) provides access to an otherwise inaccessible realm of lucidity, one where the distinction between body and thought, between matter and energy, is momentarily suspended.
> —Eleanor Kaufman, "Klossowski or Thoughts-Becoming"

Other temporalities, or atemporalities, may be found in sensation, even more obviously than in the bodily functions of breathing and heartbeat, as the brief discussion of bodily memory has already hinted. Here

THE RESURRECTION OF THE BODY

too we find rhythm to be important, though it is not, I think, the only option for eternity in somatic sensation.

Deleuze declares the relation between sensation and rhythm to be "ultimate": "What is ultimate is thus the relation between sensation and rhythm, which places in each sensation the levels and domains through which it passes. This rhythm runs through a painting just as it runs through a piece of music. It is diastole-systole: the world that seizes me by closing in around me, the self that opens onto the world and opens the world itself."[43] Rhythm contracts and opens, accelerates and stretches, builds to break the distinction between self and world and even the orderly array of the world itself, in sensation just as in sustaining life. Music, painting, and the arts more generally are paradigmatic exemplars of rhythmically structured sensation, but so too are tactile eroticism, dancing, chanting, the auditory-tactile-kinaesthetic repetition of the rosary. As with breathing and heartbeat, here too we find a sense of moving-with something outside the self; more exactly, of a rhythm that may build or may be condensed into an instant, in which self and outside cannot retain an easy distinction. Merleau-Ponty notes: "We do not possess the musical or sensible ideas, precisely because they are negativity or absence circumscribed; they possess us. The performer is no longer producing or reproducing the sonata: he feels himself, and those others feel him to be at the service of the sonata; the sonata sings through him or cries out so suddenly that he must 'dash on his bow' to follow it."[44] We may experience this in listening as in performing (though perhaps it is less rare in the performer's experience), in viewing as in painting, in following dance with our muscles as much as our eyes.

One of rhythm's powers is that of building; catching us up, it carries us not merely steadily forward but excitingly upward. It thus links to the intensifying of sensation, which has in turn some historical connection to resurrected flesh. While much of the effort of Christian asceticism has gone toward renouncing the world's pleasures, a more intense strain once devoted itself to participation in Christ's pain, particularly that of the Passion and crucifixion.[45] Pain alone is no breakthrough; on the contrary, it pins us in time, dragging out every moment. If it breaks us, we return to ourselves damaged, in need of such healing as we can find. But pain is also one measure of the intensity of sensation, and if it occurs in the context of desire or of pleasure, whether ascetic (as in many of its religious manifestations) or hedonistic (as in perverse eroticism—the distinction, of course, is seldom really so clear), the double pull of desire, into and against the intensity of sensation, is also a pull out of self, out of

145

time. The vital distinction between the agonizing endurance of misery and the transfigurative ecstasy of the instant is this doubling or tension. That is, pain without the paradoxical pull of pleasure is misery alone. The transfigurative paradox of sensation brings pleasure (which, as Kant noticed, brings with it the will to remain with) together with pain (the intensification of sensation beyond the limits of tension's release, as Freud noted).

And in this paradoxical pull, sensation can intensify to the point of breaking even its own categories, its own necessary conditions of being bounded, as Kant points out, by space and by time—which are also the conditions of subjectivity.[46] Eternity is found not only in the peculiar repetition of rhythmicity, but in the instant. We might, with Deleuze, consider this Kierkegaardian as well as Nietzschean: "When Kierkegaard speaks of repetition as the second power of consciousness," Deleuze writes, "'second' means not a second time but the infinite which belongs to a single time, the eternity which belongs to an instant."[47]

With, and only with, the added component of joyous desire, the transfiguration of sensation into ecstasy (out of the static, but also out of the enduring) becomes possible. Writing of the paintings of Francis Bacon (bear with me here), Deleuze notes: "The body exerts itself in a very precise manner, or waits to escape from itself in a very precise manner. It is not I who attempts to escape from my body, it is the body that attempts to escape from itself by means of . . . in short, a spasm: the body as plexus, and its effort or waiting for a spasm. Perhaps this is Bacon's approximation of horror or abjection."[48] It is in the most intense sensations that this curious sense of body attempting its own self-escape becomes strongest, not in weariness with the flesh but in a life in the flesh bursting the boundaries of the comprehensible, in pain, in pleasure, in the ecstatic pull between the two. But we must read this abjection in the context of a parallel that Deleuze draws between Bacon and Cézanne, where it is far from a simple negative: "Abjection becomes splendor; the horror of life becomes a very pure and intense life. 'Life is frightening,' said Cézanne, but in this cry he had already given voice to all the joys of line and color."[49] Joy, as Nietzsche notes, wants eternity[50]—joy wants the fullness of life at its most intense. Deleuze (always working under a Nietzschean influence) links Bacon's joy and splendor to this intensity: "Bacon . . . is one of those artists who, in the name of a very intense life, can call for an even more intense life. He is not a painter who 'believes' in death. His is indeed a figurative *misérabilisme*, but one that serves an increasingly powerful Figure of life."[51] Bacon, in

THE RESURRECTION OF THE BODY

this reading, seeks to capture and present sensation; not to represent its cause but to cross into the observing subject and share it. Sensation at this concentration is transfigurative in its intensity, breaking open the very subjects who would sense it.

Sensation, perception, is not distinct from flesh; the perceived quality is, Merleau-Ponty writes, "a certain node in the woof of the simultaneous and the successive."[52] In sensation as in lived rhythm, particularly but not solely in sensation marked by rhythm, we encounter in the flesh the outside of time. And in the building of rhythm, but also in the suddenness of a moment that may seem isolated—a realization of beauty, a transformative Nietzschean encounter with the landscape (such as the one that famously provoked his thought of eternal recurrence), a breakthrough in the wall of the self through a process of intensifying touch—we encounter the rupture of time, time cut through, or fragmented, or turned inside out.

The apparent opposition of this instant, which seems to stop or to shatter time, to rhythmic return may be less perfect than it seems. We have already noted one of the most interesting readings of Nietzsche's endlessly interpretable "eternal recurrence," in which Klossowski suggests that affirming recurrence (the "yes-saying" that is for Nietzsche the ethical response to the thought of infinite return) says yes not only to infinite return but to infinite loss; that is, to the return of the moment that slips, and to every possibility opened by each new instant. Each new instant can develop in any number, indeed an infinite number, of ways. As Deleuze elaborates:

> Repetition in the eternal return never means continuation, perpetuation or prolongation, nor even the discontinuous return of something which would at least be able to be prolonged in a partial cycle (an identity, an I, a Self) but, on the contrary, the reprise of pre-individual singularities. . . . Every origin is a singularity and every singularity a commencement on the horizontal line, the line of ordinary points on which it is prolonged like so many reproductions or copies which form the moments of a bare repetition. It is also, however, a recommencement on the vertical line which condenses singularities and on which is woven the other repetition, the line of the affirmation of chance.[53]

It is not only the evident repetition of rhythm but the suddenness of the cutting-through moment that suffices to eternity: it is saying yes, once or over and over again; it is living, and living more.

ETERNAL FLESH

We find in eternity the rhythm of pleasure moving into intensity, always in motion and always returning: the affirmation both of the instant and of its passage. Deleuze writes of Bacon's use of color: "Time itself seems to result from color in two ways: as time that passes, in the chromatic variation of the broken tones that compose the flesh; and as the eternity of time, that is, as *the eternity of the passage in itself*."[54] The eternity of the passage itself is the transfiguration of loss, the contraction of time to the instant and its expansion beyond all limit, an eternity that requires passage, an eternity of matter. As Nancy writes, "The point is that eternity and unity can in truth only exist in the moment, in the passage of the moment that the moment itself is."[55]

This is the eternity of our living materiality—the eternity of what slips, the spirit in the slipping. The eternity of the flesh, setting self beside itself, is nonetheless one's own; it is to myself that I return from loss, though, again, this self is never static (any more than simply ec-static); it is as this body that I live and bleed and breathe, in and out of time. This body is whole: it is all at once, contracted and gathered, as in memory, from its "dispersed and distorted state";[56] it is always, extended not within time but over it; it is the outflowing reach of desire and the pinpoint focus of will willing what is. And these eternal bodies are immortal not because they do not pass but because their passing, the slippery inherence of loss in all matter, is transfigured beyond the mere sense of loss we associate with passage. The resurrection of the flesh is a promise like that of eternal life—not endurance but intensity; not extensively infinite time, but intensively lived time, passage bound up with its own outside. It is a story of animate matter, of the living, breathing, bleeding, and sensing of flesh. We break, and we remember.

AFTERWORD
On Returning to Memory

> Rather I feel that I have done nothing but wish to speak. But if I have spoken, I have not said what I wished to say.
> —Augustine, *De Doctrina Christiana*

> [E]very word, in responding to our entreaties, eludes innumerable existences which we have dreamed or imagined, and of which we let it catch a glimpse: possibilities it could have had. You must not think words are without memory. Where we have erased everything, they are present to remind us in a stroke of lightning, a singular light, of our past, of what it could have been and what it was.
>
> Before the book, then, where we struggle without memories, elusive moments of the book inscribe themselves into its plan and expectation. . . . Between our questions and those the book asks on its own, the work is done and undone without our help.
> —Edmond Jabès, *The Book of Questions*

Without our help, says Jabès, the work of writing is done and undone, carrying within itself elusive reminders of all of the books that could have opened out from any point of it. Without our help, but with our necessary participation, as we work, unwork, and rework texts until they are ready, which is not to say that they are (ever) completed, ever finished. *Consummatum non est.* Our books do not provide answers but return to questions, with their origins in repetition; having spoken out of an urgent word-generating wish to speak (we have done nothing but wish to speak), we ask the questions again. Apparently, they were not finished; their apparent finishedness is only the start of another question, another opening.

AFTERWORD

We return not only to the questions but to ourselves, unfinished, asking. Like the work, making ourselves with the work, we are done and undone. We break apart, carrying the memory of all the selves that could have opened out from any moment of us. We "begin" in breaking; we regather; we break again. Fragmentation and redemption are not opposites but mutually inherent; memory and forgetting are not simply opposing forces, nor simply steps or stages in a process, but endlessly entangled. We remember not only when ideas and images come full force before us, but when what cannot be present or represented draws us nonetheless as what we have forgotten—when we remember the spaces. Eternity too is enfolded in the lived and living dimensions of time. Time too is unworked in its very processing.

Eternity is neither static nor total; it is not even (or not only) whole. There are fragments of it in time, complicating time's linear or cyclical progression, and it fragments time, disordering the pieces. It comes to us as every temporal dimension: in the present as joy and intensity, from the past as the gathering of memory (a converse of fragmentation implicated in turn in every other dimension of the time/eternity intersection), into the future as possibility. And it comes as time's own redemption. We live it not as totality but as breakage and incompleteness; as Mark Jordan remarks, "Fragmentation is a surer instrument of redemption" than more reassuring signs.[1] Fragmentation is as redemptive as mending, and not simply prior to it. We find the sacred not in that which simply destroys and leaves nothing but destruction in memory (or destruction of memory) but in that which, even while shattering, seduces and delights, leaving Bataillean "new knowledge" of an inherent sacred, an immanent transcendent. We fail to find it when we make our lives excessively "safe": when we keep our sensations carefully moderate, our ego boundaries fiercely secure, our futures maximally predictable, as if we could will possibility out of existence. Even to be caught up in cycling rhythms, even to attend to the breath, is already to move out of oneself, to risk.

Remembering spaces, we must feel, too, the interconnections of joy and loss. Joy is not simply compensation for mourning, nor mourning the price of joy; this pair, too, is in no simple relation of either opposition or succession. Nancy, in "Hyperion's Joy," quotes Hölderlin:

> There is a forgetting of all existence, a hush of our being, in which we feel as if we had found all.
>
> There is a hush, a forgetting of all existence, in which we feel as if we had lost all, a night of our soul.[2]

ON RETURNING TO MEMORY

In this dual hush of loss and return silence opens in our words; bodies live suspended time. The sacred is nowhere else, which is not to say that it is simply identical with the dual extensions of time and space that form experience. As Nancy points out, "Both Hegel *and* Hölderlin oppose Kant's time [which is linear, orderly, and belongs to the understanding subject whether or not it belongs to the world outside the subject] with a recapturing of time by time itself, the remembrance that restores becoming to being, the perishable to the divine."[3] The world is shot through with divinity at every point, but we can only remember this as what we have forgotten, only find it in what passes, yet does not only pass.

And so the "work" of the divine, of the space-opening sacred, is, like that of the book, unworked within itself. In another of the passages Nancy cites, Hölderlin declares, "And a desire endlessly yearns for that / Which is unbound."[4] The unboundedness, the infinity, is attributed at once to desire, which is endless, and to its object, the infinite as the only possible aim of infinite desire. And yet, in what is desired—unbound, without limit and without, one assumes, constraint—"There is," Hölderlin adds, "much to / Hold on to." And when we desire, we *do* desire to hold on, however much we may try to train ourselves in letting go; yet we desire that which is unbound, which cannot be held—and we desire it in its unboundedness. We desire the world as it slips, the infinite open, the uncertainty and promise of the future, the explosive return. Holding on is not in fact a matter of grasp: "One *must* be faithful," Hölderlin concludes. It is a question, we remember, of a certain faithfulness of memory. Fidelity to this unbounded is also fidelity to its place in the finite world: to flesh and to word, to the promise and to memory, to mourning as to pleasure—to the infinite folded within, and breaking forth.

NOTES

Introduction: *On Having Forgotten*

1. I have tried here to find a delicate balance between two forms of arrogance: assuming that the reader will have any familiarity with my own earlier work and assuming that my ideas are so fascinating that they bear reiteration in yet another text. The footnote form is something of a compromise. And so: while I have been interested in all of my books in the intersections of eternity with time, the concern is most explicit throughout *Immemorial Silence*, in the conclusion of *Counterpleasures*, and in the considerations of the fourth gospel in *Word Made Skin*, though it is present to some extent throughout that text.

2. Wolfson, *Alef, Mem, Tau*, 3.

3. Jean-Luc Nancy, "Of Divine Places," in his *The Inoperative Community*, 141. Brackets in original.

4. More fully: "Neither does eternal being become an object in time, nor is temporal being transposed into eternity. We remain in the 'in-between,' in a temporal flow of experience in which eternity is nevertheless present" (Voegelin, *Anamnesis*, 329; cited in Wolfson, *Alef, Mem, Tau*, 57).

5. Wolfson, *Alef, Mem, Tau*, 92.

6. Nietzsche, *The Anti-Christ*, section 33, 145. The title is perhaps misleading in translation, as "Antichrist" in German can mean not only "anti-Christ" but also "anti-Christian," and the latter is more true to the spirit of the text.

7. Ibid., 146.

8. Blanchot, *The Step Not Beyond*, 47.

9. Jean-Luc Nancy and Philippe Lacoue-Labarthe, "Noli Me Frangere," trans. Brian Holmes, in Nancy, *The Birth to Presence*, 266.

10. For an influential analysis of the logic of paradox, see Deleuze, *The Logic of Sense*.

11. Nancy and Lacoue-Labarthe, "Noli Me Frangere," in Nancy, *The Birth to Presence*, 267.

NOTES TO PAGES 7–12

12. Keller, *Face of The Deep*, xviii.
13. Deleuze, *Difference and Repetition*, 200.
14. Bataille, *Guilty*, 128.

1. The One and the Many

1. James, "The One and the Many," 50–51.
2. Ibid., 59.
3. Bataille, *Inner Experience*, xxxii.
4. Plato, *Theatetus*, 155d; Aristotle, *Metaphysics*, 982b12.
5. Cf. Jean-Luc Nancy: "This is not a circle: It is a conflagration. Man is the catastrophe of the One, the One is his being mortally torn apart and his life lived on" ("Hyperion's Joy", in Nancy, *The Birth to Presence*, 69). It is alternatively possible, of course, to read the equation of I and One as solipsistic (I am all that there is, and I create all that appears to be other), but to most of us this claim is at least as terrifying as the threat of ego dissolution, and deeply discouraging, besides.
6. Lenn E. Goodman, editor's introduction to *Neoplatonism and Jewish Thought*, 6.
7. See Paul, Second Letter to the Corinthians, 3:6. Cf. Romans 7:5. Unless otherwise specified, all biblical citations are from *The Catholic Study Bible* (Oxford: Oxford University Press, 1990).
8. The association with death is primarily though not entirely psychoanalytic; the Freudian death drive is fundamentally a drive to disintegration or coming apart. See Freud, *Beyond the Pleasure Principle*.
9. The first is the position of Thales, the second that of Anaximines, the third that of Anaximander. See McKirahan, "Anaximines."
10. Aside from the Neoplatonism noted later in this chapter, it is worth mentioning another Presocratic, Heraclitus, whose philosophy held that a single law united what were nonetheless oppositions in constant flux, and the fifteenth-century Nicholas of Cusa, whose ideas on implication and complication fascinatingly prefigure much later thought. Catherine Keller provocatively suggests of Cusanus that the "One" may entail something more intriguing than simple unity: "If the All is the 'all-relational,' we begin to see how this discourse may resist its own temptation to a mystical de-differentiation, with its corresponding social indifference" (Keller, *Face of the Deep*, 207).
11. I am inclined to think that our own sense of the sacred is found in the body and in language, each indicating to us the very limits of ourselves, limits we cannot comprehend because they necessarily elude the very subjects who would grasp them. This runs contrary to the usual association of divine with discorporate and of body with the brevity of time, an association particularly found where divinity is linked to eternity. Wolfson remarks of Kabbala, for instance, that "All corporeality is to be removed from the divine; consequently,

NOTES TO PAGES 12–13

God cannot be bound spatially or temporally" (*Alef, Mem, Tau*, 74). This insistence on divine discorporateness is found across the monotheistic traditions, even in Christianity, where the Incarnation presents a paradoxical complication rather than a counterargument. Without making of God a body, I want nonetheless to explore the divinity—and more specifically, the eternity—of all flesh.

12. Parmenides, *On Nature (Peri Physeos)*, Prelude, frag. 1.

13. "[H]ere we must be struck by the aptness of the poet's chosen mouthpiece. In presenting his message as the teaching of a goddess, he claims superhuman authority for it, and thereby shows a proper regard for its consistency. For a mere mortal to argue from his own speech and thought to a unique and changeless reality would be not only insufficient to prove his thesis, but blatantly at odds with it. But an immortal may argue from hers, precisely because she speaks from a superhuman perspective. Unlike a human speaker or thinker, she may claim without instant self-contradiction to be speaking and thinking of a birthless and deathless reality. Her speech and thought about it are perpetuated in Parmenides' verses: she continues to dwell upon it for all time, whether anyone heeds her words or not. Thus, her authority not only underwrites the deliverances of a mortal poet's reason; it also raises those deliverances to the only level on which they could possibly make sense" (Gallop, editor's introduction to *Parmenides of Elea: Fragments*, 28).

14. Parmenides, *On Nature (Peri Physeos)*, "Doxa," frag. 5.

15. T. S. Eliot, "East Coker," in *Four Quartets*, 23, 34.

16. Plato, *Parmenides*, 127b–e. In fact, Zeno is best known for more deliberate versions of such paradoxes, meant to deny the possibility of positional change and perhaps, in their problematizing of divisibility, even spatial extension. Most famously, the paradox of Achilles and the tortoise (which is widely attributed to him) pits the fleet-footed runner against the plodding reptile. The tortoise challenges Achilles to a race, asking only a small head start; Achilles loses, of course, because in order to catch up to the tortoise he must first close half the distance between them, while the tortoise creeps ahead, however little. Half of this new distance between them must then be covered, during which the tortoise continues to creep ahead, however little. In fact, as the tortoise argues, the distance is uncloseable; however small his head start, he must win.

It may be, as some historians of philosophy suggest, that Zeno is less monist than nihilist—not a believer in one but a nonbeliever in any: "Plato's interpretation of Zeno as supporting Parmenides is not mandatory. Eudemus, the pupil of Aristotle, read him as attacking not only pluralism but also Parmenides' One, and this alternative view of Zeno as a nihilist, rather than a monist, gained some currency (Seneca, Letters 88.44–45)" ("Zeno of Elea").

The third of the well-known Eleatic philosophers, Melissus, argues for a single One that is infinite in time and extent, homogeneous, unchanging, bodiless—and probably, like the prime matter of the Milesians, divine (Sedley, "Melissus").

17. Beyond material or numerical monism is at least one further, more distantly unitive possibility, which may be that of Parmenides and may have had an

influence upon Plato and his ideas of Forms. In her work *The Legacy of Parmenides*, Patricia Curd argues for a view of Parmenides as a "predicational" rather than a numerical monist, a believer in something like essences, or single fundamental predicates for each thing that is. Predicational monism allows for change in the illusory and insignificant sensory realm but not in Reality, which transcends the senses: "Numerical monism asserts that there exists only one thing: a complete list of entities in the universe would have only one entry. This is the kind of monism that has traditionally been attributed to Parmenides and (rightly) to Melissus. Predicational monism is the claim that each thing that is can be only one thing; and must be that in a particularly strong way. To be a genuine entity, something that is metaphysically basic, a thing must be a predicational unity, a being of a single kind . . . with a single account of what it is; but it need not be the case that there exists only one such thing. What must be the case is that the thing itself must be a unified whole" (4).

18. I take this emphasis on the method of gathering and division from Alexander Nehamas and Paul Woodruff, editors' introduction to Plato's *Phaedrus*, xlii–xlvii.

19. Ibid., xliii.

20. Ibid., xlvii.

21. Plato, *The Sophist*, 217d.

22. Plato, *Meno*, 82b–85e.

23. Plato, *Phaedrus*, 251a and following. Cf. Plato, *Symposium*, 210a–b.

24. This myth becomes especially influential on Plotinus and thus on Neoplatonism generally. In *Ennead* 1.3.1, Plotinus writes: "But what order of beings will attain the Term? Surely, as we read, those that have already seen all or most things, those who at their first birth have entered into the life germ from which is to spring a metaphysician, a musician or a born lover, the metaphysician taking to the path by instinct, the musician and the nature peculiarly susceptible to love needing outside guidance." In section three of the same *Ennead*, he picks up both on the high valuation of the life of philosophy and on the *Phaedrus*'s image of wings: "The metaphysician, equipped by that very character, winged already and not like those others, in need of disengagement, stirring of himself towards the supernal but doubting of the way, needs only a guide. He must be shown, then, and instructed, a willing wayfarer by his very temperament, all but self-directed."

Ennead 6.9 brings together the *Phaedrus* myth and the myth of two Aphrodites from Pausanias's speech in the *Symposium* (180d–181e): "So long as it is There, it holds the heavenly love; here its love is the baser; There the soul is Aphrodite of the heavens; here, turned harlot, Aphrodite of the public ways: yet the soul is always an Aphrodite. This is the intention of the myth which tells of Aphrodite's birth and Eros born with her. The soul in its nature loves God and longs to be at one with Him in the noble love of a daughter for a noble father; but coming to human birth and lured by the courtships of this sphere, she takes up with another love, a mortal, leaves her father and falls. But one day coming to hate her shame, she puts away the evil of earth, once more seeks the father, and finds her peace" (*Ennead* 6.9.9; all in *Six Enneads*).

25. Nehamas and Woodruff argue that this is the motivation for the telling of the myth: Phaedrus, who is not ready to let go of rhetorical beauty, needs to hear the third speech, which may help him along the way toward philosophy (*Phaedrus*, introduction, xli).

26. Plato, *Phaedrus*, 275D–277A.

27. Plato, *Protagoras*, 334c. I am grateful to Daniel Boyarin for inadvertently but helpfully reminding me of this line through his paper "Plato's Dialogue," delivered at the School of Criticism and Theory, Summer 2007.

28. Ramadanovic, "Plato's Forgetting," 4.

29. For what is probably the most concise presentation of this idea, see Nietzsche, *The Gay Science*, sec. 341.

30. Plotinus, *Ennead* 5, in *The Enneads*.

31. Plotinus, *Ennead* 6.9.3, in *Six Enneads*.

32. Ibid., 6.9.6.

33. Hyman, "From What Is One and Simple Only What Is One and Simple Can Come to Be," 113. His note cites *Enneads* 3.8.10, 5.1.6, cf. 5.4.1, as translated by A. H. Armstrong (Cambridge: Harvard University Press, 1988).

34. Miles, *Plotinus on Body and Beauty*, 35.

35. Ibid.

36. Hyman, 114. His note cites *Enneads* 5.4.1–2, 5.1.6, 5.2.1, cf. 3.8.10, as translated by A. H. Armstrong. Though subsequent Neoplatonists will differ considerably in their readings of the process of differentiation and whether or not to consider it in stages, the relation of one to many, and the sense of something not only puzzling but mysterious within that relation, is fundamental to all of them.

37. Miles, *Plotinus on Body and Beauty*, 16.

38. In *Word Made Skin* I develop at length this sense of interconnection, drawn in some measure from Merleau-Ponty, *The Visible and the Invisible*.

39. See, e.g.: "The pleasure demanded for the life cannot be in the enjoyments of the licentious or in any gratifications of the body" (*Ennead* 1.4.12); "It would be absurd to think that happiness begins and ends with the living-body: happiness is the possession of the good of life: it is centred therefore in Soul, is an Act of the Soul—and not of all the Soul at that: for it certainly is not characteristic of the vegetative soul, the soul of growth; that would at once connect it with the body" (1.4.14); "He that has the strength, let him arise and withdraw into himself, forgoing all that is known by the eyes, turning away for ever from the material beauty that once made his joy. When he perceives those shapes of grace that show in body, let him not pursue: he must know them for copies, vestiges, shadows, and hasten away towards That they tell of. For if anyone follow what is like a beautiful shape playing over water—is there not a myth

telling in symbol of such a dupe, how he sank into the depths of the current and was swept away to nothingness? So too, one that is held by material beauty and will not break free shall be precipitated, not in body but in Soul, down to the dark depths loathed of the Intellective-Being, where, blind even in the Lower-World, he shall have commerce only with shadows, there as here" (1.6.8, all, in *The Enneads*).

40. Cited in Miles, *Plotinus on Body and Beauty*, 79. Cf. *Ennead* 6.9.11: "The man formed by this mingling with the Supreme must—if he only remember—carry its image impressed upon him: he is become the Unity, nothing within him or without inducing any diversity; no movement now, no passion, no out-looking desire, once this ascent is achieved; reasoning is in abeyance and all Intellection and even, to dare the word, the very self; caught away, filled with God, he has in perfect stillness attained isolation; all the being calmed, he turns neither to this side nor to that, not even inwards to himself; utterly resting he has become very rest" (in *Six Enneads*).

41. Cf. Wolfson: "Surely, I am not advocating a dualism when I speak of two vectors [time and eternity] nor do I deny that kabbalistic tradition presumes an analogical relation between the two spheres such that one gains knowledge of the latent from the manifest and of the manifest from the latent—an ancient Hermetic teaching with roots in Platonic philosophy that had a profound impact on the esoteric teachings of Judaism, Christianity, and Islam as they evolved in the Middle Ages" (*Alef, Mem, Tau*, 81).

42. Aristotle develops the ideal of flourishing as the fullness of life according to one's kind in the *Nicomachean Ethics*.

43. Clyde Lee Miller, "Meister Eckhart in Nicholas of Cusa's 1456 sermon."

44. Wolfson likewise mentions a sense of a time or instant common to numerous traditions—he mentions Kabbala, Zen, and Sufism—"a time so fully present it is devoid of (re)presentation, so binding it releases one from all causal links to past or future [citing Gerald T. Elmore, *Islamic Sainthood in the Fullness of Time: Ibn al-'Arabi's Book of the Fabulous Gryphon* (Leiden: E. J. Brill, 1999), 230], a split second wherein and wherewith the superfluity of truth divests one of all memory and expectation [citing Ali ibn 'Uthman Al-Hujwiri, *Kashf al-Mahjub: The Oldest Persian Treatise on Sufism*, trans. Reynold A. Nicholson (London: E. J. W. Gibb Memorial, 1976), 367]" (*Alef, Mem, Tau*, 71).

45. Plotinus, *Ennead* 1.6.7, in *Six Enneads*.

46. See Plotinus, *Ennead* 4.4.1: "When we seize anything in the direct intellectual act there is room for nothing else than to know and to contemplate the object; and in the knowing there is not included any previous knowledge; all such assertion of stage and progress belongs to the lower and is a sign of the altered; this means that, once purely in the Intellectual, no one of us can have any memory of our experience here" (in *Six Enneads*).

47. See Plato, *Symposium*, 210a–12a.

48. Ibid., 200a–b. Compare Wolfson: "since the infinite comprises everything, it cannot be deficient in any manner, it cannot lack anything—not even lack, the potential to receive" (*Alef, Mem, Tau*, 97).

49. Ramadanovic, "Plato's Forgetting," 1.

50. Plotinus's texts, in fact, are his spoken words written down by his student Porphyry.

51. Derrida, "Sauf le nom," 35.

52. Sturken, "Narratives of Recovery," 243.

53. See esp. Nietzsche, *On the Advantage and Disadvantage of History for Life*. For an excellent discussion of this forgetting in relation to the eternal return, see Ramadanovic, "From Haunting to Trauma."

54. Augustine, under Platonic and Neoplatonic influence, makes a similar claim in *Confessions*, 10.14, 21–22.

55. Plotinus, *Ennead* 4.4.6, in *Six Enneads*.

56. Louis Mackey, "Faith and Reason in Augustine's *De Magistro*," in his *Peregrinations of the Word*, 73.

57. Compare Blanchot: "Through the movement that steals away (forgetting), we allow ourselves to turn toward what escapes (death), as though the only authentic approach to this inauthentic event belonged to forgetting. Forgetting, death: the unconditional detour. The present time of forgetting delimits the unlimited space where death reverts to the lack of presence" (*The Infinite Conversation*, 196).

58. See Klossowski, *Nietzsche and the Vicious Circle*.

59. For Nietzsche, his mother and sister formed the biggest obstacles to his own ability to think joyously of return. See *Ecce Homo*, "Why I Am So Wise," sec. 3, 11.

60. Maurice Blanchot, "The Exigency of Return (1970)," trans. Michael Holland, in *The Blanchot Reader*, 292. See also: "*Everything returns*, signifying: 'everything will return, everything returned already and once and for all, on condition that it be not, nor ever have been, present,' excludes 'everything returns,' even if it takes the form of 'nothing perhaps returns'" (ibid., 295).

61. Maurice Blanchot, "The Exigency of Return (1969)," trans. Susan Hanson, in *The Blanchot Reader*, 289.

62. Maurice Blanchot, "Thanks (Be Given) to Jacques Derrida," trans. Leslie Hill, in *The Blanchot Reader*, 321.

2. The Sin of Origin

1. Deleuze, *The Fold*, 71. My emphasis.

2. Including the variant of living eternity in Johannine Christianity—that is, the understanding of Christian eternity usually associated with the fourth gospel. Peter Manchester persuasively argues that in fact this view of Christ's temporality is compatible with Paul and the synoptic gospels as well. See Manchester, "Time in Christianity," 124–26.

3. Schelling, *Ages of the World*, 80. Cited in Wolfson, *Alef, Mem, Tau*, 42.

4. For a discussion of the difference between mortal and venial sin, see Thomas Aquinas, *Summa theologiae*, 1st part of the 2nd part, Q 88, Article 1.

5. Pseudo-Dionysius the Areopagite, *Divine Names*, in *The Mystical Theology and Divine Names*, 4.13 (106), sec. 4.

6. Meister Eckhart, German Sermon on Matthew 5:3 (DW 52), in *Selected Writings*, 204.

7. To be sure, other traditions, again especially among those labeled Gnostic, make of this disobedience an act of redemption, a rejection of the inferior creator-God in the embrace of a higher knowledge that will ultimately lead us toward the truth of the higher God.

8. *Catechism of the Catholic Church*, Second Edition, sec. 398. Notes in the text refer the reader to St. Maximus the Confessor, *Ambiguorum liber*, in J. P. Migne, ed., *Patrologia Graeca* (Paris, 1857–66), 91,1156C, and to Genesis 3:5.

9. Plotinus, *Ennead* 6.9.7, in *Six Enneads*.

10. Blanchot, *The Writing of the Disaster*, 64.

11. Augustine, *City of God*, 14, 24.

12. See ibid., 14, 15.

13. See Augustine, *Confessions*, 8.8 (20).

14. In the *Supplementum* to the *Summa*, put together by his secretaries after Thomas's death, we find the claim that "Every actual sin is caused by our will not yielding to God's law" (*Summa theologiae*, Supplement [XP], Q 2, Article 3).

15. Thus the Nicene Creed, e.g., declares, "We acknowledge one baptism for the forgiveness of sins."

16. Harent, "Original Sin."

17. See also 1 Cor. 15:22.

18. A similar suggestion is made in 1 Cor. 15:21.

19. Harent, "Original Sin."

20. Ibid.

21. Augustine's occasional opponent, John Cassian, is sometimes (mis)characterized as holding this view, though in fact he argues that redemption requires both divine and human action.

22. Augustine, *Enchiridion*, sec. 46. Curiously, a similar notion is voiced by Jonathan Edwards, http://www.jonathanedwards.com/text/osin/OS-Part%203-1.htm.

23. Jean-Luc Nancy, "Identity and Trembling," trans. Brian Holmes, in *The Birth to Presence*, 35.

24. Though not, of course, a new one; see, as one of the best examples, the Gnostic text *The Hypostasis of the Archons*. The Gnostic version depends upon a split in "god" such that the guilty god is not the highest god.

25. Again, we may compare Plotinus: "Thus the Supreme as containing no otherness is ever present with us; we with it when we put otherness away. It is not that the Supreme reaches out to us seeking our communion: we reach

towards the Supreme; it is we that become present. We are always before it: but we do not always look: thus a choir, singing set in due order about the conductor, may turn away from that centre to which all should attend: let it but face aright and it sings with beauty, present effectively. We are ever before the Supreme—cut off is utter dissolution; we can no longer be—but we do not always attend: when we look, our Term is attained; this is rest; this is the end of singing ill; effectively before Him, we lift a choral song full of God"(*Ennead* 6.9.8, in *Six Enneads*). Cf. Augustine, *Confessions*, 10, 38 (63).

26. See notes 46 and 47 below.
27. Bynum, *Fragmentation and Redemption*.
28. Plato, *Phaedrus*, 246c.
29. Ibid., 246c–d.
30. Ibid., 248c–d.
31. Blanchot, *The Step Not Beyond*, 25.
32. Plato, *Phaedrus*, 249c.
33. Meister Eckhart, Sermon on John 15:16 (DW 28), in *Selected Writings*, 122.
34. In rather different terms, this defiance of subjectivity is also famously the claim of Gilles Deleuze and Felix Guattari. See, e.g., *Anti-Oedipus* and *A Thousand Plateaus*. On the Neoplatonic element in Deleuze and Guattari, see Wyschogrod, *Saints and Postmodernism*.
35. Meister Eckhart, Sermon DW 38, in *Selected Writings*, 114.
36. In this Eckhart also echoes Origen, whose third-century theory of the Fall similarly grounds it in a lapse made possible by free will and mutually implicated with the return to the divine. See Origen, *On First Principles*, 1.3.8, 1.4.1, 1.4.5.
37. Meister Eckhart, Sermon DW 58, in *Selected Writings*, 133.
38. Augustine, *City of God*, 22, 30. See also Brown, *The Body and Society*, 231.
39. Augustine, *Enchiridion*, sec. 23.
40. Pagels, *Adam, Eve, and the Serpent*, 107, quoting Augustine, *City of God* 13, 21.
41. Augustine, *On Free Choice of the Will*.
42. Nicholas of Cusa, *The Vision of God*, 97.
43. Nietzsche, *Beyond Good and Evil*, sec. 188.
44. Meister Eckhart, "Talks of Instruction," 12, in *Selected Writings*, 22.
45. Meister Eckhart, Sermon on Luke 2:42, in ibid., 229.
46. Meister Eckhart, Sermon on Matt. 5:3, in ibid., 204–5.
47. Ibid., 290. The reference to Walshe is to M. O'C. Walshe, *Meister Eckhart: German Sermons and Treatises*, vol. 2 (London: Element Books, 1981), 271.
48. Blanchot, *The Writing of the Disaster*, 139.
49. Thomas Aquinas, *Summa theologiae*, 1st part of 2nd part, Q 81, Article 5.
50. Ibid., 1st part of 2nd part, Q 81, Article 4. Furthermore, perhaps least relevantly but also perhaps most fascinatingly, he implies that clones would be

free of original sin: "Now there is no movement to generation except by the active power of generation: so that those alone contract original sin, who are descended from Adam through the active power of generation originally derived from Adam, i.e. who are descended from him through seminal power; for the seminal power is nothing else than the active power of generation. But if anyone were to be formed by God out of human flesh, it is evident that the active power would not be derived from Adam. Consequently he would not contract original sin: even as a hand would have no part in a human sin, if it were moved, not by the man's will, but by some external power" (ibid.).

51. Holweck, "Immaculate Conception."

52. Augustine, *Enchiridion*, "Baptism and Original Sin," sec. 41.

53. The doctrine of the Immaculate Conception, declared by Pius IX in 1854, is one of very few to be declared infallible after the possibility of papal infallibility was established by Vatican I in 1870.

54. Holweck, "Immaculate Conception."

55. Brown, *The Body and Society*, 407. Brown cites *Enarratio in Ps.* 67 in J. P. Migne, ed., *Patrologia Latina* (Paris, 1857–66), 36.67–1028, citation at 21.37:826; *Sermon* 287.4 in 39:1302 and *de Trinitate* in 42.819–1098, citation at 13.18.23:42:1032; cf. *Contra Julianum, Patrologia Latina* 44.641–880, citation at 4.13.62:44:768.

56. Ibid., 417.

57. By mentioning this idea, I am not endorsing it; I find the whole notion of sexual addiction a bit dubious.

58. Augustine does argue against the Manichean reading of the Eden story, which would see it as the inverse of an original sin. He presents the Manichean version thus: "They assert, however, that Christ was the one called by our Scriptures the serpent, and they assure us that they have been given insight into this in order to open the eyes of knowledge and to distinguish between Good and Evil. Christ came in the latter days to save souls, not bodies. He did not really exist in the flesh, but in mockery of the human senses proffered the simulated appearance of fleshly form, and thereby also produced the illusion not only of death, but also of resurrection. God, who issued the Law through Moses, and who spoke through Hebrew prophets, was not the true God but one of the archons of Darkness" (Augustine, *De haeresibus ad quodvultdeum*, 46:4, in Barnstone, ed., *The Other Bible*, 41).

59. As Miles, in *Plotinus on Body and Beauty*, notes of Plotinus, if we hold that all creation comes of Good, then to be is to be beautiful.

60. Holweck, "Immaculate Conception."

61. Thomas Aquinas, *Summa theologiae*, 3rd part, Q 31, Article 1.

62. Brown, *The Body and Society*, 444.

63. For an analysis of this seduction in Augustine's *Confessions*, see my "Carthage Didn't Burn Hot Enough."

64. Miles, *Plotinus on Body and Beauty*, 40.
65. Ibid., 34.
66. Besides its links to "mystical" traditions, this self-exceeding is very close to the Nietzschean will to power, which is not a will to survive but a will to live more fully and intensely.
67. I discuss this at greater length in "Carthage Didn't Burn Hot Enough."
68. Augustine, *City of God*, 22, 30.
69. Plotinus, *Ennead* 4.4.37, cited in Miles, *Plotinus on Body and Beauty*, 83.
70. Augustine, *Confessions*, 10.19 (28).
71. Brown, *The Body and Society*, 418.
72. For Deleuze's work on repetition, see especially though not exclusively his *Difference and Repetition*.
73. In what is probably the most famous line of the *Confessions*, Augustine asks, "Lord, grant me chastity and continence, but not yet" (*Confessions*, 8.7 (17)).
74. See MacKendrick, *Counterpleasures*, "Asceticism," 65–86.
75. Wolfson, *Alef, Mem, Tau*, 93.
76. See Augustine, *Confessions*, 10.6 (8–10).
77. Rainer Maria Rilke, *Duino Elegies*, First Elegy, in *Selected Poetry*, 151.

3. From Trauma to Revelation: *Forgiveness*

1. Pope, *An Essay on Criticism*, 19.
2. Meister Eckhart, German Sermon 6, "The Just Shall Live Eternally," cited in Milem, *The Unspoken Word*, 112.
3. *Baltimore Catechism*, No. 3, Lesson 17, Q 740.
4. My sense of the temporality of the promise is drawn largely from Nancy, especially his essay "Shattered Love," trans. Lisa Garbus and Simona Sawhney, in *The Inoperative Community*, of which the next chapter will make much more.
5. Wolfson, "Fore/giveness On the Way," 154.
6. Ibid.
7. Ibid., 155.
8. Wolfson, *Alef, Mem, Tau*, 98. His note cites Charles D. Isbell, "The Divine Name *Ehyeh* as a Symbol of Presence in Israelite Tradition," *Hebrew Annual Review* 2 (1978): 101–18.
9. Willis Barnstone, ed., "Haggadah," in Barnstone, ed., *The Other Bible*, 15. From Ginzberg, ed., *The Legends of the Jews*, vol. 1, chap. 1, verse 6.
10. Ibid.
11. Ibid., Barnstone, ed., *The Other Bible*, 26; Ginzberg, ed., *The Legends of the Jews*, verse 27.
12. Wolfson, "Fore/giveness," 165. The terms of Wolfson's discussion are quite different; he goes on to explain, "for both terms signify the ultimate reintegration of the gender binary in the womb of the mother." While I have not

taken up here the gender concerns central to his analysis, I think that our concerns about time and its redemption in or by eternity overlap considerably.

13. Augustine, *Confessions*, 12.11 (11).

14. Ibid., 12.12 (15).

15. Barnstone, ed., *The Other Bible*, 15; Ginzberg, ed., *The Legends of the Jews*, verse 6.

16. Mackey, "From Autobiography to Theology: Augustine's *Confessiones*," in *Peregrinations of the Word*, 7–55:44.

17. Wolfson, "Fore/giveness," 163.

18. Mackey, "From Autobiography to Theology," 27.

19. In *Beyond Good and Evil*, Nietzsche places the sacrifice of God at the pinnacle of sacrificial possibilities: "There is a great ladder of religious cruelty with many rungs; but three are most important. At one time one sacrificed human beings to one's god, perhaps precisely those most loved. There was sacrifice of the first-born in prehistoric religions, or the sacrifice of the Emperor Tiberius in Mithras' grotto at Capri. Then, in the moral epoch of mankind, one sacrificed to one's god the strongest instincts one possessed; one's 'nature.' Finally, what was left to be sacrificed? Did one not have to sacrifice God himself, and worship nothingness?" (sec. 55). This need not, of course, refer to the crucifixion, but polyvalence is a Nietzschean specialty.

20. As Joseph Martos notes, penance, often lengthy and sometimes severe, was originally imposed *prior* to absolution; however, increasing concern over long periods of penitence, including the question of what might happen to the soul of one who died before completing her penance, eventually led (between the eleventh and thirteenth centuries) to the current practice of granting absolution at confession, with the presumption that the much briefer penance will follow. Indeed, the catechismic formula stops at *willingness* to complete the penance, as we have seen. (Martos, *Doors to the Sacred*, 224–335).

21. Perhaps relevantly and at least intriguingly, the Greek *aphiemi* and Latin *dimittere*, among these languages' roots of "forgive," imply release or unbinding.

22. Hanna, "Sacrament of Penance."

23. *Catechism of the Catholic Church*, sec. 1871. The text cites Augustine, *Faust* 22, in J. P. Migne, ed., *Patrologia Latina* (Paris, 1857–66), 42.

24. Cf. *Catechism of the Catholic Church*, section 977: "Baptism is the first and chief sacrament of forgiveness of sins because it unites us to Christ" (255). Also see ibid., sec. 1446, 1459, 1462, 1468.

25. Ibid., secs. 1450–60 (364–67). The increasing legalism of penance (or later reconciliation) comes about as bishops take on increasingly legislative or judicial roles in the fourth century, and sin, perhaps correspondingly, comes to be understood more and more legalistically. "Long and severe penances were often seen in the same light as criminal sentences: they were needed to satisfy the demands of the law, to expiate or pay for the offense committed, to fulfill the requirements of divine justice" (Martos, *Doors to the Sacred*, 321).

26. Martos, *Doors to the Sacred*, 309.
27. Arendt, *Eichmann in Jerusalem*, 296.
28. See *Catechism of the Catholic Church*, sec. 1440–45. Along these lines, Erich Loewy, writing in response to Simon Wiesenthal's *The Sunflower*, suggests that the soldier who asks for forgiveness in the story may want just this human integration: "By his behavior Wiesenthal tacitly admits the SS man back into a human community from which such a person must, when the truth strikes, feel himself permanently excluded. That is a form of acceptance, of acceptance of common humanity if not forgiveness or even understanding. One wonders if, rather than the empty words of forgiveness, such human acceptance was not far more what the SS man truly wanted and hoped for" (in Wiesenthal, *The Sunflower*, 204–5).
29. Blanchot, *The Writing of the Disaster*, 53.
30. "[W]here sin increased, grace overflowed all the more" (Rom. 5:20).
31. Blanchot, *The Writing of the Disaster*, 53.
32. Krog, *Country of My Skull*, 276.
33. Nietzsche, *On the Genealogy of Morality*, 2.4, 40. Nietzsche argues (2.4–6) that the creditor's right to extract satisfaction by inflicting pain is in turn influential upon the formation of memory, pain being the best mnemonic, and that our entire notion of future obligation and promise keeping is grounded upon this contractual relationship.
34. Ibid., 2.4, 39.
35. Ibid., 2.16, 57.
36. Michel Foucault, "Nietzsche, Genealogy, History," in *Language, Counter-memory, Practice*, 151.
37. See Baudrillard, *Seduction*, 131–53.
38. Lang, *The Future of the Holocaust*, 140.
39. Wolfson, "Fore/giveness," 153.
40. Ibid.
41. Cf. Wolfson, *Alef, Mem, Tau*, 137: "to look ahead one must turn back, a restoration to a past that is always yet to come in the present of the future."
42. Kushner, response, in Wiesenthal, *The Sunflower*, 186.
43. Lang, *The Future of the Holocaust*, 134.
44. There is a possible exception to this, in that such forgiveness may allow the one forgiven to avoid a consequence that would have happened had the forgiveness not occurred; however, she will not know that she has avoided it. The scriptural "Father, forgive them; they know not what they do" (Luke 23:34) suggests just such preemptive amnesty.
45. Krog, *Country of My Skull*, 96.
46. Martos, *Doors to the Sacred*, 335. In quite another tradition, Calvin suggests that "Scripture does not specify anyone to whom we should unburden ourselves and so it leaves us free to choose from among the faithful someone who seems worthy to hear our confession. Nevertheless, because pastors must above all be

suited for this, it is better for us to address ourselves to them" (*Institutes* 3, 4, 12; cited in ibid., 349).

47. Nancy, "Corpus," trans. Claudette Sartiliot, in *The Birth to Presence*, 189–90.

48. For a fabulous fictional version of this notion, see James Morrow, "Bible Stories for Adults, no. 20: The Tower," in *Bible Stories for Adults*, 61–84. Most people follow Augustine (generally not intentionally) in viewing perfect human communication as an impossibility: "Communication is a necessary condition for community; but direct communication between human minds, a transparency of mutual understanding, is not possible in the fallen human condition" (Markus, *Signs and Meanings*, 110; his note cites Augustine, *De Genesi contra Manicheos*, 2.4.5). Augustine argues that transparent communication will be restored to resurrected humanity (*City of God*, 22, 29.6).

49. "Forgiveness is not, it *should not be*, normal, normative, normalizing. It *should* remain exceptional and extraordinary, in the face of the impossible: as if it interrupted the ordinary course of historical temporality.... If there is something to forgive, it would be what in religious language is called mortal sin, the worst, the unforgivable crime or harm. From which comes the aporia, which can be described in its dry and implacable formality, without mercy: forgiveness forgives only the unforgivable. One cannot, or should not, forgive; there is only forgiveness, if there is any, where there is the unforgivable" (Derrida, *On Cosmopolitanism and Forgiveness*, 32–33).

50. Nietzsche, *The Gay Science*, sec. 287.

51. Arendt, *Eichmann in Jerusalem*, 251–52.

52. Moreton, *The Journey Is Home*, 129.

53. Cf. Keller, "Some respond more *responsibly* than others to the cosmic desire.... The creature either responds in creative sensitivity to its own context; or it blocks the flux of its own becoming" (*Face of the Deep*, 181).

54. As Lang writes, "On this Dialectical Model, it takes (at least) two to remember, that is—in a corollary of Wittgenstein's private language arguments—that the act of remembrance is not only a construct (as Nietzsche had memorably described it) but also a social construct, depending for its expression on a principle of exchange and collaboration. No one memory, in other words, without two" (*The Future of the Holocaust*, 9).

55. As Krog writes, "But there is also the invisible audience—the imagined audience on the horizon somewhere—the narrator's family, colleagues, the new government. And every listener decodes the story in terms of truth. Telling is therefore never neutral, and the selection and ordering try to determine the interpretation" (*Country of My Skull*, 107). Cf. Arendt: "Eichmann was on the stand from June 20 to July 24, for a total of thirty-three and a half sessions. Almost twice as many sessions, sixty-two out of a total of a hundred and twenty-one, were spent on a hundred prosecution witnesses who, country after country, told their tales of horrors" (*Eichmann in Jerusalem*, 223).

56. Van Alphen, "Symptoms of Discursivity," 26.
57. Mieke Bal, Introduction, in Bal, Crewe, and Spitzer, eds., *Acts of Memory*, viii.
58. See Freud, *Beyond the Pleasure Principle*, sec. 2.
59. Ibid., sec. 3.
60. Lear, *Happiness, Death, and the Remainder of Life*, 45.
61. Bal, Introduction, in Bal, Crewe, and Spitzer, eds., *Acts of Memory*, ix.
62. Ibid., xi.
63. Cf. Wolfson, *Alef, Mem, Tau*, 52. "Time is indicative of a narrative telling, a diachronic plot whose synchronic crux is open-ended, yielding a rhetoric of temporality characterized by a confluence of repetition and change too complex for simplistic binary opposition [Wolfson's note: "My thinking here reflects the analysis of Dominick Lacapra, 'The Temporality of Rhetoric,' in *Chronotypes: The Construction of Time*, ed. John Bender and David E. Wellbery (Stanford: Stanford University Press, 1991), pp. 118–47, esp. 137)"], a past determined by a future that anticipates the past as a word spoken in the dialogue between the same and other, the question and response."
64. Michel Foucault, Preface, *Madness and Civilization*, x–xi.
65. Along these lines, a fellow inmate with whom Simon Wiesenthal discusses his difficult encounter with the dying Nazi soldier suggests that the act of listening might be of primary importance, even without forgiveness: "Through his confession, as you surely know . . . his conscience was liberated and he died in peace because you had listened to him" (Wiesenthal, *The Sunflower*, 80).
66. Virginia Burrus, "Shameful Confessions," in *Saving Shame*, 111.
67. Ibid., 112.
68. Ibid., 115.
69. Ibid., 116–17.
70. Elizabeth Grosz, "Thinking the New: Of Futures Yet Unthought," in Grosz, ed., *Becomings*, 15–28:18.
71. Bataille, *Guilty*, 74.
72. Manchester, "Time in Christianity," 110.
73. Ibid., 118.
74. Ibid., 120.
75. Ibid., 124.
76. Wolfson, "Fore/giveness," 163.
77. Manchester, "Time in Christianity," 129.
78. Ibid.
79. Ibid., 133.
80. A thought I steal from Bruce Milem, personal communication.

4. Poppies and Rosemary: *Love*

1. See Matt. 22:37–40, Mark 12:30–31, Luke 10:27; see also Romans 13:10, Galatians 5:14, James 2:8.

2. Meister Eckhart, German Sermon on 2 Tim. 4:2, 5 (DW 30), in *Selected Writings*, 125.

3. *A Catechism of Christian Doctrine*, Question 1128.

4. Augustine, *Confessions*, 7.17 (23).

5. Blanchot, *The Unavowable Community*, 40.

6. It may fit, though, with a Nietzschean ethics of human flourishing, if not so well with an Aristotelian version, where moderation is emphasized. Then, too, Aristotle certainly values the love inherent in friendship, and his idea of moderation has considerable flexibility to it. See Aristotle, *Nicomachean Ethics*, bk. 8.

7. Jordan, *Blessing Same-Sex Unions*, 157.

8. Barthes, *A Lover's Discourse*, 14.

9. Irigaray, *The Way of Love*.

10. Nancy, "Identity and Trembling," trans. Brian Holmes, in *The Birth to Presence*, 30.

11. This idea can be traced back at least as far as Aristophanes' speech in Plato's *Symposium* (189c–93e). One of its most elegant formulations appears in Nicholas of Cusa: "For what were more foolish than to entreat that Thou shouldest give Thyself to me when Thou art All in all? And how wilt Thou give Thyself to me if Thou do not with Thyself give me heaven and earth and all that in them are? Nay more, how wilt Thou give me Thyself if Thou hast not given me mine own self also?" (*The Vision of God*, 31).

12. Nancy, "Shattered Love," trans. Lisa Garbus and Simona Sawhney, in *The Inoperative Community*, 93.

13. Ibid., 100.

14. Ibid., 101.

15. Ibid., 100.

16. Blanchot, *The Step Not Beyond*, 24–25.

17. See also: 2 Corinthians 3:6, "for the letter brings death, but the Spirit gives life"; Romans 6:23, "For the wages of sin is death, but the gift of God is eternal life in Christ Jesus our Lord," and 8:2, "For the law of the spirit of life in Christ Jesus has freed you from the law of sin and death."

18. "For now death had a 'legal hold over us' due to our willingness to slip into corruption" (Keller, *Face of the Deep*, 59).

19. Blanchot, *The Step Not Beyond*, 24.

20. Ibid., 25–26.

21. Blanchot, *The Unavowable Community*, 42.

22. The heresies regarding relations among persons of the Trinity are difficult to navigate; it would certainly be (and has been) heretical to suggest that at the crucifixion the Father simply dies; however, that there is some self- as well as son-sacrifice seems to me a defensible if perhaps imperfectly orthodox proposition. In Hans Urs von Balthasar's influential interpretation, Christ is the constant self-giving of God; the crucifixion is a real suffering in time, but time is more

importantly taken up into eternity. We must guard against the tendency to focus on the Passion and crucifixion only, but we mustn't lose sight of them either. "All the contingent 'abasements' of God in the economy of salvation are forever included and outstripped in the eternal event of Love. And so what, in the temporal economy, appears as the (most real) suffering of the Cross is only the manifestation of the (Trinitarian) Eucharist of the Son: he will be forever the slain Lamb, on the throne of the Father's glory, and his Eucharist—the Body shared out, the Blood poured forth—will never be abolished, since the Eucharist it is which must gather all creation back into his body. What the Father has given, he will never take back" (*Mysterium Paschale*, ix). There is much that is delightful in this interpretation; I would hesitate only at von Balthasar's remark that "the very contradiction between human treason and the love of God in giving his Son must be bonded together with the 'contradiction of the cross' and there find its resolution" (*Mysterium Paschale*, 112). Precisely the irresolvability of this tension puts it in the position of love, which promises the future, absolutely, firmly, and yet can never guarantee it.

Martos notes connections between the emphasis on sacrifice and the understanding of the Eucharist: "The patristic emphasis on the sacrificial nature of the liturgy also contributed to the trend away from communion, since a sacrifice could be offered to God without everyone partaking of the sacred food. The bishop offered the sacrifice on behalf of the people, and in this sense it was always an offering of the entire congregation whether or not they ate the bread and drank the wine. And the sacrificial victim was the second person of the blessed Trinity, so there could be no doubt that it was a worthy and acceptable sacrifice. . . . The idea that in the liturgy Christ was both priest and victim was not lost, but gradually the role of Christ as priest became more associated with the actions of the bishop and the role of Christ as victim became more associated with the bread and wine which were offered and then 'destroyed' by being consumed" (*Doors to the Sacred*, 258).

23. The peculiar complexities possible here are most strongly indicated in the fourth gospel, in which Christ tells his disciples: "Whoever has seen me has seen the Father. How can you say, 'Show us the Father?' Do you not believe that I am in the Father and the Father is in me? The words that I speak to you I do not speak on my own. The Father who dwells in me is doing his works. Believe me that I am in the Father and the Father is in me, or else, believe because of the works themselves" (John 14:9–11).

24. "Grace is unjust, an unjustified gift that does not take what is right into consideration, while confirming it nonetheless. The law, without grace, would be impossible to respect . . . even at a distance" (Blanchot, *The Step Not Beyond*, 24).

25. Ibid., 25.

26. Nietzsche, Third Essay, in *On the Genealogy of Morality*, 67–118.

27. See John 19:4–22.

28. "[T]he Lord Jesus, on the night he was handed over, took bread, and, after he had given thanks, broke it and said, 'This is my body that is for you. Do this in remembrance of me.' In the same way also the cup, after supper, saying, 'This cup is the new covenant in my blood. Do this, as often as you drink it, in remembrance of me.' For as often as you eat this bread and drink the cup, you proclaim the death of the Lord until he comes" (1 Corinthians 11:23–26).

29. Turner, "The Darkness of God and the Light of Christ," 149.

30. Here, again, we find conceptual resonance with the traditions of Kabbala, where "Time marks the pulsation of absence coming into presence" (Wolfson, *Alef, Mem, Tau*, 98).

31. As Hélène Cixous has noted, apropos of Moses' hope to see the promised land, there is a sense in which mourning, the loss of or the failure to attain the desired, is also the sustaining of desire ("Promised Belief").

32. The centrality of the Eucharist or the communion rite varies across Christianity. Fergus Kerr cites Michael Dummett: "When Orthodox and Catholic Christians . . . speak of 'going to church' . . . they mean, primarily, attending the celebration of the Eucharist *with or without receiving communion*. For Protestants . . . going to church means taking part in some service of prayers, hymns and psalms" (Michael Dummett, "The Intelligibility of Eucharistic Doctrine," in *The Rationality of Religious Belief: Essays in Honour of Basil Mitchell*, ed. William J. Abraham and Steven W. Holzer [Oxford: Oxford University Press, 1987], 237); cited in Kerr, "Transubstantiation after Wittgenstein," 122.

33. See Kerr, "Transubstantiation after Wittgenstein," 117: "*The Catechism of the Catholic Church* (1994), discussing the Eucharistic presence of Christ, makes no appeal to a metaphysics of substance (London: Geoffrey Chapman, 1994, secs. 1371–81). Indeed, it has been criticized for *not* saying something about the various theories" (he cites Raymond Moloney, S.J., *Commentary on the Catechism of the Catholic Church*, ed. Michael J. Walsh [London: Geoffrey Chapman, 1994], 269). Cf. Martos: "The term *transubstantiation* was first used by Hildebert of Tours early in the thirteenth century and within decades it was in common usage at the University of Paris. The Fourth Lateran Council even used Hildebert's terminology in saying that the bread and wine were 'transubstantiated' into the body and blood of Christ, but at the time no one took it as an ecclesiastical endorsement of the philosophical view that went under that name. The view can be summarized as proposing that the reality or substance of the elements changed while their appearances remained those of bread and wine" (*Doors to the Sacred*, 271).

34. The belief that the substance of body and blood *and* the substance of bread and wine are present simultaneously.

35. Interestingly, Martos argues that "most of the sacraments were instituted not by direct invention but by transignification: Christ changed the significance that existing rituals had for those who believed in him and in so doing changed the realities that they embodied and revealed" (*Doors to the Sacred*, 300).

36. See Kerr, "Transubstantiation after Wittgenstein," 126: "The transignification theory, relying on the unwarrantedly generalized philosophical principle that the nature of things like bread and wine is determined by the meaning they have for human beings, allows—even requires—us to say that, since the bread and wine, after the consecration, are *treated* differently, as being the Body and Blood of Christ, that is what they are. Even an atheist could understand that." Herbert McCabe argues for a more subtle version of the Eucharist as involving a linguistic or conventional transformation, declaring that "the body of Christ is present in the Eucharist as the meaning is present in a word" and "The Eucharist is the creative language of God, his eternal Word made flesh" ("The Eucharist as Language," 132).

McCabe also writes, "Since it was generally agreed by advocates of both transubstantiation and of transignification that the consecration of the bread and wine made no chemical or physical or other scientifically detectable difference to these elements, the choice seemed to be between a deeper metaphysical transformation of the elements or a change in *our* interpretation of their significance. Of course, for transignificationists this change in our perception was an act of faith, a supernatural activity in us of the Holy Sprit, but it seemed to be something that had to do with us, in us, rather than with the bread and wine themselves. It sounded like nominalism" (ibid., 133).

See also Martos, who argues that part of the ground for accepting transignification, despite the difficulties of the subjectivity of "meaning" or "significance," is a change in the theology of the mass, including the recovery of earlier forms of Eucharistic practice, which precede the doctrine of transubstantiation (*Doors to the Sacred*, 300–301).

37. Anscombe, "On Transubstantiation," 110–11. Cited in Kerr, "Transubstantiation after Wittgenstein," 120.

38. Matt. 26:39, "yet, not as I will, but as you will"; Mark 14:36, "but not what I will but what you will"; Luke 22:42, "not my will but yours be done." Cf. John 18:11.

39. Roughly, the belief that the persons of father and son in God are so identified—being merely aspects of one being—that God the father may be said to have suffered on the cross.

40. See n. 22, above. Note also: "the divine 'essence' . . . is forever 'given' in the self-gift of the Father. . . . We shall never know how to express the abyss-like depths of the Father's self-giving, that Father who, in an eternal 'super-Kenosis,' makes himself 'destitute' of all that he is and can be so as to bring forth a consubstantial divinity, the Son" (Von Balthasar, *Mysterium Paschale*, viii).

41. MacKendrick, "Word Made Flesh," 25–47 in *Word Made Skin*.

42. Eliot, "Burnt Norton," in *Four Quartets*, 19.

43. Kerr, "Transubstantiation after Wittgenstein," 139: "With the irony or paradox typical of the New Testament, [the Eucharist] is a celebratory feast which is about a defeat and death. It is both about the world of sin and about the

redemption of this world. . . . It is misunderstood if either of these is forgotten or played down." Cf. Turner, "The Darkness of God and the Light of Christ," 157.

44. Nancy, "Identity and Trembling," in *The Birth to Presence*, 41.

45. In the fourth gospel's story of Thomas, the open wounds are mentioned as convincing evidence of his identity (John 21:27–28).

46. MacKendrick, "Cut," 137–60 in *Word Made Skin*.

47. Pohle, "The Real Presence of Christ in the Eucharist."

48. See McMahon, "Perpetual Adoration."

49. Cf. Micah 6:3.

50. Blanchot, *The Writing of the Disaster*, 121.

51. Wallace Stevens, "Sunday Morning," in *The Collected Poems*, 66–70.

52. Freud, "On Transience."

53. Ibid.

54. *Glukupikron*, literally "sweet-bitter." For an extended consideration of Sappho's treatment of Eros, as well as Plato's, see Carson, *Eros the Bittersweet*.

55. In "On Transience," Freud also provides a concise encapsulation of this part of libido theory: "libido . . . in the earliest stages of development is directed towards our own ego. Later, . . . this libido is diverted from the ego on to objects, which are thus in a sense taken into our ego. If the objects are destroyed or if they are lost to us, our capacity for love (our libido) is once more liberated, and it can then either take other objects instead or can temporarily return to the ego. But why it is that the detachment of libido from its objects should be such a painful process is a mystery to us and we have not . . . been able to frame any hypothesis to account for it. We only see that the libido clings to its objects and will not renounce those that are lost even when a substitute lies ready to hand. Such then is mourning." That the death of a loved one provokes fear of one's own death is an ancient idea; we find it beautifully developed as far back as the Sumerian tale of Gilgamesh.

56. Nancy, Introduction, in *The Birth to Presence*, 3.

57. Jabès, *The Book of Questions*, vol. 2, 10.

58. Burrus, *The Sex Lives of Saints*, 16.

59. Blanchot, *The Step Not Beyond*, 24.

60. Bataille, *Erotism*, 11.

61. Nancy, "Shattered Love," 106–7.

62. Augustine, *Confessions*, 4.7 (8). I would differ from Augustine in my approval of this madness. For him, the recognition of this investment as mad, impossible, or likely to lead to mourning is an argument for turning all of one's love toward the undying God.

63. Cf. Wolfson: "The intrinsic linking of alterity and temporality underscores as well the texture of the erotic fabric that envelops time. The fecundity of eros signifies the desire for the other in the mystery of the other's essential inessentiality" (*Alef, Mem, Tau*, 52).

64. Blanchot, *The Infinite Conversation*, 192–93.
65. Hölderlin, "To the Fates," 7.
66. Cf. Bataille, *Inner Experience*, 59.
67. An image drawn from Bataille, *Erotism*, 12–13.
68. Continuity and boundary blurring belong only to self-loss; as Bataille writes, "for us, discontinuous beings that we are, death means continuity of being" (Bataille, *Erotism*, 12).
69. Cixous, "Promised Belief."

5. Dismembered Divinity: *Saints' Relics*

1. Patricia Cox Miller, "Subtle Embodiments," 7.
2. Otera Bada, "Why Does the Church Continue to Canonize People?"
3. Ibid.
4. Keating and McCarthy, "Moral Theology with the Saints," 204; they cite *Vatican Council II, Lumen Gentium (Dogmatic Constitution on the Church, 1964)*, no. 50.
5. Ibid.; they cite William Thompson, *Fire and Light: The Saints and Theology* (New York: Paulist Press, 1987), and Donna Orsuto, "The Saint as Moral Paradigm," in *Spirituality and Morality: Integrating Prayer and Action*, ed. Dennis Billy and Donna Orsuto (New York: Paulist Press, 1996), 127–39.
6. To oversimplify the distinction, Catholicism has tended to be slightly more comfortable with the idea of joining with God, though even that, occurring as it does in the context of "mystical" experience, can be problematic. Orthodox Christianities, however, have been more accepting of theosis or divinization, giving it both a more clearly accepted and a more central role.
7. Dooley, "Church Law on Sacred Relics," 66–67.
8. In answer to a query voiced by a few of my friends, living people who touch saints' bodies do not become third-class relics, or indeed relics at all, at least in the saintly sense. More seriously, although canon law forbids the sale of first- and second-class relics, it does not forbid the sale of *reliquaries*, the often elaborate containers in which relics are kept. As these may or may not contain relics when they are sold, the trade in first- and second-class relics remains technically possible through this loophole.
9. Bynum, *Fragmentation and Redemption*, 272.
10. Augustine, *City of God*, 8, 27.
11. See, e.g., Thurston, "Relics." Or see Geary, *Furta Sacra*, 33.
12. Augustine, *City of God*, 22, 8.
13. Ibid.
14. In exceptional cases, or in the case of martyrs, this requirement may be dispensed with (Beccari, "Canonization and Beatification").
15. Patricia Cox Miller, "Subtle Embodiments," 5.
16. Thomas Aquinas, *Summa theologiae*, III, Q 25, Article 6; cited in Dooley, "Church Law on Sacred Relics," 9.

17. Ibid.
18. See Geary, *Furta Sacra*, 37, 39.
19. For those unfamiliar with them, kneelers resemble two benches. One is near floor level and is generally padded so that it can be knelt upon; in front of it is the second, which will be around waist or chest level, depending upon the height of the kneeling person, allowing the arms or elbows to rest on it as the hands are folded. The relic may be placed under glass in the top surface of this taller "bench" or low table.
20. Bynum, *Fragmentation and Redemption*, 144, 185.
21. Canon 1198 sec.4; cited in Dooley, "Church Law on Sacred Relics," 117. See also Geary, *Furta Sacra*, 42.
22. "We have decreed that all temples consecrated without the relics of martyrs must have sacred relics deposited therein, . . . A bishop who hereafter consecrates a temple without relics is to be deposed, as being one who has transgressed ecclesiastical traditions" (quoted in Dooley, "Church Law and Sacred Relics," 116).
23. Ibid.
24. Bynum, *Fragmentation and Redemption*, 276.
25. Briefly, the mind-body problem is this: if the mind (identical in most older accounts with the soul) and the body are not the same thing or at least the same kind of thing (e.g., matter), how can they possibly interact or be related to one another?
26. Gregory of Nyssa, "On the Soul and Resurrection." Once more compare Plotinus, who says of the soul, "it feels the corporeal conditions at every point of its being, and is thereby enabled to assign every condition to the exact spot at which the wound or pain occurs. Being present as a whole at every point of the body, if it were itself affected the pain would take it at every point, and it would suffer as one entire being, so that it could not know, or make known, the spot affected; it could say only that at the place of its presence there existed pain—and the place of its presence is the entire human being. As things are, when the finger pains the man is in pain because one of his members is in pain; we class him as suffering, from his finger being painful, just as we class him as fair from his eyes being blue" (*Ennead* 4.4.19, in *Six Enneads*).
27. Descartes, *Meditations on First Philosophy*, Meditation 6.
28. Gregory of Nyssa, "On the Soul and Resurrection."
29. Ibid.
30. Pohle, "The Real Presence of Christ in the Eucharist."
31. Ibid.
32. Patricia Cox Miller, "Subtle Embodiments," 5, citing Rowan Williams, "Troubled Breasts: The Holy Body in Hagiography," in *Portraits of Spiritual Authority: Religious Power in Early Christianity, Byzantium and the Christian Orient*, ed. Jan Willem Drijvers and John W. Watt (Leiden: E. J. Brill, 1999), 68, 73.

33. Blanchot, *The Writing of the Disaster*, 105.
34. See: Schopen, "Relic," 257; Geary, *Furta Sacra*, 152; Patricia Cox Miller, "'Differential Networks,'" 123.
35. On faith as seduction, see Baudrillard, *Seduction*, 142.
36. It does seem that a nearly whole body missing some parts might well be more unsettling than parts of a body more widely scattered. Perhaps this is because the latter create in us no expectation of wholeness, an expectation violated in the former by those few missing bits.
37. Lacan, "The Mirror Stage."
38. Jean-Luc Nancy, "Finite History," in *The Birth to Presence*, 143.
39. Keating and McCarthy, "Moral Theology with the Saints," 206.
40. Geary, *Furta Sacra*, 162.
41. Brown, *The Cult of the Saints*, 96. See also 100: "hence the miracles which Gregory of Tours treasured at the festival of Saint Martin were miracles of reintegration into the community. The barriers that had held the individual back from the *consensus omnium* were removed." Likewise ibid.: "The demons loose the bonds by which they had held the paralyzed and the possessed at a distance from their fellow men." And 112: "Hence the drama of exorcism was not merely a drama of authority: it was a drama of reintegration. The human being who had been swept far away from the human community was solemnly reinstated among the warm mass of his fellows. . . . Hence the imaginative importance of the great prayers of exorcism that maintained and articulated, in liturgical form, the expectations of the group at the shrine. These stressed the solemn ordering of the universe at the Creation, the position of the sufferer as a temple of God, and the awesome reentry of God into his temple."
42. Keating and McCarthy, "Moral Theology with the Saints," 211.
43. John Paul II, "I Entrust the World to Divine Mercy."
44. Louth, *Discerning the Mystery*, 145; cited in Keating and McCarthy, "Moral Theology with the Saints," 206–7.
45. Brown, *The Cult of the Saints*, 80.
46. Ibid., 78.
47. I must in honesty admit, however, that the copies I have seen of the image have tended toward kitsch: the wavy-haired Christ is too benevolently smiling; the light-stream representing blood is invariably pink.
48. See, e.g., Matt. 9:20–22, Mark 3:10 and 8:22–25, Luke 6:19, John 9:6, etc.
49. Bynum, *Fragmentation and Redemption*, 296.
50. See Harries, "Death and the Dead in the Late Roman West," 59, 65.
51. For the foundational discussion of this leap beyond ethics, see Kierkegaard, *Fear and Trembling*. I find Kierkegaard's ideas enormously important and useful, though I would argue with his sense that the religious realm is necessarily teleological.

6. Eternal Flesh: *The Resurrection of the Body*

1. The idea that time is a necessary category of the understanding, and so all that we understand is necessarily understood in temporal terms, is set forth most clearly by Kant in *The Critique of Pure Reason*.

2. Nancy, "Hyperion's Joy," trans. Christine Laennec and Michael Syrotinski, in *The Birth to Presence*, 68; Nancy cites Hölderlin, "Über Religion," in *Werke und Briefe* 2:638.

3. Augustine, *Enchiridion*, chap. 84.

4. Maas, "General Resurrection."

5. MacKendrick, "Word Made Flesh" in *Word Made Skin*.

6. Augustine, *On the Merits and Forgiveness of Sins, and on the Baptism of Infants*.

7. See Drury, "Gregory of Nyssa's Dialogue with Macrina," esp. 220–21.

8. Augustine, *Enchiridion*, chap. 21, "Unbaptized Infants Damned, but Most Lightly; the Penalty of Adam's Sin, the Grace of His Body Lost."

9. For a persuasive argument to this effect, see Dawson, "Transcendence as Embodiment."

10. See John 20:17.

11. Nancy and Lacoue-Labarthe, "Noli Me Frangere," trans. Brian Holmes, in *The Birth to Presence*, 274–75.

12. Augustine, *Confessions* 12, 3 (3).

13. Ibid., 12, 6 (6).

14. Ibid., 12, 15 (18) and 19 (28).

15. Ibid., 12, 19 (28).

16. Ibid., 12, 29 (40).

17. Deleuze, *Difference and Repetition*, 79. I am not being faithful to Deleuze's system of time's syntheses here, but his senses of enfolded times, vertical repetition, and rhythm are all relevant to my discussion.

18. Merleau-Ponty, *The Visible and the Invisible*, 147.

19. Ibid., 268. This sense of enfolding and opening onto is recurrent in Merleau-Ponty's philosophy of the flesh.

20. Wolfson, *Alef, Mem, Tau*, 115.

21. Nancy, Introduction, *The Birth to Presence*, 2.

22. Meister Eckhart, German sermon on Luke 1:26, 1:28 (DW 38, W 29), in *Selected Writings*, 112–13. The image of divine birth in the soul is further developed in the German sermon on Matt. 2.2 (W 2, PF 2, DP 58), 215–22.

23. Ibid., 113.

24. Ibid., 114.

25. Nancy, *The Birth to Presence*, Introduction, 4.

26. "Thus it is a simple historical fact that those who defined orthodox Christian belief about the incarnation universally held that God is non-temporal" (Leftow, "A Timeless God Incarnate," 273). Leftow specifically identifies the presumption of divine atemporality with Augustine (274).

NOTES TO PAGES 138–48

27. This is one option Leftow mentions in considering possible solutions to the paradox of an eternal God in a body (see 292f.).
28. Plotinus, *Ennead* 6.9.9, in *Six Enneads*.
29. Genesis 2:4–7.
30. Psyche, pneuma, anima, and spirit can all refer to breath, to life, or to soul, though not all equally or indifferently so.
31. Augustine, *Confessions*, 10, 22 (38).
32. Burrus, *The Sex Lives of Saints*, 160.
33. Deleuze, *Difference and Repetition*, 21.
34. Ibid., 201. "Repetition is this emission of singularities, always with an echo or resonance which makes each the double of the other."
35. Ibid., 287.
36. Keller, *Face of the Deep*, 23.
37. Nancy, "Abandoned Being," trans. Brian Holmes, in *The Birth to Presence*, 42.
38. See, for several examples, "Sacred Hearts," in MacKendrick, *Word Made Skin*, 115–36.
39. Jacques Derrida, "Le toucher: Touch / To Touch Him," 131.
40. Nietzsche, *The Gay Science*, section 84, 138–40.
41. Plotinus, *Ennead* 1.1.1, in *Six Enneads*.
42. In his essay "Masochism: Coldness and Cruelty," Deleuze distinguishes repetition in the instant from repetition before the instant (Deleuze and von Sacher-Masoch, *"Masochism: Coldness, and Cruelty" and Venus in Furs*, 114).
43. Deleuze, *Francis Bacon*, 37.
44. Merleau-Ponty, *The Visible and the Invisible*, 151.
45. The phenomenon of stigmata, attributed to several saints though not counted as a miracle toward beatification or canonization, provides us with particularly vivid instances of such participation.
46. This is a one-line version of an argument developed over several chapters of MacKendrick, *Counterpleasures*. The long version is perhaps more convincing. For Kant's account of space and time, in which he links time to subjectivity (the addition of space is not his but results from an increased emphasis on the body), see Kant, *Critique of Pure Reason*.
47. Deleuze, *Difference and Repetition*, 8.
48. Deleuze, *Francis Bacon*, 15, ellipsis in original.
49. Ibid., 45.
50. "Doch alle Lust will Ewigkeit." Ambiguous between pleasure and desire, *lust* is here rendered as "joy": "But joys all want eternity" (Nietzsche, *Thus Spake Zarathustra*, section 79).
51. Deleuze, *Francis Bacon*, 53.
52. Merleau-Ponty, *The Visible and the Invisible*, 132.
53. Deleuze, *Difference and Repetition*, 201–2.
54. Deleuze, *Francis Bacon*, 115; my italics.

55. Nancy, "Hyperion's Joy," in *The Birth to Presence*, 71.
56. Augustine, *Confessions*, 12, 16 (23).

Afterword: *On Returning to Memory*

1. Jordan, *Blessing Same-Sex Unions*, 154.
2. Nancy, "Hyperion's Joy," in *The Birth to Presence*, 64; quoting Friedrich Hölderlin, *Hyperion*, trans. Willard R. Trask (New York: Frederick Ungar, 1965), 54.
3. Ibid., 74.
4. Ibid., 81; quoting Friedrich Hölderlin, "Reflexion," in *Werke und Briefe*, 2:604.

WORKS CITED

Alphen, Ernst van. "Symptoms of Discursivity: Experience, Memory, and Trauma." In *Acts of Memory: Cultural Recall in the Present*, ed. Mieke Bal, Jonathan Crewe, and Leo Spitzer, 124–38. Hanover: Dartmouth College Press, 1999.

Anscombe, G. E. M. "On Transubstantiation." London: Catholic Truth Society, 1974. In *The Collected Philosophical Papers of G. E. M. Anscombe*, vol. 3, *Ethics, Religion and Politics*, 107–12. Oxford: Basil Blackwell, 1981.

Arendt, Hannah. *Eichmann in Jerusalem: A Report on the Banality of Evil*. New York: Viking Press, 1963.

Aristotle. *Metaphysics*. Trans. Richard Hope. Ann Arbor: University of Michigan Press, 1960.

———. *Nicomachean Ethics*. Trans. Terence Irwin. Indianapolis: Hackett Publishing,1999.

Augustine, Saint. *City of God*. Trans. Henry Bettenson. New York: Penguin Books, 1984.

———. *Confessions*. Trans. Henry Chadwick. New York: Oxford University Press, 1991.

———. *The Enchiridion on Faith, Hope and Love*. Trans. J. F. Shaw. Excerpted from *Nicene and Post-Nicene Fathers*, first series, vol. 3. Ed. Philip Schaff. Peabody, Mass.: Hendrickson Publishers, 1989. Also available online at http://www.newadvent.org/fathers/1302.htm. K. Knight, 2004.

———. *On Free Choice of the Will*. Trans. Thomas Williams. Indianapolis: Hackett Publishing Co, 1993.

———. *On the Merits and Forgiveness of Sins, and on the Baptism of Infants*. Excerpted from *Nicene and Post-Nicene Fathers*, first series, vol. 5. Ed. Philip Schaff, 1887. Also available online at http://www.newadvent.org/fathers/15011.htm. K. Knight, 2005.

WORKS CITED

Bal, Mieke, Jonathan Crewe, and Leo Spitzer, eds. *Acts of Memory: Cultural Recall in the Present*. Hanover: Dartmouth College Press, 1999.

The Baltimore Catechism. Baltimore: Baltimore Plenary Council, 1974. Available online at http://www.ewtn.com/faith/teachings and at http://www.truecatholic.org/baltcont.htm.

Balthasar, Hans Urs von. *Mysterium Paschale*. Trans. Aiden Nichols, O.P. Grand Rapids, Mich.: William B. Eerdmans Publishing Company, 1990.

Barnstone, Willis, ed. *The Other Bible*. San Francisco: Harper San Francisco, 1984.

Barthes, Roland. *A Lover's Discourse: Fragments*. Trans. Richard Howard. New York: Noonday Press, 1978.

Bataille, Georges. *Erotism: Death and Sensuality*. Trans. Mary Dalwood. San Francisco: City Lights, 1986.

———. *Guilty*. Trans. Bruce Boone. Venice, Calif.: Lapis Press, 1988.

———. *Inner Experience*. Trans. Leslie Anne Boldt. Albany: State University of New York Press, 1988.

Baudrillard, Jean. *Seduction*. Trans. Brian Singer. New York: St. Martin's Press, 1990.

Beccari, Camillus. "Canonization and Beatification." *The Catholic Encyclopedia*, vol. 2. New York: Robert Appleton Co, 1907. Available online at http://www.newadvent.org/cathen/02364b.htm. K. Knight, 2003.

Blanchot, Maurice. *The Blanchot Reader*. Ed. Michael Holland. Oxford: Basil Blackwell, 1995.

———. *The Infinite Conversation*. Trans. Susan Hanson. Minneapolis: University of Minnesota Press, 1993.

———. *The Unavowable Community*. Trans. Pierre Joris. Barrytown, N.Y.: Station Hill Press, 1988.

———. *The Step Not Beyond*. Trans. Lycette Nelson. Albany: State University of New York Press, 1992.

———. *The Writing of the Disaster*. Trans. Ann Smock. Lincoln: University of Nebraska Press, 1996.

Brown, Peter. *The Body and Society: Men, Women, and Sexual Renunciation in Early Christianity*. New York: Columbia University Press, 1988.

———. *The Cult of the Saints*. Chicago: University of Chicago Press, 1981.

Burrus, Virginia. *Saving Shame: Martyrs, Saints, and Other Abject Subjects*. Philadelphia: University of Pennsylvania Press, 2008.

———. *The Sex Lives of Saints: An Erotics of Ancient Hagiography*. Philadelphia: University of Pennsylvania Press, 2004.

Bynum, Carolyn Walker. *Fragmentation and Redemption: Essays on Gender and the Human Body in Medieval Religion*. New York: Zone Books, 1996.

Carson, Anne. *Eros the Bittersweet*. Normal, Ill.: Dalkey Archive Press, 1998.

Catechism of the Catholic Church, Second Edition. Washington, D.C.: United States Catholic Conference, Inc., 1994.

WORKS CITED

Catholic Study Bible. Oxford: Oxford University Press, 1990.

Cixous, Hélène. "Promised Belief." Address at Postmodernism, Culture, and Religion 2. Syracuse University, Syracuse, N.Y., April 2007.

Curd, Patricia. *The Legacy of Parmenides: Eleatic Monism and Later Presocratic Thought*. Princeton: Princeton University Press, 1998.

Dawson, David. "Transcendence as Embodiment: Augustine's Domestication of Gnosis." *Modern Theology* 10 (1994): 1–26.

Deleuze, Gilles. *Difference and Repetition*. Trans. Paul Patton. New York: Columbia University Press, 1995.

———. *The Fold: Leibniz and the Baroque*. Trans. Tom Conley. Minneapolis: University of Minnesota Press, 1993.

———. *Francis Bacon: The Logic of Sensation*. Trans. Daniel W. Smith. Minneapolis: University of Minnesota Press, 2003.

———. *The Logic of Sense*. Trans. Mark Lester and Charles Stivale. New York: Columbia University Press, 1990.

——— and Félix Guattari. *Anti-Oedipus: Capitalism and Schizophrenia*. Trans. Robert Hurley, Mark Seem, and Helen R. Lane. Minneapolis: University of Minnesota Press, 1983.

——— and Félix Guattari. *A Thousand Plateaus*. Trans. Brian Massumi. Minneapolis: University of Minnesota Press. 1987.

——— and Leopold von Sacher-Masoch. *"Masochism: Coldness, and Cruelty" and Venus in Furs*. New York: Zone Books, 1991.

Derrida, Jacques. "Le toucher: Touch / To Touch Him." Trans. Peggy Kamuf. *Paragraph* 16, no. 2 (July 1993): 122–57.

———. *On Cosmpolitanism and Forgiveness*. Trans. Mark Dooley and Michael Hughes. London: Routlege, 2001.

———. "Sauf le nom." Trans. John P. Leavey, Jr. In *On the Name*, ed. Thomas Dutoit, 33–85. Stanford, Calif.: Stanford University Press, 1995.

Descartes, René. *Meditations on First Philosophy*. Trans. George Heffernan. Notre Dame, Ind.: Notre Dame University Press, 1992.

Dooley, Eugene A., J.C.L. "Church Law on Sacred Relics." Ph.D. dissertation. Washington, D.C.: Catholic University of America, 1931.

Drury, John L. "Gregory of Nyssa's Dialogue with Macrina: The Compatibility of Resurrection of the Body and Immortality of the Soul." *Theology Today* 62 (2005): 210–22.

Eckhart, Meister Johannes. *Meister Eckhart: Selected Writings*. Trans. and ed. Oliver Davies. New York: Penguin Books, 1994.

Eliot, T. S. *Four Quartets*. New York: Harcourt, Brace, Jovanovich, 1943.

Foucault, Michel. *Language, Countermemory, Practice: Selected Essays and Interviews*. Ed. Donald F. Bouchard. Ithaca, N.Y.: Cornell University Press, 1977.

———. *Madness and Civilization: A History of Insanity in the Age of Reason*. New York: Vintage Books, 1988.

Freud, Sigmund. *Beyond the Pleasure Principle*. Trans. James Strachey. New York: W. W. Norton and Company, 1961.

WORKS CITED

———. "On Transience." Trans. James Strachey. New York: Riverhead Books, 2005. Available online at http://www.freuds-requiem.com/transience.html.

Geary, Patrick J. *Furta Sacra: Thefts of Relics in the Middle Ages*. Princeton: Princeton University Press, 1978.

Ginzberg, Louis, ed. *The Legends of the Jews*. Trans. Henrietta Szold. Available online at http://www.sacred-texts.com/jud/lotj/.

Goodman, Lenn E., ed. *Neoplatonism and Jewish Thought*. Albany: State University of New York Press, 1992.

Gregory of Nyssa. "On the Soul and Resurrection." Available online at http://www.tparents.org/Library/Religion/Christian/Fathers/NPNF2-05/Npnf2-05-37.htm#P3516_2250208.

Grosz, Elizabeth, ed. *Becomings: Explorations in Time, Memory, and Futures*. Ithaca, N.Y.: Cornell University Press, 1999.

Hanna, Edward J. "The Sacrament of Penance." In *The Catholic Encyclopedia*, vol. 11. New York; Robert Appleton, 1911. Available online at http://www.newadvent.org/cathen/11618c.htm. K. Knight, 2003.

Harent, S. "Original Sin." In *The Catholic Encyclopedia*, vol. 11. New York: Robert Appleton Company, 1911. Available online at http://www.newadvent.org/cathen/11312a.htm K. Knight, 2005.

Harries, Jill. "Death and the Dead in the Late Roman West." In *Death in Towns: Urban Responses to Dying and the Dead, 100–1600*, ed. Steven Bassett, 56–67. Leicester: Leicester University Press, 1992.

Hölderlin, Friedrich. "To the Fates." In *Selected Poems and Fragments*, trans. Michael Hamburger. New York: Penguin Books, 1994.

Holweck, Frederick G. "Immaculate Conception." In *The Catholic Encyclopedia*, vol. 7. New York: Robert Appleton Company, 1910. Available online at http://www.newadvent.org/cathen/07674d.htm. K. Knight, 2003.

Hyman, Arthur. "From What Is One and Simple Only What Is One and Simple Can Come to Be." In *Neoplatonism and Jewish Thought*, ed. Lenn E. Goodman, 111–35. Albany: State University of New York Press, 1992.

The Hypostasis of the Archons. Trans. Roger A. Bullard and Bentley Layton. In *Nag Hammadi Library in English*, ed. James M. Robinson, 161–69. Leiden: E. J. Brill, 1988.

Irigaray, Luce. *The Way of Love*. Trans. Heidi Bostic and Stephen Pluhácek. London: Continuum, 2002.

Jabès, Edmond. *The Book of Questions*, vol. 2. Trans. Rosmarie Waldrop. Middletown, Conn.: Wesleyan University Press, 1991.

James, William. "The One and the Many." In *Pragmatism: A New Name for Some Old Ways of Thinking*, 49–63. New York: Longman Green and Co., 1907.

John Paul II. "Urbi et Orbi." December 25, 2000. Available online at http://www.catholic-forum.com/saints/pope0264lg.htm, October 25, 2005.

———. "I Entrust the World to Divine Mercy." Available online at http://www.catholicculture.org/library/view.cfm?recnum=4484.

WORKS CITED

Jordan, Mark. *Blessing Same-Sex Unions: The Perils of Queer Romance and the Confusions of Christian Marriage*. Chicago: University of Chicago Press, 2005.

Kant, Immanuel. *Critique of Pure Reason*. Trans. Paul Guyer. Cambridge: Cambridge University Press, 1999.

Keating, James, and David M. McCarthy. "Moral Theology with the Saints." *Modern Theology* 19, no. 2 (April 2001): 203–18.

Keller, Catherine. *Face of the Deep: A Theology of Becoming*. New York: Routledge, 2004.

Kerr, Fergus. "Transubstantiation after Wittgenstein." *Modern Theology* 15, no.2 (April 1999): 115–30.

Kierkegaard, Søren. *Fear and Trembling*. Trans. Alastair Hannay. New York: Penguin Books, 1985.

Klossowski, Pierre. *Nietzsche and the Vicious Circle*. Trans. Daniel W. Smith. Chicago: University of Chicago Press, 1998.

Krog, Antjie. *Country of My Skull: Guilt, Sorrow, and the Limits of Revenge in the New South Africa*. New York: Three Rivers Press, 2000.

Kushner, Harold S. Response. In Simon Wiesenthal, *The Sunflower: On the Possibilities and Limits of Forgiveness*, with a symposium edited by Harry James Cargas and Bonny V. Fetterman, 183–85. New York: Schocken Books, 1998.

Lacan, Jacques. "The Mirror Stage as Formative of the I Function, as Revealed in Psychoanalytic Experience." In *Écrits: A Selection*. Trans. Bruce Fink et al., 3–9. New York: W. W. Norton and Company, 2004.

Lang. Berel. *The Future of the Holocaust: Between History and Memory*. Ithaca, N.Y.: Cornell University Press, 1999.

Lear, Jonathan. *Happiness, Death, and the Remainder of Life*. Cambridge: Harvard University Press, 2000.

Leftow, Brian. "A Timeless God Incarnate." In *The Incarnation: An Interdisciplinary Symposium on the Incarnation of the Son of God*, ed. Stephen Davis, Daniel Kendall, S.J., and Gerald O'Collins, S.J., 273–300. Oxford: Oxford University Press, 2002.

Louth, Andrew. *Discerning the Mystery: An Essay on the Nature of Theology*. New York: Oxford University Press, 1983.

Maas, A. J. "General Resurrection." In *The Catholic Encyclopedia*, vol. 12. New York: Robert Appleton Company, 1911. Available online at http://www.newadvent.org/cathen/12792a.htm. K. Knight., 2005.

McCabe, Herbert, O.P. "The Eucharist as Language." *Modern Theology* 15, no. 2 (April 1999): 131–41.

MacKendrick, Karmen. *Counterpleasures*. Albany: State University of New York Press, 1999.

———. *Immemorial Silence*. Albany: State University of New York Press, 2001.

———. *Word Made Skin: Figuring Language at the Surface of Flesh*. New York: Fordham University Press, 2004.

WORKS CITED

———. "Carthage Didn't Burn Hot Enough." In *Toward a Theology of Eros*, ed. Virginia Burrus and Catherine Keller, 205–17. New York: Fordham University Press, 2006.

Mackey, Louis. *Peregrinations of the Word*. Ann Arbor: University of Michigan Press, 1997.

McKirahan, Richard. "Anaximines." In *Routledge Encyclopedia of Philosophy*, ed. E. Craig. London: Routledge, 1998. Available online at http://www.rep.routledge.com/article/A011SECT1.

McMahon, Joseph H. "Perpetual Adoration." In *The Catholic Encyclopedia*, vol. 1. New York: Robert Appleton Company, 1907. Available online at http://www.newadvent.org/cathen/01152a.htm. K. Knight, 2006.

Makin, Stephen. "Zeno of Elea." In *Routledge Encyclopedia of Philosophy*, ed. E. Craig. London: Routledge, 1998. Available online at http://www.rep.routledge.com/article/A123SECT2.

Manchester, Peter. "Time in Christianity." In *Religion and Time*, ed. A. N. Balslev and J. N. Mohanty, 109–37. Leiden: Brill, 1993.

Markus, R. A. *Signs and Meanings: World and Text in Ancient Christianity*. Liverpool: Liverpool University Press, 1996.

Martos, Joseph. *Doors to the Sacred: A Historical Introduction to Sacraments in the Catholic Church*. New York: Image Books, 1982.

Merleau-Ponty, Maurice. *The Visible and the Invisible*. Trans. Alphonso Lingis. Evanston, Ill.: Northwestern University Press, 1968.

Milem, Bruce. *The Unspoken Word: Negative Theology in Meister Eckhart's German Sermons*. Washington, D.C.: Catholic University of America Press, 2002.

Miles, Margaret R. *Plotinus on Body and Beauty*. Oxford: Basil Blackwell, 1999.

Miller, Clyde Lee. "Meister Eckhart in Nicholas of Cusa's 1456 sermon: 'Ubi est qui natus est rex Iudeorum?'" (November 11, 2001). Available online at Stony Brook Philosophy Department website http://www.sunysb.edu/philosophy/research/miller_2.html.

Miller, Patricia Cox. "'Differential Networks': Relics and Other Fragments in Late Antiquity." *Journal of Early Christian Studies* 6, no. 1 (1998): 113–38.

———. "Subtle Embodiments: Imagining the Holy in Late Antiquity." In *Apophatic Bodies*, ed. Chris Boesel and Catherine Keller. New York: Fordham University Press, forthcoming.

Moreton, Nelle. *The Journey Is Home*. Boston: Beacon Press, 1985.

Morrow, James. *Bible Stories for Adults*. New York: Harvest Books, 1996.

Nancy, Jean-Luc. *The Birth to Presence*. Trans. Brian Holmes and others. Stanford, Calif.: Stanford University Press, 1993.

———. *The Inoperative Community*. Ed. Peter Connor. Minneapolis: University of Minnesota Press, 1991.

Nicholas of Cusa. *The Vision of God*. Trans. Emma Gurney Salter. New York: Frederick Ungar Publishing, 1928.

Nietzsche, Friedrich. *The Anti-Christ*. In *The Twilight of the Idols and The Anti-Christ*. Trans. R. J. Hollingdale. New York: Penguin Books, 1968.

WORKS CITED

———. *Beyond Good and Evil: Prelude to a Philosophy of the Future*. Trans. Walter Kaufmann. New York: Vintage Books, 1989.
———. *Ecce Homo*. Trans. R. J. Hollingdale. New York: Penguin Books, 1982.
———. *The Gay Science*. Trans. Walter Kaufman. New York: Vintage Books, 1974.
———. *On the Advantage and Disadvantage of History for Life*. Trans. Peter Preuss. Indianapolis: Hackett Publishing, 1980.
———. *On the Genealogy of Morality*. Trans. Maudemarie Clark and Alan J. Swensen. Indianapolis: Hackett Publishing, 1998.
———. *Thus Spake Zarathustra*. Trans. Thomas Common. New York: Random House, undated.
Origen. *On First Principles*. Trans. G. W. Butterworth. Gloucester, Mass.: Peter Smith, 1973.
Otera Bada, José M. "Why Does the Church Continue to Canonize People?" Opus Dei Website. http://www.opusdei.org/art.php?w=32&p=3943. Opus Dei Information Office, 2006.
Pagels, Elaine. *Adam, Eve, and the Serpent*. New York: Vintage Books, 1989.
Parmenides. *Parmenides of Elea: Fragments*. Trans. and Introd. David Gallop. Toronto: University of Toronto Press, 1984.
———. *On Nature (Peri Physeos)*. Ed. Allan F. Randal. From translations by David Gallop, Richard D. McKirahan, Jr., Jonathan Barnes, John Mansley Robinson, et al. Available online at http://home.ican.net/~arandall/Parmenides/.
Plato. *Meno*. Trans. W. K. C. Guthrie. In *The Collected Dialogues of Plato*, ed. Edith Hamilton and Huntington Cairns, 353–84. Princeton: Princeton University Press, 1961.
———. *Parmenides*. Trans. F. M. Cornford. In *Collected Dialogues of Plato*, 920–56.
———. *Phaedrus*. Ed. and trans. Alexander Nehamas and Paul Woodruff. Indianapolis: Hackett Publishing Co., 1995.
———. *Protagoras*. Trans. W. K. C. Guthrie. In *Collected Dialogues of Plato*, 308–52.
———. *Republic*. Trans. Paul Shorey. In *Collected Dialogues of Plato*, 575–844.
———. *The Sophist*. Trans. F. M. Cornford. In *Collected Dialogues of Plato*, 957–1017.
———. *Symposium*. Trans. Michael Joyce. In *Collected Dialogues of Plato*, 526–74.
———. *Theatetus*. Trans. F. M. Cornford. In *Collected Dialogues of Plato*, 845–919.
Plotinus. *The Enneads*. Trans. Stephen MacKenna. New York: Penguin Books, 1991.
———. *Six Enneads*. Trans. Stephen MacKenna and B. S. Page. Chicago: William Benton, 1990. Available online at Internet Classics Archive at http://classics.mit.edu/Plotinus/enneads.1.first.html.

WORKS CITED

Pohle, J. "The Real Presence of Christ in the Eucharist." In *The Catholic Encyclopedia*, vol. 5. New York: Robert Appleton Company, 1909. Available online at http://www.newadvent.org/cathen/05573a.htm.

Pope, Alexander. *An Essay on Criticism*. Whitefield, Mont.: Kessinger Publishing, 2004.

Pseudo-Dionysius the Areopagite. *The Mystical Theology and Divine Names*. Trans. C. E. Rolt. Mineola, N.Y.: Dover Publications, 2004.

Ramadanovic, Petar. "Plato's Forgetting: Theatetus and Phaedrus." *Tympanum: A Journal of Comparative Literary Studies* 4 (2000). Available online at http://www.usc.edu/dept/comp-lit/tympanum/4/ramadanovic.html.

———. "From Haunting to Trauma: Nietzsche's Active Forgetting and Blanchot's Writing of the Disaster." *Postmodern Culture* 11, no. 2 (January 2001). Available online at http://www3.iath.virginia.edu/pmc/text-only/issue.101/11.2ramadanovic.txt.

Rilke, Rainer Maria. *The Selected Poetry of Rainer Maria Rilke*. Trans. Stephen Mitchell. New York: Vintage Books, 1989.

Schelling, Friedrich W. J. *Ages of the World*, Third Version. Trans. and Introd. Joseph M. Wirth. Albany: State University of New York Press, 2000.

Schopen, Gregory. "Relic." In *Critical Terms for Religious Studies*, ed. Mark C. Taylor, 256–68. Chicago: University of Chicago Press, 1998.

Sedley, David. "Melissus." In *Routledge Encyclopedia of Philosophy*, ed. E. Craig. London: Routledge, 1998. Available online at http://www.rep.routledge.com/article/A070.

Stevens, Wallace. "Sunday Morning." In *The Collected Poems of Wallace Stevens*, 66–70. New York: Vintage, 1990.

Sturken, Marita. "Narratives of Recovery: Repressed Memory as Cultural Memory." In *Acts of Memory: Cultural Recall in the Present*, ed. Mieke Bal, Jonathan Crewe, and Leo Spitzer, 231–48. Hanover: Dartmouth College Press, 1999.

Tertullian. "The Resurrection of the Flesh." Trans. A. J. Maas. Excerpted from *Ante-Nicene Fathers*, vol. 3, ed. Alexander Roberts and James Donaldson. New York: Christian Literature Company, 1885. In *The Catholic Encyclopedia*, vol. 12. New York: Robert Appleton Company, 1911. Available online at http://www.newadvent.org/cathen/12789a.htm. K. Knight, 2003.

Thomas Aquinas, Saint. *Summa theologiae*. New York: Benzinger Brothers, 1947. Available online at http://www.newadvent.org/summa/. New Advent, 1995, 1996.

Thurston, Herbert. "Relics." In *The Catholic Encyclopedia*, vol. 12. New York: Robert Appleton Company, 1911. Available online at http://www.newadvent.org/cathen/12734a.htm. K. Knight, 2003.

Turner, Denys. "The Darkness of God and the Light of Christ: Negative Theology and Eucharistic Presence." *Modern Theology* 15, no. 2 (April 1999): 143–58.

WORKS CITED

Voegelin, Eric. *Anamnesis: On the Theory of History and Politics*. Trans. M. J. Hanak, based on the abbreviated version translated by Gerhart Niemeyer. Ed. and Introd. David Walsh. Columbia, Mo.: University of Missouri Press, 2000.

Wiesenthal, Simon. *The Sunflower: On the Possibilities and Limits of Forgiveness*, with a symposium edited by Harry James Cargas and Bonny V. Fetterman. New York: Schocken Books, 1998.

Wolfson, Elliot R. *Alef, Mem, Tau: Kabbalistic Musings on Time, Truth, and Death*. Berkeley: University of California Press, 2006.

———. "Fore/giveness on the Way: Nesting in the Womb of Response." In *Graven Images: Studies in Culture, Law and the Sacred* 4 (1988): 153–69.

Wyschogrod, Edith. *Saints and Postmodernism: Revisioning Moral Philosophy*. Chicago: University of Chicago Press, 1990.

INDEX

absolution, 55, 62, 65, 164n20
Achilles, 155n16
Adam, 32–48 passim, 135
Aletheia, 104
Alexander (Pope), 56
Anaximander, 154n9
Anaximines, 154n9
Anscombe, Elizabeth, 95
Anselm, Saint, 139
Anti-Christ (Nietzsche), 5
Antony and Cleopatra (Shakespeare), 49
Aphrodite, 156n24
aporia, 26, 166n49
Apostles' Creed, 134
Archive Fever: A Freudian Impression (Derrida), 55, 112
Arendt, Hannah, 63–64, 68, 72, 166n55
Aristophanes, 168n11
Aristotelianism, 129
Aristotle, 10, 13, 25, 168n6
asceticism, 53–54, 145
Athanasian Creed, 134
atonement, 56, 58, 59, 63, 65, 72
Augustine, Saint, 4; and beauty, 54; and Christianity, 27, 81; and communication, 166n48; and confession, 78; and continence, 53; and creation, 58–59, 136; and God, 51, 54, 85; and language, 28; and love, 102; and martyrs, 110; and memory, 24, 52, 133, 143, 159n54; and miracles, 111; and original sin, 32–54 passim, 135; and pleasure, 48; and resurrection, 133–34; and revelation, 80; and will, 44, 48, 50
Augustine, Saint (quoted), 42, 149

Bacon, Francis, 146–47, 148
Bal, Mieke, 74, 75
Balthasar, Hans Urs von, 95, 168–69n22
Baltimore Catechism, 3, 9. *See also A Catechism of Christian Doctrine*
baptism, 36, 38, 43, 55, 62–63
Barthes, Roland, 86, 87, 92
Bataille, Georges, 7, 10, 79, 102, 150
beauty, 13, 16, 17, 22, 158n39; and death, 99–103; and Plato, 20, 24–25, 40; and Plotinus, 50; and relics, 129; and rhythm, 143, 147
Benedict XVI, 108
Beyond Good and Evil (Nietzsche), 164n19
birth, 38, 138, 139; of Christ, 47, 49
Blanchot, Maurice, 1, 20, 45–46, 66, 73, 115; and death, 101–2, 159n57; and forgiveness, 64–65; and law, 40–41, 89, 90, 91; and love, 86, 99; and original sin, 36; and return, 29–30; and writing, 2, 6
blessedness, 5–6
body, 23, 40, 53, 61, 74, 97, 114, 123, 129, 130; and Augustine, 135; of Christ, 23,

189

INDEX

70, 93, 95, 98, 99, 102, 129–30; and the Eucharist, 144; and Immaculate Conception, 48–49; and relics, 106–28 passim; and resurrection, 132–48; and time, 139–48. *See also* corporeality; mind-body
The Book of Questions (Jabès), 70, 89, 103, 149
breath, 139–42, 150
Brown, Peter, 47–49, 122–23, 127
"Burnt Norton" (Eliot), 27
Burrus, Virginia, 77, 101, 123, 140
Bynum, Carolyn Walker, 39, 110, 112–13, 129

Cabrini, Frances Xavier, Saint, 110, 117–18, 121
canonization, 107–8, 111, 124, 125, 177n45
Carmelites, 122
Carroll, Lewis, 103
Cassian, John, 77, 160n21
A Catechism of Christian Doctrine, 9, 32, 55, 56, 84, 85, 106, 132
Catherine, Saint, 53, 129
Catholicism, 37, 108
Catholics, 95, 170n32. *See also* saints
Celan, Paul, 99
chance, 79, 82, 147
Christ, 129, 142, 162n58; and death, 89–90, 91; and the Eucharist, 92–99, 105, 114, 169n22; and Immaculate Conception, 47–49; and love, 87; pain of, 145; and resurrection, 80, 134, 136; and suffering, 124
Christianity, 3–4, 22–24, 27, 81, 158n41; and body, 124, 129, 155n11; and the Eucharist, 170n32; and forgiveness, 60; and love, 53; and original sin, 37; and penance, 61; and resurrection, 48, 134; and revelation, 80; and the Trinity, 108–9
Christology, 108
City of God (Augustine), 43, 51, 110
Cixous, Hélène, 105, 170n31
Clement VIII, 112
Cloisters, 116–17
commandments, 84–89, 103

communication, 71, 94, 120, 166n48
community, 61, 62, 107, 119–20, 120–23, 125, 128
conception. *See* Immaculate Conception
concupiscence, 35, 36–37, 50
condemnation, 65, 72, 80, 82
confession, 62, 70–71, 72–73, 77–78
Confessions (Augustine), 42, 136
configuration, 80, 81, 135–36
Congregation for the Causes of Saints, 107, 108
consciousness, 73, 76, 78, 146
consubstantiation, 94
continence, 53
continuity, 101, 104, 105
contrition, 65, 77
conversion, 44, 58, 59, 77
Cordovero, Moses, 5
"Corona" (Celan), 99
corporeality, 5, 17, 23, 131, 135, 136, 138, 139, 144, 154n4; Christ's, 49, 134; and eternity, 132–33; and the Eucharist, 93, 97; and materiality, 22; and penance, 61; and relics, 109, 111, 112, 116, 127, 129; and resurrection, 135. *See also* body
Council of Trent, 37, 111
creation, 39, 45, 57, 58–59, 136, 139, 175n41; and redemption, 60
crucifixion, 53, 60, 61, 91, 97, 124, 145, 168–69n22
Curd, Patricia, 156n17
Cusanus, Nicholas. *See* Nicholas, of Cusa

damnation, 32–34, 72, 83; eternal, 60; and forgiveness, 63; and grace, 33, 49; and Leibniz, 32, 45, 49, 81, 82; and trauma, 77, 79, 81
Davies, Oliver, 45
death, 11, 41, 66, 85, 88, 90, 91, 105, 159n57; and beauty, 99–103; and Christ, 94, 95–96, 97; future as, 104; and God, 92; and law, 66, 85, 88–89, 90, 99; and love, 98–99, 100; and relics, 112, 113, 124, 125, 128, 130; and resurrection, 134; and sin, 37
decomposition, 85, 88, 124

190

INDEX

Deleuze, Giles: and damnation, 32, 33; and forgiveness, 56; and repetition, 5, 7, 29, 53, 141–42, 143, 146, 147, 148; and rhythm, 141–42, 145; and sensation, 5, 145; and sin, 4, 34; and time, 136–37
Derrida, Jacques, 26, 55, 71, 112, 142
Descartes, René, 113, 127
desecration, 110
desire, 17, 33, 41, 45–46, 86, 99, 105, 148, 151, 170n31; and breath, 140; and death, 100–102; and freedom, 44; and Immaculate Conception, 47; and joy, 22, 24, 51, 146; and law, 90; limitation of, 49; and original sin, 34–39, 43, 72, 77; and pain, 145; redemptive, 49–54, 65; and return, 142, 144; and sacred, 54
determination, 44, 64, 88, 119
Deuteronomy, 30
dialogue, 74, 82; and confession, 77; and forgiveness, 67, 70–73
Difference and Repetition (Deleuze), 137
discipline, 37, 50
disobedience, 36, 37, 42, 43
divinity, 3, 30, 39, 40, 42, 50, 133, 140, 142, 151; and Christ, 138; and desire, 35, 41, 51, 54, 99; and eternity, 154n11; and forgiveness, 58, 83; and guilt, 60; and joy, 33; and love, 33, 100; and materiality, 12, 22; and original sin, 135; and return, 29, 59, 73; and sacred, 12, 35; and saint's relics, 106–31, 119; and time, 61, 143; and the Trinity, 91; and will, 46
De Doctrina Christiana (Augustine), 149
Duino Elegy (Rilke), 79
Dummett, Michael, 170n32
durchbrechen (breaking through), 29

"East Coker" (Eliot), 13
Eckhart, Meister, 52, 59; and Christ, 138; and divinity, 42; and love, 44–45, 84–85; and origin, 35; and Plato, 41; and return, 29
Eichmann, Adolf, 68, 72, 166n55
Eliot, T. S., 12–13, 27, 96
emanation, 21–22, 23, 24, 29
Enchiridion (Augustine), 133

endurance, 88, 97, 133, 134, 137–39, 144, 146, 148
Enneads (Plotinus), 21, 156n24
Eros, 39, 101, 104
eroticism, 86, 102, 145
eternity, 3, 5–6, 7, 12, 23–24; and Augustine, 58; and damnation, 32–33; and death, 96; and divinity, 154n11; and forgiveness, 56, 66, 77, 82; and future, 81; and joy, 51; and love, 85, 88, 101, 103; and original sin, 34, 36, 49; and pleasure, 39, 148; and present, 32, 34, 61, 66, 115; and resurrection, 132–36, 143; and rhythm, 145, 146, 147–48; and time, 33, 34, 61, 80, 92, 132–33, 135, 137–38, 140, 144, 150. *See also* recurrence, eternal
ethics, 11, 86, 130, 168n6
Ethics and Infinity (Levinas), 46
Eucharist, 5, 28, 92–99, 105, 114, 169n22
Eudemus, 155n16
Eve, 35, 36, 43, 46, 47, 48
evil, 43, 48, 61, 72, 82; and guilt, 64–65; and trauma, 78
Exodus, 30
exorcism, 175n41
Ezekiel, 140

Face of the Deep (Keller), 20, 55
faith, 25–26, 81, 97, 98, 129; and relics, 116, 127, 130
Faustina. *See* Maria Faustina, Saint
Finnegans Wake (Joyce), 28
flourishing, 24, 26
The Fold (Deleuze), 32
"Fore/giveness on the Way: Nesting in the Womb of Response" (Wolfson), 56
forgiveness, 4, 36, 55–83, 88, 137; divine, 103; and love, 84–85; and promise, 86
Forms, 13–16, 156n17
Foucault, Michel, 9, 32, 40, 62, 66, 76, 77, 115
Fourth Lateran Council, 170n33
Frances X. Cabrini, Saint, 110
freedom, 42–46, 50, 78–79
free will. *See* will, free
Freud, Sigmund, 74, 100, 101, 138, 146, 172n55

191

INDEX

future, 67, 71, 78–79, 93, 138, 150, 151; as death, 104; and the Eucharist, 93, 94; and forgiveness, 56, 57, 61, 63, 64, 66, 68, 70, 72; and love, 85, 88, 100, 103, 169n22; and mutability, 136; and past, 30; and present, 57, 67, 79; and repetition, 30, 81, 83; and return, 30; and sin, 60; and time, 79–83; and trauma, 74, 76

gathering, 2, 13, 15, 28, 101, 150
Geary, Patrick, 121
Genesis, 35, 37, 39, 58, 60, 136, 139
Gervasisus, 111
Gilgamesh, 172n55
Gnostic traditions, 23, 24, 160nn7, 24
goodness, 13, 21, 22, 36, 57; and God, 34, 48; and saints, 123
grace, 66; and damnation, 33, 49; and forgiveness, 64, 65; of God, 58; and law, 89, 91, 169n24; and Mary, 47; and original sin, 37, 38, 43, 82, 135; and saints, 109
Graham, Martha, 141
Gregory, of Nyssa, 113–14, 115, 127, 135
Gregory, of Tours, 175n41
Grosz, Elizabeth, 79
guilt, 33, 39, 52, 54, 60, 63–64; and damnation, 33; and forgiveness, 65, 70; and original sin, 38, 43, 45

Hamlet (Shakespeare), 84
Harries, Jill, 130
hate, 33–34, 68, 72, 78, 100; and God, 32, 82, 99
hearing, 76–77
Hegel, Georg Wilhelm Friedrich, 151
Heraclitus, 154n10
Hildebert of Tours, 170n33
history: and relics, 115–20
Hölderlin, Friedrich, 105, 133, 151
Holy Spirit, 93, 108–9
hope, 52, 81, 94, 140, 143
Hopkins, Gerard Manley, 126, 139
Hyman, Arthur, 21
"Hyperion's Joy" (Nancy), 20, 150–51

identity, 5, 18, 26, 35, 38, 41, 44, 97; and community, 122; and love, 86; and saints, 107, 109
Immaculate Conception, 46–49, 108
immortality, 20, 58, 132, 135, 137–38; and resurrection, 134; of the soul, 127
incarnation, 49, 51, 60, 129, 139, 155n11; and forgiveness, 61
"The Inoperative Community" (Nancy), 120
integration, 64, 74, 143
intellect, 21–22
Irigaray, Luce, 86–87
Islam, 158n61

Jabès, Edmond, 70, 89, 101, 103, 149
James, William, 10
Jesuits, 122
Jesus. *See* Christ
Job, 139–40
John (Gospel), 60, 87
John Paul II, 107–8, 109, 125, 140
John XV, 107
Jordan, Mark, 86, 150
joy, 50, 105; and desire, 22, 24, 51, 146; and divinity, 33; and the Eucharist, 92; and future, 71; and loss, 138, 150; and love, 87, 102; and original sin, 34, 39; and pain, 17, 128; and Plotinus, 21–22, 24; and will, 45, 48
Joyce, James, 28
Judaism, 158n41
Jude, Saint, 125
justice, 57, 63–64, 65, 66, 70, 83, 89, 91, 92

Kabbala, 56, 58, 80, 154n11, 158n44, 170n30
Kant, Immanuel, 146, 151
Kaufman, Eleanor, 144
Keating, James, 120, 123
Keller, Catherine, 7, 20, 55
Kerr, Fergus, 171n36
Kierkegaard, Søren, 80, 81, 146, 175n51
Klossowski, Pierre, 20, 29, 147
"Klossowski or Thoughts-Becoming" (Kaufman), 144
kneelers, 111–12, 121

INDEX

knowledge, 11, 16, 17, 20, 23, 26, 150; and trauma, 78; tree of, 35, 36
Kowalska, Maria Faustina. *See* Maria Faustina, Saint
Krog, Antje, 65, 69, 166n55
Kushner, Harold, 68, 70

Lacoue-Labarthe, Philippe, 6, 136
Lang, Berel, 66, 68, 166n54
language, 27–28, 75, 77–78, 127
law, 11, 33, 38, 40–41, 72, 102; and death, 66, 85, 88–89, 90, 99; and forgiveness, 62–66, 67; and guilt, 60; and love, 85–86, 88, 101; and relics, 130; and sacrifice, 89–92
Lear, Jonathan, 75
Leftow, Brian, 176n26, 177n27
The Legacy of Parmenides (Curd), 156n17
Leibniz, Gottfried, 4, 33–34, 56, 70; and damnation, 32, 45, 49, 81, 82
Lethe, 104
Levinas, Emmanuel, 46, 77
Leviticus, 84
libido, 100, 172n55
liturgy. *See* Eucharist
Loewy, Erich, 165n28
Lombard, Peter, 71
loss, 11, 24, 27, 28, 31, 38, 54, 67, 73, 134; and the Eucharist, 95, 96, 97, 98, 99; and joy, 138, 150; and love, 85, 91, 100, 101, 102, 103, 104; and original sin, 36, 37, 44; of Paradise, 35; and relics, 127; and saints, 120; of self, 34, 52–53, 82, 125, 130; and time, 59, 79, 137–38, 148
Louth, Andrew, 126
love, 4–5, 16, 17–18, 22, 24–25, 44–45, 49, 84–105, 137, 169n22; and Christianity, 53; and crucifixion, 60; divine, 52, 53, 103; and forgiveness, 83; human, 52; and Leibniz, 33; and memory, 103–5; and original sin, 34, 51; of self, 39, 42
A Lover's Discourse: Fragments (Barthes), 92
Lucifer, 43
Luke (Gospel), 84, 92–93, 96
Lutgarde, Saint, 53

Lutherans, 194
Lysias, 16, 17, 18

Mackey, Louis, 27, 59, 60
Macrina, 113–14
Madness and Civilization (Foucault), 76
Manchester, Peter, 80, 81, 159n2
Manichean, 46, 48
Maria Faustina, Saint, 120–21, 125, 128
Mark (Gospel), 93
marriage, 86, 89
Martins, Cardinal José, 108
Martos, Joseph, 35, 164n20, 169n22, 170nn33, 35, 171n36
martyrs, 110, 111, 127
Mary, Mother, 47–48, 49, 108
Mary Magdalene, 126
materiality, 12, 22, 136, 148; and relics, 106; and resurrection, 133
Matthew (Gospel), 93
McCabe, Herbert, 171n36
McCarthy, David, 120, 123
Melissus, 155n16, 156n17
Meno (Plato), 16
mercy, 57, 63–64, 83, 89, 90
Merleau-Ponty, Maurice, 137, 145, 147
metonymy, 115
Miles, Margaret, 21–22, 23
Miller, C. Lee, 24
Miller, Patricia Cox, 106, 111
mind-body, 113–14, 127. *See also* body; corporeality
miracles, 110–11, 113, 124, 175n41, 177n45; and relics, 129
monism, 10–12, 21, 156n17
Moreton, Nelle, 72
mortality, 36, 37, 40, 135; and law, 92; and love, 82, 85, 100, 101, 103, 104
Moses, 30, 170n31
motion, 13, 15, 21, 134, 136
mourning, 5, 151, 172n62; and the Eucharist, 92, 94; and joy, 138, 150; and love, 96, 98, 100–103, 105; and relics, 127
multiplicity, 11, 12, 13, 15, 21, 26, 28, 29, 30–31, 81; and dialogue, 71; and return, 99; and unity, 22, 24
music, 145

193

INDEX

mutability, 58, 136
mysticism, 41, 53–54

Nancy, Jean-Luc, 1, 3–4, 6, 20, 38, 56, 71, 120, 136, 138, 150–51; and community, 119, 122; and eternity, 133, 148; and joy, 102; and love, 4–5, 87, 88–89, 96, 105; and mourning, 101; and promise, 89; and rhythm, 142
National Shrine of Divine Mercy, 125
National Shrine of Our Lady of Mt. Carmel, 121–22
Nehamas, Alexander, 14, 15
Neoplatonism, 12, 20–26, 29, 56, 59, 135, 137, 156n24
Neumann, Bishop John, 117, 118–19, 120, 126
Nicene Creed, 134
Nicholas, of Cusa, 44, 84, 154n10, 168n11
Nietzsche, Friedrich, 29, 66, 147, 163n66, 164n19; and Christ, 5; and death, 92; and ethics, 168n6; and forgetting, 26; and freedom, 44; and future, 71; and guilt, 65; and joy, 146; and return, 20, 81, 82, 147; and rhythm, 143
"Nietzsche, Genealogy, History" (Foucault), 9, 32, 40, 61, 115
nihilists, 155n16
"Noli Me Frangere," 6, 7

obedience, 44, 48, 103
"Of Divine Places" (Nancy), 3–4
"On Beauty" (Plotinus), 24–25
"On Transience" (Freud), 100, 172n55
Origen, 161n36
origin, 24, 29, 80, 124, 136, 139, 141
original sin, 32–54; and resurrection, 4, 60, 72, 75, 77, 81–82, 89, 134, 135, 143; and law, 90. *See also* sin

Pagels, Elaine, 43–44
pain, 145–46
Parmenides (philosopher), 12–13, 15, 21, 23
Parmenides (Plato), 13, 14
Passion, 145
past, 25, 56–83 passim, 128, 149, 150; and damnation, 32; and the Eucharist, 94;
and forgiveness, 88; and future, 30; and love, 85; and memory, 26, 41, 93, 112, 143, 144
Patrick, Saint, 122
Patripassianism, 95
Paul, Saint, 37, 89, 90, 91, 93, 94
Paul IV, 108
Pausanias, 156n24
Pelagius, 43
penance, 55, 56, 61, 62, 63, 83
"Peter Quince at the Clavier" (Stevens), 132
Phaedrus (character), 17–18, 19
Phaedrus (Plato), 15, 16, 20, 22, 24, 25, 27, 30, 59, 156n24; and original sin, 40–42
Philebus (Plato), 14
philosophy, 7, 10–12, 25
Pius IX, 47
Plato, 9–20, 22, 26, 30, 41, 54, 143
Platonism, 22, 26, 129
"Plato's Forgetting" (Ramadanovic), 20
pleasure, 47, 48, 54, 90, 145–46, 148, 151; absence of, 82
Plotinus, 12, 26, 156n24, 160n25; and beauty, 24–25, 50, 54, 162n59; and God, 35, 51; and Neoplatonism, 21, 22, 23; and rhythm, 139, 143; and soul, 174n26
poetry, 14, 143
polyvalence, 164n19
prayer, 1, 4, 61, 111
predestination, 33
present, 5, 26, 28–31, 137–38, 143, 144, 147, 150; and divinity, 39; and eternity, 32, 34, 61, 66, 115; and the Eucharist, 92, 93, 94, 98, 99, 114; and future, 57, 67, 79; and love, 81, 85, 99; and relics, 112–18, 125; and trauma, 74–75, 82
promise, 55–62, 63, 83, 86, 101; and law, 89; and love, 85, 88–89, 92, 105
Protasius, 111
Protestantism, 108
Protestants, 95, 170n32
Pseudo-Dionysisus the Aeropagite, 34
Pytel, Father Ronald, 120

Ramadanovic, Peter, 20, 25
reality, 5, 6, 13, 19, 22, 23, 27, 76, 135, 156n17

194

INDEX

recollection, 4, 6, 15, 30, 41, 94; and loss, 95; and love, 103, 105; and Plotinus, 24; and speaking, 27

reconciliation, 56, 61, 62, 63, 64

recurrence, 12, 30, 31, 86, 137, 141, 144; eternal, 25, 29, 102, 147

redemption, 5, 101, 150; and baptism, 38; and body, 144; and Christ, 48; and creation, 60; and forgiveness, 59, 61, 65, 82; and original sin, 49, 51; and repentance, 58; and time, 30, 137, 138; and wholeness, 39

redemptive desire, 49–54, 65

relics, 5, 106–31, 137; defined, 109–10; and fragmentation, 126–31

reliquaries, 111–12, 116–17, 118, 119, 125, 127, 173n8

repentance, 58, 59, 77

repetition, 3, 78, 79, 97, 145, 149; and damnation, 33–34, 82; and Deleuze, 5, 7, 29, 53, 141–42, 143, 146, 147, 148; and forgiveness, 20; and fragmentation, 25, 28–29; and future, 30, 81, 83; and trauma, 73, 74, 75, 76, 77

Republic (Plato), 13

restitution, 63, 65, 83

resurrection, 5, 53, 90, 94, 96, 97, 104; and body, 48, 49, 114, 129, 132–48; and martyrs, 127; and original sin, 4, 60, 72, 75, 77, 81–82, 89, 134, 135, 143; and revelation, 80; and soul, 113–14; and time, 92

"The Resurrection of the Flesh" (Tertullian), 134

return, 23, 24, 38, 58, 64, 65, 69, 71, 101; and Blanchot, 29–30; and desire, 142, 144; and divinity, 29, 59, 73; and Eckhart, 29; eternal, 103, 104, 147; and the Eucharist, 97–99; and future, 30; infinite, 97, 147; and love, 105; and Nietzsche, 20, 81, 82, 147; and origin, 80; and time, 139–44

revelation, 24, 50, 55–83, 119

rhetoric, 16, 28

"The Rhetoric of Ethics as Excess: A Christian Theological Response to Emmanuel Levinas" (Webb), 70

rhythm, 139–48, 150

Rilke, Rainer Maria, 54, 79

Romans (book of Bible), 37

sacred, 5, 78, 150, 151, 154n11; and desire, 54; and divinity, 12, 35; and forgiveness, 64, 72, 80, 83; and love, 100, 101; and original sin, 49; and relics, 107, 108, 112, 117, 119, 123–26, 127, 128, 130

sacred heart, 142

sacrifice, 53, 60, 61, 63, 103, 110, 138; and law, 89–92

sainthood, 107, 109, 119, 120

saints, 106–31

salvation, 54, 58, 60, 61

Santayana, George, 79

Sappho, 101

Second Vatican Council, 108, 112

seduction theory, 50

seminal transmission, 46, 47

sensation, 5, 144–48, 150

separation, 32–39, 41, 42, 45, 49, 77, 80, 82; and resurrection, 135

Seton, Elizabeth Ann, 116, 117, 121

sex, 86

The Sex Lives of Saints (Burrus), 123

Shakespeare, William, 49, 84

sin, 4, 36, 46, 60, 61, 70, 77, 81–82, 144; and death, 37; and forgiveness, 55, 62–63; inability to, 43, 44; and law, 90; mortal, 166n49. *See also* original sin

singularity, 26

Socrates, 14, 15, 16, 17–19, 20, 28, 40

solitude, 38–39

Sophist (Plato), 15

sophists, 19

sorting, 14

soul, 14, 47–48, 138; and Augustine, 43, 46, 52; and body, 61, 113–14, 127, 129, 130, 135, 157–58n39; and damnation, 32, 33; and Eckhart, 42, 138; and original sin, 37, 49; in *Phaedras*, 16–17, 20, 27, 40–41; and Plotinus, 21–24, 26; and resurrection, 134

speaking, 1, 16, 18–19, 25–26, 27–28, 76–78, 149

"Spelt From Sibyl's Leaves" (Hopkins), 126

INDEX

spirit, 48, 89, 90, 96, 130, 135, 136, 137, 140, 148. *See also* Holy Spirit
spirituality, 46, 79
Stephen, Saint, 111
The Step Not Beyond (Blanchot), 89
Stevens, Wallace, 99, 100, 132
stigmata, 177n45
Sturken, Marita, 26
subjectivity, 26, 45, 52, 54, 64, 146
suffering, 10, 124, 127
Sufism, 158n44
"Sunday Morning" (Stevens), 99
The Sunflower (Wiesenthal), 165n28
Symposium (Plato), 22, 156n24, 168n11

Teresa, Saint, 53, 116
Tertullian, 134
Thales, 154n9
Thamos, King, 19
Theatetus, 16
theology, 2, 7, 8, 27, 51, 53, 86, 108
Therese, Saint, 122, 123–24, 126
Theuth, 19
"Thinking the New: Of Futures Yet Unthought" (Grosz), 79
Thomas, Apostle, Saint, 142
Thomas, Aquinas, Saint, 37, 46, 48, 63, 110, 111
Through the Looking Glass (Carroll), 103
time, 2, 4, 5, 12, 23, 24, 25, 29, 30, 51, 52, 53, 54, 86, 102–3, 128, 151; and body, 139–48; and death, 96; and divinity, 61, 143; and eternity, 33, 34, 61, 80, 92, 132–33, 135, 137–38, 140, 144, 150; and the Eucharist, 94; and forgiveness, 55–62, 72, 77; and future, 79–83; and loss, 59, 79, 137–38, 148; and love, 85; and redemption, 30, 137, 138; and relics, 112; and resurrection, 92; and return, 139–44; and trauma, 73, 75
"To Possess Truth in One Soul and One Body" (Nancy), 1
Torah, 57–58
transfiguration, 62, 68, 71, 78, 80, 82, 94–95, 129; of loss, 148; of sensation, 146, 147; and time, 138

transformation, 69, 70, 71, 75, 78, 92, 94–95, 147; and forgiveness, 80, 81, 82
transience, 100, 101, 138
transignification, 94–95
transubstantiation, 93, 94–95, 112, 125, 171n36
trauma, 4, 50, 55–83, 144
Trinity, 91, 96, 97, 108
truth, 12, 13–14, 16, 26, 27, 78
Truth and Reconciliation Commission, 65, 68, 69
Turner, Denys, 94

The Unavowable Community (Blanchot), 86
Urbi et Orbi (John Paul II), 140

Vatican II, 108, 112
veneration, 110, 114
Victricius, 122
violence, 62, 66, 119, 126, 128
The Visible and the Invisible (Merleau-Ponty), 137
The Vision of God (Cusanus), 84
visions, 128

Webb, Stephen H., 70
Wiesenthal, Simon, 165n28, 167n65
will, 36–46 passim, 49, 50, 51, 96, 148; divine, 53, 60, 135; eternal, 61; and flesh, 48; free, 33, 43, 44, 45; God's, 95; and resurrection, 135
Williams, Rowan, 114
Wolfson, Elliot, 2, 4, 5, 137, 154n11, 158n44, 167n63; and forgiveness, 56–57, 58, 59, 67, 80
Woodruff, Paul, 14, 15
worship, 106, 108, 110, 112
"The Wreck of the *Deutschland*" (Hopkins), 139
writing, 1–2, 6–7, 16, 18–19, 25–26, 30, 149
The Writing of the Disaster (Blanchot), 1, 64–65, 66, 73

Yom Kippur, 56

Zen, 158n44
Zeno, 13, 15